Television, Power, and the

The Russian media are widely seen to be increasingly controlled by the government. Leaders buy up dissenting television channels and pour money in as fast as it hemorrhages out. As a result, TV news has become narrower in scope and in the range of viewpoints which it reflects: leaders demand assimilation and shut down dissenting stations. Using original and extensive focus group research and new developments in cognitive theory, Ellen Mickiewicz unveils a profound mismatch between the complacent assumption of Russian leaders that the country will absorb their messages, and the viewers on the other side of the screen. This is the first book to reveal what the Russian audience really thinks of its news and the mental strategies they use to process it. The focus on ordinary people, rather than elites, makes a strong contribution to the study of post-communist societies and the individual's relationship to the media.

ELLEN MICKIEWICZ is James R. Shepley Professor of Public Policy Studies in the Terry Sanford Institute of Public Policy and Professor of Political Science at Duke University. She is a leading authority on Russian news media, and her previous publications include *Changing Channels: Television and the Struggle for Power in Russia* (1999) and *Split Signals: Television and Politics in the Soviet Union* (1988).

Television, Power, and the Public in Russia

ELLEN MICKIEWICZ

CAMBRIDGE
UNIVERSITY PRESS

CAMBRIDGE UNIVERSITY PRESS
Cambridge, New York, Melbourne, Madrid, Cape Town, Singapore, São Paulo, Delhi

Cambridge University Press
The Edinburgh Building, Cambridge CB2 8RU, UK

Published in the United States of America by Cambridge University Press,
New York

www.cambridge.org
Information on this title: www.cambridge.org/9780521716758

First published 2008

Printed in the United Kingdom at the University Press, Cambridge

A catalogue record for this publication is available from the British Library

Library of Congress Cataloguing in Publication data
Mickiewicz, Ellen Propper.
Television, power, and the public in Russia / Ellen Mickiewicz.
    p.   cm.
ISBN 978-0-521-88856-1
1. Television broadcasting of news – Russia (Federation)   2. Television and
politics – Russia (Federation)   I. Title.
PN5277.T4M54   2008
070.4'30947–dc22   2007052899

ISBN 978-0-521-88856-1 hardback
ISBN 978-0-521-71675-8 paperback

Contents

Figures

Preface

As new heads of television were announced and revamped news operations put in place, or when the state moved in and began to prevent stations from projecting any point of view that did not actively support the Kremlin's, it always seemed to me that there was one element most took for granted: the public. Put the material before them, and they will assimilate it. Or run mass-public opinion surveys and see the "big picture." But no one much cared about the ordinary, average viewer watching the screen in the provinces. Only Moscow mattered. Yet it was a mistake to assert so confidently what viewers were thinking and talking about as the news came on. This study examines precisely that question: how did ordinary viewers come to their conclusions? More specifically, what were the tools they used to take apart positive stories to meet the standards of the questioning public? This is the final link in the circle of the most powerful medium in Russia: not why people thought certain programs popular or unpopular but, drilling down, how, what did they rely on, what instruments did they use – and, unquestionably, some had many more than others – to process what they saw.

During the course of writing this book, I came to know from transcripts and films these ordinary viewers gathered in focus groups in four Russian cities. They were lively, passionate, angry, funny, and some diffident. They were interesting and most, regardless of the level of education they had attained, quite sophisticated. They had a lot to say and would have surprised and probably troubled the state-controlled television apparatus. This is a study, then, of the methods and strategies the Russian television public engages in, not always consciously, as compared to the working assumptions that the powerful have about them.

I should like to acknowledge here the help of some people whom I was fortunate enough to know for many years. Leila Vasilieva is one of the most skilled and experienced facilitators of focus groups in

Russia. She personally moderated all of the groups; that meant traveling to Rostov-on-the-Don in the south, to Volgograd, to Nizhny Novgorod, and Moscow, and in the course of these trips to conduct four focus groups in each city. She had to do it within a limited time frame, so that the results would be comparable. It is because of her willingness to conduct all the groups that we do not have to worry about the possible effects of differing methods and cues. Olga Oslon, who has worked on audience research, was always wise and imaginative and knew the medium and its public through and through.

It is essential in running such focus groups to avoid many words, even seemingly innocuous ones, that could cue Soviet-style answers. The Soviet ideology disseminated repeated formulations, and if we invoked them accidentally we could be sure that almost unthinking habit would take over and nullify our attempt to get to the layers of greater candor. Peter Hart, one of America's leading pollsters, provided ideas about pulling participants out of their unthinking or formulaic, automatic responses, and I am grateful for his ideas.

I thank Sarah Oates, Senior Lecturer at University of Glasgow and specialist on Russian media, for many interesting and knowledgeable conversations, and Robert Orttung and Danielle Lussier, specialists on the regions of Russia, whose expertise was very valuable. Without doubt among my academic colleagues, it is Doris Graber whose work has introduced to the field new ways of thinking and new research on political psychology and cognitive science.

At Duke University, this project benefited greatly from conversations with John Transue of the Political Science Department. I am also grateful to Kevin M. Carragee and to the two anonymous reviewers for the Cambridge University Press. All contributed perceptive and detailed comments and observations.

Victoria Frolova, a graduate student in the Political Science Department, has been a superb research assistant. To Melissa Solomon I express my gratitude for her careful and sensitive reading of some of the chapters in the book.

The research was funded in part by a grant from the Markle Foundation and by my research fund at Duke University.

1 | *The missing term in the equation*

When almost an entire population depends on television for its news, and its political leaders accord almost miraculous powers to the medium, *and* gobble one commercial channel after another, wouldn't those political leaders want anxiously to know what viewers make of the news? Isn't viewer-processing as vital to their strategy as message-creation? In today's Russia these are vital questions, on which careers and huge resources can ride – and, strangely enough, the answer to both these questions is "no." The other side of the television screen – the one where the viewers are arrayed – is invisible. Agreement with the message is assumed. Hence, the question: what if the "reception" on the other side of the screen was actually confounding and contradicting the leaders' assumptions every day, and by what method are viewers able to do thus?

These are the research problems that drive this study. The findings may vary for young and old, for citizens of Volgograd, or Rostov, or Nizhny Novgorod, or Moscow, for the college-educated and for those who stopped after high school. In the end, the invisible viewers take shape. Concepts of Russian television have been the subject of numerous studies: there is much information on ownership of television channels, both national and regional. There is, equally, a good deal of scholarship on the content of television news and entertainment. The findings run from anecdotal snapshots by journalists and tourists, to extremely labor-intensive quantifications of the features of each news story, to all-embracing narratives of culture and power. But there is an underresearched missing link: the viewers. There are statements and studies that speak *for* the viewers, but ordinary citizens are a missing term – taken for granted by the powerful, routinely underestimated as an undifferentiated mass, and granted little ability to follow a learning curve, penetrate content strategies, and develop in their minds alternatives that they, as citizens, would prefer. But, come election time, they can cast a vote that in effect says "I vote against the whole lot of them," and this option has begun to grow significantly. The rash of

1

"against-all" votes may be one manifestation of this dissatisfaction, as chapter 3 suggests. The demographics of the "against-all" voters have changed radically over the years, moving from the "marginal" citizens of little education, old age, and low income, to those of the young, high education, and high professional status. The government has been concerned enough to delete "against-all" from the ballot choices.

This is not an investigation of the decisions citizens make using mental shortcuts. It does not seek linkages between processing the news and thereafter choosing to take action or desist from it. Not enough is known about the very first step in the process: processing comes first, and must have certain characteristics if the message is to become part of memory and help to provide a mental shortcut to interpreting yet other messages. Post-Soviet Russia is a useful laboratory for this study. It is a nation of television viewers, and, except for a few far-flung rural dwellings in Siberia, almost every family has a set. The sudden collapse of the Soviet Union, and the introduction of a post-Soviet reality happened very quickly and across the whole country. Whatever the arguments about whether or how democracy is exportable, no one today would suggest that the habits of democracy seen in advanced Western democracies were, or could be, simply imprinted on a blank slate. There is no blank slate in human affairs, or clarity about what exactly "democracy" means to Russians. Most have lived through a period called "the transition to democracy." It has been full of contradictions: the relaxation of control of the economy and speech, private ownership, opportunities to travel, job choice, as well as food shortages and financial collapse, health catastrophes, corruption and crime; not to mention the plight of the elderly, their fixed pensions swallowed up by the new inflation, sometimes driven by hunger to suicide, and often tricked or threatened out of their former state-owned apartments.

We want to know what viewers actually make of a news story. How will they process the information that comes at them from the television set? People usually do not watch alone, so how do they talk to each other about what they get from news stories? Crucially, this work is not a popularity or ratings study: whether people like this program, or that host, or that studio anchor can change from one program to another. We are concerned here with how the brain itself forms ways to process information, uses heuristics, and depends on mental shortcuts. This process tends not to change over long periods of time. Political heuristics are most often connected to political decision-making by voters as a way of categorizing a candidate or policy with respect to one's own preferences, without having acquired all the knowledge that is available. In the present study, the use of heuristics in the focus groups is of interest not for viewer action or voting action, but for the extent that it is used by viewers to process news stories. (For an interesting election case, see chapter 3.) This is a much more difficult task than it might seem at first glance. The volume of news and its presentation deliberately conceals or skews all but the government's view of events. The presentation is in viewer-unfriendly formats – such as, among others, rapidly running through lists of numbers and producing evidence without context or comparison. The news is highly Moscow-centric and power-centric and is constructed to please the Kremlin more than to connect with viewers.

Yet news is central to the viewer's day and is widely watched. Russians have methods to process this news and to emerge at the end of the story with a very different interpretation, one that is much expanded from the original. In the United States, for example, political heuristics may be party labels, evidence of personal character with which to draw conclusions about political character, and positions of interest groups, among others.[1] In Russia, political parties have not reached the level of maturity to provide material for heuristics. Nor do most candidates focus in detail on the policy and projects they would sponsor were they to be elected. In fact, one of the complaints of viewers is that candidates in the news say nothing about policy plans, their connection with constituents, or about promises to be accountable and efficient on their behalf.

Kuklinski and Quirk (2000) acknowledge that politicians debating in the United States are likely to distort judgment by the isolated facts they choose and the way they frame issues, adding up to misleading and manipulative rhetoric. Whatever uninformative or emotional diversions are produced by these debates, they are still in the zone of the contending parties. It is that basic advantage that vanished from Russia with the closing down of TV-6 in 2002.

So it is crucial to consider the mental processes Russian viewers rely on to make sense of the welter of information broadcast to them every

[1] J. H. Kuklinski and P. J. Quirk, "Reconsidering the Rational Public: Cognition, Heuristics, and Mass Opinion," in A. Lupia, M. D. McCubbins, and S. L. Popkin (eds.), *Elements of Reason: Cognition, Choice and the Bounds of Rationality*. Cambridge, Cambridge University Press, 2000.

day. What instruments in their cognitive tool boxes do Russian viewers use to form their own meaning? It is clear that some of these instruments have been preserved since Soviet times, and with differing levels of success can be one asset applied to a very changed information system – including, for example, the Internet. The Internet is growing fast in the large Russian cities. In our focus groups, it is used mainly at the place of work, but as use grows it is increasingly clear that the Internet is protean. In March 2007, President Putin signed a decree merging two agencies: a technical Information Technologies Agency and the Federal Service for Media Law Compliance Ministry, one of the weakest members of the government bureaucracy. The new entity is charged with making new regulations, especially for the Internet. Any proposed form of control over such a massive body of information and freedom of personal expression concerns the "*Internetchiki*" (Internet surfers), but the new agency is generally dismissed as unlikely to be able to perform its mission.

The new Russia watches news, but there has been very little understanding about *how* they do – and, equally, why they might "cut out" from a story, or say that this is precisely the moment they would go to put the kettle on for tea. Audiences also differ in the number and array of tools available to them, and in the feelings that play such an important part in memory. Do ordinary viewers have ways to process what is unfamiliar? Where do their minds search for some navigation tools? These keys to processing information are related to memory, and it should be emphasized that they are quite durable and change slowly. In chapter 6 we give some examples of the mutability of memory under specific circumstances (its capacity to rewrite itself as a person changes), but the basic processing tools, unlike the more superficial popularity contests for television's favorite anchor or program, go very deep, and for the most part remain the same.

One often hears that the only explanation is the skill built up in Soviet times of "reading between the lines." But this is a misleading and quite insufficient explanation; it is not in fact an explanation at all; it simply pushes back the research question to another stage that must itself be explored. "Reading between the lines" does not tell us the *content* of that reading. There will be as many variations as there are news consumers. Nor does "reading between the lines" tell us how the viewer came to a certain conclusion: was it by use of certain heuristics? That, in turn, depends on how richly the viewers were endowed with experiences and memories available for making sense of the news. Not everyone can "read between the lines" with the same degree of accuracy, depth, or overarching society-wide generalization. Skills, experiences, memories, formal education, and "life education" differ significantly among people, and reflections from "reading between the lines" would be as varied, or contradictory, or multi-leveled, as any response to a televised message. It seems to me that once the results of "reading between the lines" have been tallied up, one must then embark on a real analysis: all that this much-used term means is that during the Soviet period many viewers employed their own correctives to counter the steady flow of positive bureaucratic news that came from the television set. So-called "reading between the lines" is of little use in looking at what conclusions viewers come to, and via what mechanism. We are more interested in the mechanisms, the differences that demographics might make, and the differences that education and life in the country or capital make to the viewers who sit in front of the set (as one of our viewers does, ten hours a day), but who may process very little.

Nor is this a study of persuasion and the efficacy of the Kremlin's strategy. This book follows how the viewer absorbs or does not absorb; processes the information for later retrieval or fails to retain it; and what kinds of factors, such as trust, relate to any of these strategies. Some of the viewers in the focus groups say that a news story can be both objective *and* planted. Going through the process of understanding why that phrase is not an oxymoron reveals a pragmatic and very labor-intensive processing of news stories by viewers. Elections have become the most important part of political life for the Kremlin. Televised election news turns out to be a dramatic mismatch between viewers' interpretations and the message sent from Moscow.

Chapter 3 is about the way television covers election campaigns in Russia and what the viewers make of the coverage; what purpose elections serve in Russia's stunted democracy; and what they ought to be if the elected are to be fully accountable to the citizens.

All of the intimidation of journalists, the violent takeover of television stations in the regions and in Moscow, the particular fragility of pre-election periods when televised dissent is out of order, and all of the strong-arm techniques undermining the democratic free press, have been made in the name of the viewers. To keep them from becoming opposition voters has meant reining in television at any cost and imposing like-minded allies of the elites. As the following pages show, these strategies have been implemented with near-total incomprehension of how the public really does process the news and the likelihood that many of these coercive moves and homogenizing efforts will turn out to have been counter-productive.

Too often, consciously or by habit, those who control the television agenda and images operate in the belief that the audience assimilates the message precisely as it is transmitted: this assumes a kind of homogenization in the most heterogenous audience for any medium of communication. Television's mass-audience are the well and poorly educated, the highly literate and the functionally illiterate; housewives, elderly people, and young families who have few other affordable choices. Reasoning from content to its assumed internalization by viewers is the way the networks function, but crucially, it fails to take seriously enough diverse viewers, each with different psychological baggage and life experiences, and must surely be recognized as thoroughly inadequate, resting on a flawed assumption and with no real interest in the domestic television public.

A note on methods

This study was conducted in Russia in January 2002, the last period in which diversity in television news was clearly present on a national scale. It was also a relatively normal time, chosen deliberately – without national election campaigns either ongoing or about to begin, without an immediate crisis looming. To see how cognitive methods were employed, and which were chosen, the potential distractions and divisiveness of exogenous claims on viewers' attention were reduced as far as possible. Sites for the focus groups were chosen after considerable reflection. Sixteen focus groups, a total of 158 participants, were invited to participate in four cities: Rostov, Volgograd, Nizhny Novgorod, and Moscow. Each of these cities represents a different political and media environment.[2] When the focus groups were in the field, the four cities had the following characteristics:[3]

---

[2] I thank Danielle Lussier for her knowledgeable comments on these regional features, and Robert Orttung for his expert assistance.

[3] see http://www.isn.ethz.ch/researchpub/publihouse/rrr; Obshchestvennaya expertiza, 2000; J. Wishnevsky, *The Evolution of the Russian Communist Party*, E. Teague ed. Washington, DC: The Jamestown Foundation, 1999.

- The *Volgograd Region* borders Kazakhstan, is roughly 300 miles from Chechnya, and has a stagnating economy with a weak private sector. It has traditionally been part of Russia's "red belt," strong enough in its allegiance to be called its "buckle." In media pluralism and editorial autonomy, the city ranks lowest among the four and media density is low.

- *Rostov*, on the river Don, is the capital of the Southern Federal District, one of seven administrative units that President Putin created for the Russian Federation. Long-serving, investor-friendly governor Vladimir Chub, backed by the pro-Putin party, was re-elected in the fall of 2001 by 78 percent of the voters; his strongest competitor, a Communist Party leader, had been disqualified on the dubious charge of having too many invalid signatures. Rostov has reasonably high media density, especially in radio and television, and government efforts to control the media have often met with private-sector resistance.

- *Nizhny Novgorod*, 250 miles east of Moscow, was called Gorky in Soviet times, and it was to Gorky that Andrei Sakharov was exiled until Gorbachev allowed him to return to Moscow. Until 1991, it was a "closed city," a defense industry powerhouse. Now it is capital of the Volga Federal District. The market reforms of the first governor, Boris Nemtsov, slowed significantly under his successors, and foreign investment dropped sharply. The media market is relatively large, with a strong private sector in electronic media, notwithstanding the attempts of the government to interfere.

- *Moscow* is by far the most educated region of the four, and residents can access a very large number of television stations: over-the-air, cable, and DBS (satellite television). In this, it exceeds by an order of magnitude any of the other three cities: at the time of the focus groups, Volgograd had the narrowest range of nonstate television choices of the cities outside Moscow – Nizhny Novgorod had 8 commercial channel choices; Rostov, 7; and Volgograd, only 2.5.[4] All of the cities except Moscow are situated within a large and populous area (home to 37 percent of Russia's population) of the adjacent Volga and Southern Federal Districts, thus reducing confounding

[4] I count as "commercial channels" those that broadcast entirely on a channel or share the broadcast time with another channel and whose audiences are large enough to ensure reasonable ratings.

differences that more dissimilar population points would produce. Focus groups were differentiated by college and secondary education, a pattern shown by pilot studies to enhance participation. There were twice as many college-educated groups, reflecting their current and future centrality to the political and economic development of Russia.

To address the generational question – will Soviet-era information processing patterns be lost, altered, or continue? – one focus group in each city was restricted to post-Soviet participants – that is, they were too young to be watching typically Soviet (pre-Gorbachev) news. The average post-Soviet participant was born in 1980; old-style Soviet television began to change markedly in 1985. If there are differences, we cannot know if they are related to youth as a stage of life or to a genuine generational change; it is a first cut at the question. Young people also were mixed in with the other groups, but the post-Soviet groups consisted only of young people. To limit the variability of context, the groups were all conducted by a single experienced specialist from the Public Opinion Foundation (a Russian survey organization headquartered in Moscow). It was important to present an original way of posing theoretical questions about processing information without cueing any Soviet-era concepts that might then be brought out as a rote response. New and different forms of questions and graphs were used for the first time in the experience of the focus groups: television news clips of different channels' treatments of the same event were also used (see chapters 3 and 4). Needless to say, I was not present during the focus groups, as there could be no easier way to contaminate or nullify the discussion than having a foreigner, even a Russian-speaking foreigner, sitting in the room.[5] As is customary in focus groups, everything was done to make the discussion among ten strangers (with nametags showing only a first name, not the real one) as casual and comfortable as possible. Discussions tended to be very lively and went on for two hours. Beforehand, participants were asked to fill out a short questionnaire on age, employment, education, media use, and a pair of short attitudinal questions about the market economy and about tolerance. There were two factual questions to find out something about political knowledge.

---

[5] I thank Peter Hart for his brilliant counsel on these subjects.

In response to the criticism that focus group members discuss topics animatedly but may not think them important when surveyed, Lunt and Livingstone (1996)[6] note that: "people do not talk at length or with interest about an issue on which they have nothing meaningful to say." These were lively discussions. On two occasions during the session the participants were shown three to four treatments of a single event. This was actual footage from actual news programs, but without network identification; in addition, there were no pictures of anchors, microphones with logos, sign-offs by reporters, or anything else that might identify the station, including stage sets; all of the stories were reported from the field. The participants did not indicate they had seen the stories before. After each story, there was a vigorous discussion about what they had just seen.

One hundred and fifty-eight Russians participated in the total set of sixteen focus groups in the four cities. Slightly more than half were women (53 percent). About 50 percent were aged 30 and under; 25 percent were 31–45, and the remaining 25 percent were over 45. There were many young people – we call them "post-Soviet," because as we have seen one group in each city was just for young people, so that they could speak to their generation and in their generation's language. That accounts for 25 percent of the total. Another 25 percent were also young people who happened to fall into two other groups put together by level of education (high school and university). We wanted to have more people with higher education who would comprise an equal proportion, because from these groups come leaders, opinion-makers at the local level, and the pool from which upward-mobility-bound individuals are drawn. Two groups in each city were devoted to people with university education.

Before the focus groups began, we had asked participants about their patterns of media consumption. Over half said they consumed the news every day (51 percent); another 29 percent said they did so three to four times a week, and 20 percent only once or twice a week. If we term "heavy viewers" those who consumed news daily or three to four times a week, which is certainly reasonable, then among this group 80 percent could be counted as heavy news viewers. We were curious where they got most of this news from. Knowing that we had to refer

[6] P. Lunt and S. Livingstone, "Rethinking the Focus Group in Media Communications Research," *Journal of Communication*, 46, 1996: 79–98, p. 91.

to subjects that were on television and that were of importance across the regions of our groups, we asked where they preferred to go for news of the President and where they went for news of Chechnya. For the former, 85 percent went to the handful of Moscow-based networks. It is reassuring that this is precisely the pattern found in a 2006 national poll by VTsIOM in Moscow: "the overwhelming majority of Russian citizens – 85 percent – prefer to receive information from central television broadcasts."[7] We must stress, however, that the national poll used a random sample and is generalizable; our focus groups are not, but this coincidence of results shows that the habit of watching television news and watching it on one of the very few national outlets available is shared by the whole country.

We also asked about sources of news about Chechnya. To this, 81 percent said that they tuned in to the national news channels. What is interesting is the composition of the "other sources," which respondents were allowed to specify: 19 percent of the focus group participants wrote "other." Of this 19 percent, 60 percent said "people who fought there" and "other people."

Perhaps because the television audiences are not seen and are so often taken for granted, I wanted to let these groups of viewers explain at length and in considerable depth exactly how they understand the news, how their lives are lived, and what their values are. This book is not a study of media effects: it does not research the degree to which viewers are persuaded by the officials' news agenda on television. Nor is it a monitoring study: it does not seek to keep a running check, or track the audience's preferences, on television, their favorite anchors, their favorite shows, and how that has changed over time with new program repertories. Rather, it seeks to understand something that goes much deeper, changes far more slowly, and, in the end, is far more powerful. This question is: how do Russians process the news? To put it differently, Russian viewers are flooded every day with material coming from the television set. What methods have they devised to manage the volume, categorize, and store what is important to them, and recall it when needed? They obviously do not and can not proceed in this fashion

---

[7] *Johnson's Russia List*, 229, October 11, 2006, 2, "Russian Citizens' Use of Internet, Other Media Surveyed"; *Rossiyskaya Gazeta*, October 11, 2006, report by Yelena Yakovleva: "The Internet and the Person: Where Russia's Citizens Get their Information."

with every bit of information – or even most of it – to which they are exposed. Therefore, what mental processes distinguish what is to be stored or focused on with concentrated attention, and what happens to information that does not pass that threshold? Russian viewers may be sitting in front of the set watching the news, but that is far from invoking the instruments needed for processing it from the considerable resources in their tool box.

We know little to nothing about this critical first stage of processing. Yet the Russian government, the natural resource giants, and the moneyed bosses all behave as if they do know, and engage in practices that severely limit the information market and stifle the necessary diversity for democratic governance – and at a high price. Television is expensive, and most of these stations are hemorrhaging money.

Focus groups are disadvantaged in one important dimension in particular. They are not representative of the city, region, or country from which they are drawn. The mass-public opinion survey can make this claim, which is what makes it so valuable in tracking changes in candidate likeability or support for war, for example. In addition, surveying the number of "eyes" determines the ratings, which then form the basis of advertising revenue. Doris Graber[8] writes about mass surveys: "In the ordinary interview situation, where closed-ended questions predominate, people's thought processes are guided only in a limited number of directions. The few cues that are provided to assist in memory searches may not resonate at all with the respondents' memory structure." Focus groups, conversely, show that the typical interpretation of responses to key survey questions – to take one example, trust in state television and the desire for positive news – is quite flawed and that respondents often intend more or less the reverse of what they say. The rationale for the use of focus groups in cases like these is well described by Gamson, citing Morgan: " '[Focus groups] are useful when it comes to investigating what participants think, but they excel at uncovering why participants think as they do.' ."[9]

For our research, the mass-survey lacks the advantages of the focus group, even though it has the advantage of representativeness. For all

[8] Doris Graber, *Processing Politics: Learning from Television in the Internet Age.* Chicago, University of Chicago Press, 2001: 50–51.
[9] "Does 'Trust' Mean Attention, Comprehension and Acceptance? Paradoxes of Russian Viewers' News Processing," in K. Voltmer (ed.), *Mass Media and New Democracies.* London, Routledge, 2006.

their impressive contributions, some aspects of mass-surveys are inevitably problematic, as one finds with most methodologies. For example, self-reporting of exposure to television tends to be unreliable because of fading memory or revision as a result of subsequent events. Recall of exposure to partisan political material tends to be associated with support for the candidate. In any case, exposure, even if it could be reliably measured, cannot be equated with reception. Focus groups are particularly helpful in the analysis of viewers' construction of meaning from political messages. Chapter 6 shows that trust does not have the meaning one might suppose and is assumed in surveys, where it is usually a one-off question. Surveys, in addition to the usual problems of degradation of memory, have respondents trying to please the interviewer and "retrospective" answers that correct inattention to social duties (nonvoting turned into voting, for example). There are seemingly innocuous terms and questions that do not cross borders easily – especially when personal experience of commonly used abstract terminology denoting forms of democracy, checks and balances in government, categories of rights, etc. has so little in common with ordinary Western usage. Finally, the survey is a one-time question-and-answer (Q and A), with a stranger at your door or on your phone. The focus groups on which we base much of this study have a social setting, closer to life, where people do talk over questions and live in contact with each other. Over the course of two hours, the ten participants got to know each other fairly well.

The circle of the day: how important is television in Russians' lives?

Before anything can be concluded about television audiences, we must establish how important television is in the lives of ordinary people. One could look at the ratings numbers. The deficiencies of this approach are the missing qualitative dimensions: is anyone actually watching or making tea in another room; do viewers "talk back" to their sets in the words of Johnson (1970), arguing and disagreeing?[10] Or are they bored, vacant, diffident, and intermittent watchers? All of these options provide some information, but none tells us enough about the place of television in competition with other preferences in the lives of ordinary people.

[10] N. Johnson, *How to Talk Back to Your Television Set*. Boston, MA, Little, Brown, 1970.

In Russia, where television has very deep penetration, virtually every household has at least one set. If television is really important to people, it should be proven by its part of an entire system of daily activities. In other words, asking only about television-watching rips the activity out of context and it may not be possible to grasp what people would rather do and where television falls among the other priorities of daily life. To identify this study as an examination of why and when people watch television would push that activity into the forefront of their thinking and dampen the effects of other activities at work or home in daily life. It was especially critical to have the facilitator avoid cues that provoked instant replies and clichés, or yesterday's headlines, or typical formulae of the former Soviet era.

We therefore started with an introduction explaining that the discussion was to be about their lives and how they filled their time, and would prefer to fill it. There was no special emphasis on television. Life's everyday activities were displayed in the form of a large circle divided into seven equal wedges marked:

- *Work*
- *Reading newspapers*
- *Watching television*
- *Housework*
- *Going to movies and theater*
- *Using Internet (at work and/or at home)*
- *Spending time with children* (figure 1.1)

By giving each activity an equal part of the circle of their lives, the participants were stimulated to instruct the facilitator to increase or decrease the segments, depending on the life each one led. The circle had another advantage, as well: it brought up the question of *substitution*. To find out the real "costs" of any of the activities in the circle of life there has to be an understanding that time is not elastic, and that the expansion of one element results in the decrease of another. That brings up what will later be examined as *tradeoffs*. If one substitutes television for something else, what is it? Or if, on the other hand, the slice representing movie-going is reduced to enlarge watching television, is it possible to understand what activities come at the cost of others and how devoted the respondent is to them? It is more realistic to analyze television audiences in this fashion than to consider television in a world by itself and not within a system of competing activities and desires.

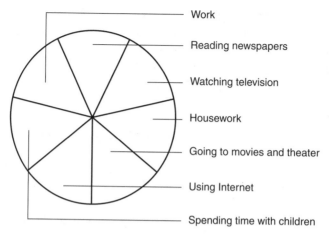

Work

Reading newspapers

Watching television

Housework

Going to movies and theater

Using Internet

Spending time with children

Figure 1.1 The circle of the day

Use of the Internet in Russia is increasing, especially in large cities: the largest proportions of people who use the Internet frequently as a source of information live in Moscow and St. Petersburg. Nonetheless, about a quarter of Russia's citizens use the Internet. Of them, 5 percent use the resources of the Worldwide Web daily, another 8 percent do so a few times a week, 6 percent a few times a month, and 4 percent only occasionally.[11]

Post-Soviets: youth, energy, and opportunities

Post-Soviet focus groups, presumably more carefree than their elders, should have the widest "play" among the slices of the circle, and that is true to a certain extent.

In *Moscow*, watching TV is listed by all; it usually comes in second or third. Most put work or (for college students) study in first place. In second place is newspaper reading and then using the Internet which, for most of them, is accessible only at their place of work. These last two mark them as different from other groups. They have more money relative to their expenses and more opportunities to consume newspapers and use computers. For all the young women in the group, housework is a major preoccupation, and, if they have children, taking

---

[11] W. Gamson, *Talking About Politics*. Cambridge, Cambridge University Press, 1992: 192.

care of them. Maxim (history teacher) and Viktor (tour manager) want to go to movies and plays but "unfortunately in recent times going to movies and theater doesn't work out." Then there is Oleg (man-about-Moscow), who does just about everything: he's an evening student and works and studies. "Then work around the house, reading newspapers, watching television. And sometimes I go to movies and theater because it's hard to have time on my hands."

Young people in *Nizhny Novgorod* are less likely to use the Internet (only two of them do). Work is always first, housework and watching television are next. Movies and plays are "periodically" available. Sergei (college student) says twice a week; Marina (a nurse) says once a week; Boris (a jurist) says once every two weeks; Alena (a math teacher) says once a month – "I wish it were more."

Going south to *Rostov* the young people have different preferences and many more constraints, especially time constraints. Work continues to be number one, then housework, then television or taking care of children. There isn't much else. These are young people, but they give the impression of older individuals, more loaded down with obligations. Dima (college student) says: "Well, probably work, work around the house and for all the rest either there's no time or one doesn't have children [yet]." Natalia (25, housewife taking care of her young child), says: "and then work, housework, of course, for that you don't always have to allocate time. Housework, you're on the go all the time." Two of the men mention looking for work as a major focus of their time. Three mention going to the movies, but one of them says he does it "very rarely."

Finally, there is *Volgograd*, where life for these young people seems very distant from Moscow. Alexander (21, college student) wants to go to movies and plays, "but it doesn't always work out." When asked how often he actually goes, he responds, "rarely." Vera (24, teacher) finds housework absorbing her time: "without washing dishes and floors; it's very hard to avoid." "Watching TV, it's on sometimes as though parallel to the whole rest of the day and sometimes we don't pay much or enough attention ... although I dig out of there some pieces from several programs." As for reading newspapers, "It works out, but not as much as I would want. Say, in a week, I can cut out a piece of time [for papers]. But going to movies and plays, that's generally a misfortune, a problem." For Misha (college student), television is substituted for plays and theater, "because there's not enough money, time, and opportunities." Evgeny (25, in the military), says that "work takes up practically all my time. Then television, but work around the house too. Then nothing. Reading newspapers – only in the tram do you have time, free time." Two members regard newspaper reading as part of their "minority" time, but they do it. Only two members of the group use the Internet. For almost everybody, it's the same three activities that take up the whole circle: work, housework or taking care of children, and television.

There are substantial differences among the opportunities these young people have. Volgograd was least endowed with political change and a vigorous media market. Television has a very high place in the lives of its young people. It is free, in the home where the children and housework are, and it can easily be consumed as a secondary activity, unlike the newspaper, which claims full attention. We move next to a less mobile group: high-school graduates.

High-school-educated participants: the day dims

It is *Moscow* where the post-Soviet younger generation enjoys much of what the metropolis now has to offer. The groups in this section have gone no further than high school; their career prospects and likely future earnings do not promise much mobility. These Muscovites sound very different from the young ones describing the segments of their lives. Here is how they adjust the circle of life: Lena (61, pensioner): "housework ... a lot"; Katya (53, housewife): "for me, too, basically housework"; Oksana (24, property surveyor): "TV"; Maxim (53, bookkeeper): "work"; Natasha (37, housewife): "work [understood as] housework"; Viktor (47, computer technician): "majority [of what he does] is work around the house"; Oleg (27, unemployed): "TV and work around the house."

As the group discussion proceeds, Galya (45, programmer) says: "Everything except using the Internet"; Yura (29, trainer/instructor) says the same: "also everything, except using the Internet"; Lena adds that she goes to plays; Oleg goes to movies; Yura goes to theater and watches television. Maxim, without indicating his own practice, says "movies are more expensive than plays"; Oksana lists housework and the Internet in equal shares and Maxim uses the Internet at work.

In *Nizhny Novgorod*, few in the group read newspapers, and if they do, they qualify it as "rarely." Only Alexei (30, working in industry) uses the computer as an aid to his study, but not, he says, the Internet. Viktor (62, a pensioner) has consigned his life to watching television: 10 hours of it daily. Going out? Going to the movies?: "Going to the movies? I don't remember when the last time was that I went. Television takes up everything." Zoya (61, pensioner) puts down her main activity as: "watching television. Sometimes, very rarely, I go to the movies. I read the paper very rarely." Only Anatoly (24, apartment handyman) spends his time mainly at work and then work around the house, says he doesn't watch television or movies.

The high-school-educated in our *Rostov* group has a simple trio of activities to fill up the circle: work, spending time with children (or housework), and watching television. As is so common with households everywhere, the television set is always on: it serves as company in an empty apartment; it is left on in case something interesting comes up; it is ideally suited to the performance of other activities around the house. As Olya (31, instructor in a women's health gym) puts it: "Even if I don't sit focused in front of the television, it's working in the background. My husband watches. The television [is on] all the time." For several, going to the movies and plays is said to be desirable, but when asked how often it actually happens, it can be none at all: as Igor (30) says: "for theater and movies very little time remains." One acknowledged it was once every three months. No one mentions the Internet.

In *Volgograd*, we see the same or even a greater narrowing of the circle. The trio prevails: work, housework (or time with children), and television. Alexander (63, pensioner) tells the group that he has a good deal of free time and spends it with his children and grandchildren.

College-educated participants: a better life, more options, and still devotion to television

From post-Soviets and high-school graduates, there are viewers with higher education and greater prospects for mobility. A college education is a significant step up the social mobility ladder in all four cities. With college education can come a better job and more money.

Moscow offers the most options, though work is still in first place by a sizable margin. Volodya (30, teacher) works 16–18 hours a day; Igor (37) 12 hours; Sveta (36, teacher) 10 hours; Maxim (23, systems operator currently out of work) usually works 8–10 hours a day. When the facilitator asks if they would prefer more or less time at work, all answer less, though Yura (22) qualifies his wish for less work by adding that "my work satisfies me so I don't experience any discomfort." Katya (31, secretary) says she's an "active woman" and would like more work.

When prompted about the place of the other segments of the circle, watching television and reading newspapers, the answers are practically those of addicts, except for Yura the iconoclast:

Oksana (45, dispatcher): Watching is usually constant, especially on holidays. It's that way because of the big New Year's [programs] . . . I'm simply sorry to miss something, especially movies. There are some interesting ones. And generally there is a demand to watch television, especially the news.

Ira (54, housewife): I watch every evening.

Lena (65, pensioner): So do I.

Maxim (28, entrepreneur): Television all the time. I can't live without it. I can't imagine myself without television.

Galya (43, supplier): Yes. Absolutely. As soon as I cross the threshold.

Katya: Absolutely.

Viktor (46, merchant marine captain): Everybody of course spends the time [watching].

Yura (22, student, with a novel approach): To my huge satisfaction it broke last year. I don't have it fixed on purpose. Because of this I have a lot of time, but in this case I try to watch sports news or some interesting programs in other places . . . at guests or at relatives.

There is something sobering about the dependence on television of these well-educated Muscovites. They live in the capital city; much is on offer; they acknowledge the time that both work and television absorb them. Yura tries to live without it, but still goes visiting to watch television.

Reading newspapers has nothing like the same emotion and thrill. For some, newspapers are still very expensive. Lena, who does read them, says: "I'd like it if newspapers were cheaper." Several others read them – or parts of them – at work or commuting on the subway.

Going to movies and plays is not difficult in Moscow, and most of the participants say they like such entertainment. Two women in the group say they go out to movies or plays. But that is far from the norm in these groups. In the Soviet era, plays and films – of defined content – were considered part of high culture, no longer the privilege of only the bourgeoisie but available to all. With that opening to the population came the obligation to attend. I recall a vivid example of this cultural evangelism: the great pianist, Emil Gilels, had to give a concert in the unattractive auditorium of a provincial cement factory just before the winter holidays. The local Communist Party secretary came on stage, stuck his chest out and proudly introduced the master, trailing behind him – and continued to talk – and talk. Soon it was no longer about Gilels but about the Party, the production plans, the shining light of socialism. Gilels was now impatient. The audience of workers, shamed and embarrassed, solved it themselves. As soon as the Party Secretary intoned a sentence, wild applause broke out. Evidently pleased, the secretary continued, but to his surprise, the applause came back while he was speaking. He was unable to speak through the massive waves of noise (yet could not object or punish). The burly pianist threw his arm around the politician's shoulder and forcibly walked him off the stage. The ovation from the audience was spontaneous and deafening.

The concert was an example of what all social classes *should* be brought to understand and appreciate. But it was not to everyone's taste. Actually hardly any of the cement workers seemed to like it. It was the end of the week; the winter holidays were approaching, and the workers were anxious to have their own parties, apparently starting right after the concert. They talked and walked up and down the aisles while the concert was going on. Gilels appeared to take no notice and gamely went on with his program.

Many focus group participants still retain this normative outlook from the Soviet era, but do nothing about it – except rhetorically. They continue to call it "important" to go to movies and plays, but behavior diverges for many:

Volodya: For me it's important . . . [it doesn't work out] probably sometimes because of laziness.
Maxim: I'd like to, but it doesn't work out.
Igor: You know, in general it's important. But it's necessary to find the time.
Natasha: It's necessary to go to theaters and movies. Movie theaters are not significantly fewer. It's more I think the youth who go . . . in the past century [one went] practically every week. That is, no matter how tired you were it was necessary for our generation . . .; . . . it was necessary.
Oksana: It's all important, only it doesn't work out for me. I even wanted to complain that I wanted to go more often but it doesn't work out.

In *Nizhny Novgorod*, unlike the groups in Moscow, the Internet figures in the discourse. Tanya (50, teacher) reads electronic versions of newspapers; Antonina (24, graduate student) uses the Internet; Alexander (48, state employee) uses the Internet at work, because he has access to a computer there; Andrei (35, engineer/programmer) has as his priorities work, Internet, television, and work around the house; Marina (43, employee) has almost the same mix: work, television, housework; then Internet, newspapers, movies and theater get "about 1–2 percent." Liuda (52, physician), unlike anyone else, does everything in the circle, although she's given up newspapers to read fiction and political analysis. She gave up reading newspapers, she says: "because, honestly speaking, I hardly trust our newspapers at all." A different Liuda (40, children's teacher) has largely replaced the newspaper with television:

Probably, the use of the Internet and going to movies and theater so often have been sharply reduced. And I read newspapers once or twice a week, but not daily. As for the rest, it's naturally, daily … I prefer the news [on television]. I like NTV a lot. I watch it with pleasure. So from 7:00 p.m., I'm freed from housework and I can freely turn on the television and watch what happened today. Before, we read newspapers daily, but now I can read newspapers only about twice a week, but I watch the news daily.

These are markedly different people than either the post-Soviet or the high-school-educated participants. They have a much wider involvement in the world around them – especially in Moscow – not least, because so many have a computer at work from which they can access the Internet. Yet, for all their education and access to more resources housework and looking after children for women and long hours of work for men and women limit their consumption of most of the activities in the circle of daily life. Only television requires neither money nor constant attention, and it sits in the top trio of occupations.

The *Rostov* groups had a heavier concentration of participants who named only work, housework, and television. Natasha (28, teacher) put it this way: "work – practically all work, practically all the rest of the time is housework. There is nothing whatever left for going to cultural programs." The workplace can also offer a devious way to read the newspaper, which is read in company time and without spending money. Angela (31, operator) says: "at work you can read the newspapers, I won't hide that, but not watch television." Some of the participants from other groups confessed that they read the newspaper while appearing to work.

In *Volgograd* the winters are long and harsh: the snow that falls in October may never melt until spring. Thoroughly rebuilt after its destruction in the Second World War, the streets are wide beyond human proportions and the first-floor windows of the massive buildings are higher than one's head. Yet Volgograd is an active, if overly traditional city, still tied to its long Communist Party leadership. It is also not faring well in the new market-competitive atmosphere of the country. Among the well educated, there is a pattern. Alexei (22) gives as his top three activities, work, the Internet, and watching television. He says he cannot live without them. Using the Internet is part of his job. Mikhail (52, programmer) also uses the Internet, but the rest do not. For them, with minor variations, it is work, housework and looking after children, and television. Galina (32, economist/manager) has a husband who "likes television very much," she says, "and living with him, sometimes I get very overwhelmingly tired of television and my husband ... I get very tired of TV, because it's practically never off. I have to do all this work around the house accompanied by watching TV. I pay attention but only a little." Sergei (41, employee), the ultimate fan, says that television is among his top activities: "since there is a TV set in each room and even in the kitchen, so that there is time to watch television before work and also in the evening when there's time to watch." Movies and theater get limited attention.

Why do Russians consume unsatisfying news so avidly?

Russians, as most television consumers, choose both entertainment (including sports, game shows, documentaries, films, and all the rest) and news. Most people enjoy a mix. Some people cannot bear to watch the news, either because of the depressing pictures they see or the boring repetition of items they know and care little about. On the whole, Russians consume a great deal of news. It is common to hear elites in Russia, perhaps especially those in the industry, say that people are tired of news and want to relax with entertainment, and that the proportion of news transmitted should be reduced. Yet, as the ratings show, national news does very well across the whole of Russia and in Moscow. Why? Is this a matter of outdated socialization or of contemporary preferences?

Looking first at the post-Soviets in Moscow, the main division is between entertainment programming and news. Katya (23, cashier for a publisher) opts for news over all else, because of the uncertainty and violence of life:

Basically to get some given information. That is, really when in recent times in Russia, something happens and not only in politics and economics, but even simply elemental catastrophes and so forth, crises, conflicts, etc. In principle, I need these data to know what's going on. Usually, for this reason. Sometimes I simply like to watch a film that's really worth it. And very rarely entertainment programs.

Julia (20, student) watches the news unless she can see an entertaining film on her day off. Oleg (25, working and studying) watches "basically the news." He says it's important to know what's happening and when asked why, he says: "to evaluate the situation helps one to live." Julia adds a more dire reason: "Suddenly the country is destroyed while we're sitting." Lena (24, translator) ponders the larger issue of the news she watches:

In the news, lots of different things happen, but, you know, somehow the theme changes more quickly, the coverage changes, because you don't have time to experience a deep [feeling] of shame for the people who appear. Although sometimes they also show some politician or other of ours, who, frankly, talks such nonsense. You think, it would be better to turn it off right away. But because we are watching news, personally I watch from curiosity. But at the same time it gives me nothing practical. I don't understand the economics; I don't get the politics. And when they show about the president, I love to watch the interviewers. There they are, meeting in all those palaces . . .

All of the group watch the news; even when they're watching a film, the news comes on regularly. So far, they have expressed their interest in the news in terms of personal utility – to be better prepared for unexpected changes in the political and economic environment; the price of foreign currency or, as Maxim (23, history teacher) asserts: "there is a natural pull toward knowledge." Ivan (21, studying jurisprudence) watches the news, because he can't help it; the television set is literally ". . . on all the time. It constantly works . . . By habit we turn it on, and it's very difficult to turn it off. That's our habit."

In chapter 4 among some post-Soviet viewers – especially in Moscow – there is a disturbing lack of empathy or even downright contempt for others in Russia who are the subjects of natural disaster stories. There have been numberless cases of mining catastrophes, floods, and plane crashes, so the daily scene is often a *cri de coeur*, but perhaps that

constant diet has encouraged the sense of preferred isolation in which
the capital basks. That alienation and feeling of superiority come out in
our questions as well. Lena is annoyed by the constant menu of explosions and floods on television news. The facilitator asks if they (those
affected) are responsible for the floods. Lena:

Of course, because it turned out they were not ready for winter. They weren't
even ready for floods from melting snow. It's like that all the time ... Yes,
it's them – it's them. I, for example, absolutely do not feel anything in
common, nor with the people who live in our South, where the Kuban
overflowed ...

I am I. I live in Moscow. I consider that Moscow is a state within a state. It
has nothing in common with the rest of Russia. That's why when I say "we"
I have in mind Muscovites. When foreigners ask, say, what is your opinion
there or what is your average wage, or do you have something or other,
I answer them, without a second's hesitation, I answer: "well, that isn't true
because I don't have an understanding either about what they think, or about
what they say, not about Yekaterinburg, or about Sakhalin. What they get,
how they live, I haven't the faintest idea."

Boris (25, the jurist from Nizhny Novgorod) tries to explain why he
watches: "for me it's important, of course, to know what's going on in
the country and the world. Why? To know; I don't know ... to put it
coarsely: a war could start and I wouldn't know, it's illustrative ... I'm
just saying that something new happens in the country and I don't
know anything. Except for work, I don't see anything." Even if some
would rather watch light entertainment, there is a sense of obligation.

Rostov post-Soviets have a wider range of programs that they watch.
They like movies; one says that once he surfs to MTV, he's mesmerized
and can't leave it. Some would rather be entertained than watch the
news. Yet there is a sense of obligation and even guilt about missing the
news. Natalia says that "in our house the day is lost if you don't watch
the news. You already begin to feel ill at ease."

The young Volgograders prefer movies, serials, and entertainment
programs. Denis, Evgeny, and Alexandra all want to relax. Vera sometimes comes home "in such a mood" and "our news is mostly negative
stuff," that she wants to watch an entertainment program. On week-
ends and days off, they are particularly interested in entertainment. If
Denis spends about half of his television time watching the news,
Alexandra spends only 10 percent, and Vera perhaps 20 percent, and
certainly not as a daily news consumer. The most motivated is Misha

(24, student in an institution of higher education in Volgograd), who lives in the countryside without television and who is desperate to see the news whenever he's a guest of someone with a set. He figures it works out two to three times a week that he can see *some* news. His passion for the news – a scarce element for him – elevates it to the highest importance.

The college-educated

Participants talk about their *preference* for news in spite of the *constrained* time making their viewing limited. To put this in context, they were asked how important housework was for them. Lena, Volodya, Olga, Maxim, and Irina (all Muscovites) say it's absolutely "required," "the most basic [task]," and (from a man) "it's not only for women that it's important."

Andrei (35, engineer and programmer from Nizhny Novgorod) has the temperament and experience of a "news detective." Whether a holdover from the past, or an adjustment to new and unpopular policies, some members of focus groups spoke specifically about their procedures for putting together data that was clearly insufficient in one source – and may not be solved by several – so that some degree of information discovery can take place. Andrei watches all the different newscasts on different channels he can in order to "create for himself some kind of picture." He also usually buys two newspapers. Vladimir (59, unemployed, from Nizhny Novgorod), who watches a number of different news programs to form his own picture, says: "I can't miss the news." Liuda (52, doctor, from Nizhny Novgorod) is the same kind of "news detective": she watches the news at home daily on three channels (two from Moscow) "to create for herself some kind of representation because they present the news differently." Olya (47, bookkeeper, from Nizhny Novgorod) watches the news even when she's busy: "to learn something, what happened in the country on this day." Oksana from Moscow watches the news on different channels to compare them. Vika (41, biologist) has a son in Rostov who is another "news detective." He is 17 and expects to be treated as an equal. So, for them, watching the news is not a passive activity, as Vika says: "basically, we watch the news together, information programs, information analysis. We discuss it, we fight about it, we agree." They talk about the news soberly and without affect. Television as a secondary activity, as a background drone, is pervasive, especially for the person (usually, not always, the woman) tied to housework and child care. Mostly, watching television is a 50–50 affair: half news, half entertainment.

It's good to be young and live in Moscow. It's better if you haven't started a family yet. There are plays and wide-screen movies on offer; there are bars and clubs; people congregate at night. It is these young people who can sample most of the activities in the day's circle of possibilities. A combination of place, age, and obligations provide access. Moscow is one of the most expensive cities in the world; the many options that young Muscovites sample in the big city are not so available to others. As some of these young people say, they consider themselves to live on an island detached from the rest of Russia, and they have no interest whatever in what goes on outside their island of superior opportunities and taste. Is this outlook a matter of age and the life cycle? In these groups, the participants also declare their interest in going to the movies, the theater, and reading newspapers. Some manage to do it, but for most it is once a month or once every three months, if at all. As one of the participants remarked, movies are expensive. This is no longer the subsidized world of Soviet days, when all forms of entertainment carried messages of political education and were priced to be available to all. In the other cities there are fewer choices: it is television that fills in their lives, with its feature films and sports, news, and analysis programs.

At the very beginning of the session, when the focus groups first saw the big circle, participants pointed out which activities they liked to do. Many of them have jobs where they must use a computer, and some go beyond their work requirements to explore the Internet. There are others who cite very high Internet usage, who prefer to read newspapers online. They are not a majority of the groups but most of the time when they talk about Internet use they put it at the top of their preferences, perhaps first or second. All of the other activities were named, especially going to movies and theater. These were virtually compulsory during the Soviet era. When individuals began to talk about how they spent their time, *movies or plays* no longer featured in the conversation. Sometimes they would then explain that it was too expensive or difficult to go very often; sometimes the facilitator would prompt by asking how often they went and the answer might be very little. Here again, the first answer that emerged came from the decades-long Soviet-era value hierarchy assigning entertainment forms from low to high culture. Patience, endurance, and hard work are essential; the participants, except for Moscow youth, are themselves sobered by their own accounts of their lives – the endless work on the job or at home, looking after children, a family budget too tight to go out to the movies. The one joyful and engaging activity costs nothing, it fits in a box. Only focus groups could deliver this world, a large part of which was very emotional.

It is patently clear that whatever the city of residence or level of education or gender, television is such a central part of life that only work and taking care of one's children can make a greater demand on the Russians in our groups. Being young and in Moscow and unencumbered by familial responsibilities can broaden the choices and Moscow, the most dynamic city in the country, has more to offer. It is, thus, especially fitting that we investigate how ordinary Russians watch television and what cognitive practices help them to process the news. Russians are wholly wrapped up in this medium, far more than any other medium and more than any other activity in their lives.

The media landscape in Russia

Newspapers

Unpacking the processes used by television news viewers would be of less importance if viewers were intermittent and unenquiring television watchers. That is not what we see in the focus groups. Television is at the center of the time available during any twenty-four-hour period. For most people, especially outside the capital, television trumps newspapers, even though participants appear slightly ashamed when they say they rarely read the paper. The newspaper occupied a place of great honor and importance during the years of Soviet rule; it is what Lenin used to mobilize readers into a party. Newspapers were posted on boards for anyone to read; each firm or factory had its own "wall newspaper." Newspapers now have two disadvantages: they demand full attention to texts, and the extremely heavy subsidies that made the big newspapers so cheap in Soviet times have been withdrawn. Nor are there discounts for distribution by mail. All that makes newspapers relatively expensive – a purchase that one must think about. It is true that some newspapers are partially subsidized by the government, but not the politically interesting ones in Moscow.

There are newspapers that have had iconic status (like *Pravda* in Soviet times) or *Moscow News* (in the glasnost reforms under Gorbachev). Russians traditionally have been a nation of readers. For decades, entering the subway felt like entering a library. At a meeting in 2006 in Moscow, world press leaders criticized President Putin for narrowing press freedoms. Putin responded robustly: "'I have different data,'" he said. "'The state's share in the Russian press market has continually declined, which is easy to verify, whereas the number of publications is continuing to grow.' He asserted that there were 53,000 periodicals in Russia today. 'It was simply impossible to control all of them, although he admitted there was an ongoing struggle between the state's interests and freedom of speech.'"[12] Immediately, articles surfaced about the true status of those tens of thousands of "politically free" newspapers.

Included in the figure of 53,000 used by Putin, there are only five newspapers with a decent circulation. Most are owned by friends or clients of the government, i.e. large companies. They may even be considered to be in government hands, because the owners are so close to the government. The picture looks like this:

- *Rossiskaya Gazeta*: pro-Kremlin, circulation 374,000
- *Izvestia*: pro-Kremlin, circulation 209,000
- *Komsomolskaya Pravda*: pro-Kremlin, circulation 686,000
- *Argumenty i Fakty*: pro-Kremlin, circulation 2.9 million
- *Moskovsky Komsomolets*: pro-Kremlin, circulation 800,000.

By and large the main newspapers have been bought by friends of the Kremlin, except for one foreign-owned group that publishes two free English-language papers of high quality and a daily business paper. As for the rest of the thousands of publications, some of the most respected observers in Russia stress that the Kremlin cares little about most of them: "'The vast majority of periodicals the President was referring to are of an entertainment nature and do not need to be controlled by the government,' said Igor Yakovenko, head of the Russian Union of Journalists."[13] Alexei Simonov, the authoritative head of the Glasnost Foundation, noted that the smaller papers received much of the money they needed from regional governments

---

[12] *Johnson's Russia List*, 229; *Rossiyskaya Gazeta*, October 11.
[13] RIA Novosti, "Putin Urges Greater Media Responsibility at Moscow Press Summit," June 5, 2006. Reprinted in *Johnson's Russia List*, 130, June 6, 2006.

(also supporting government policy). One could add that another source of revenue and influence in the region are big firms operating there (often exploiting natural resources). Simonov singled out from this vast group three regional papers able to retain independence: "'*Chelyabinsky Rabochy*, AltaPress, and Leonid Levin's Yakutia-based media group'." In another corrective note to the expansive picture drawn by President Putin, well-known journalist Evgenia Albats compared her professional life as a reporter in the late 1980s with today, the sense of going after any story earlier, but being more careful under the present government: "'Now when newspapers report the news, they do it with a great deal of caution, and it is now impossible for reporters to conduct any investigations since there is no access to information of any governmental agencies'."[14] Even Rafael Akopov, one of the biggest newspaper publishers, said that up to 90 percent of the Russian newspapers are subsidized by state structures or private investors. And the sponsors usually treat the publications as a political resource and do not require that their projects pay for themselves.[15]

Radio

Radio has portability, like a newspaper, and can be used as a secondary activity, like television, and these are valuable features for a medium used while driving. A poll conducted by a respected Moscow firm found that 75 percent of the polled preferred television to other mass-media sources, mainly Channel One and Channel Rossiya (Channel Two); another 15 percent preferred radio stations; and 10 percent preferred newspapers, magazines, books, and the Internet.[16]

Radio has found niche audiences, as it has in the United States; different kinds of music appeal to different age groups and sexes. Is radio a competitor? Can it attract large populations to whatever news is produced (and it is mainly headlines)? Radio was once in the glasnost *avant garde*; it broadcast provocative and hard-headed commentary; it

---

[14] J. Page, "Fears for a Free Press as Chelsea Boss 'Takes over Paper'," *The Times (UK)* June 8, 2006. Reprinted in *Johnson's Russia List*, 132, June 8, 2006, 12.

[15] *Johnson's Russia List*, 229; *Rossiyskaya Gazeta*, October 11.

[16] O. Yablokova, "Newspapers Passing into Hands of Kremlin Allies," *Moscow Times*, June 7, 2006. Reprinted in *Johnson's Russia List*, 131, June 7, 2006, 1.

was a fighter for glasnost and, in the words of the mythical Monty Python: "knew how not to be seen." That is no longer its goal; music is. In general, local media are under pressure from both the political and economic powers in the region. The station Echo of Moscow is completely different: even though the natural gas industry giant Gazprom owns it, its stubbornly principled director has refused to give in to censorship and organizes debates and gives time to all parts of the political spectrum. Alexei Venediktov should be recognized for carrying out the most intelligent balancing act of total integrity. He has chosen "to be seen," and his wild hair, as though electrically charged, classifies him as a *bona fide* public intellectual. As always in the Russian media sector, time horizons are notoriously short. Always excepting the Echo of Moscow, radio is not a real competitor for the public when compared to television, and no other mass-medium is either.

Television

It is television – no matter how middle- or low-brow – that captures the largest and most heterogenous audience. As such, it has had a highly charged history packed into a very short period. In 1993, the Soviet-style state-operated and state-owned television system became a limited market in which, for the first time, the state competed with commercially run networks. By 2002, when this study was in the field, the television news landscape was dominated by six Moscow-based networks: Channel One, theoretically a public–private hybrid but actually a state-controlled station with the greatest penetration and ratings; Channel Two, directly owned and operated by the state; Center Television, the station owned and controlled by the city of Moscow – or, rather, by its very powerful mayor – with limited national penetration; NTV, the largest commercial network; TV-6, another commercial, less widely received station; and REN TV, the channel with the least penetration. In 2000, NTV was forcibly taken over by its largest stockholder, Gazprom, an ally of Russia's president. Many of NTV's staff went over to TV-6, then under tycoon Boris Berezovsky's control, and became the transplanted opposition arm of television news. It, too, was crushed by presidential disapproval, hasty court decisions, bankruptcy, and closure. Months later, it tried to re-emerge as TVS, with the same leadership and some of the familiar on-screen personalities but with an inadequate set of quarreling investor–directors, a hugely reduced audience, and perilously low advertising revenue. By the summer of 2003, after TVS had closed down, all that was left of national network television news were three channels (One, Two, and NTV), all owned either wholly or in part by the state or by large energy companies close to it. When this study was in the field, there were still four networks, and it was still possible for viewers to access external diversity in the news.

The dominance of the national networks over news consumption has remained remarkable. As noted above, the weakness and limited penetration of the newspaper market has contributed to the dependence on television for news and information for the mass-audience.[17]

The landscape would not be complete without some sense of the legal culture in which it operates. For the media to function effectively as producers of news and public affairs, legal protections and the legal culture that supports them should be in place. At its most developed point, diversity of viewpoints on Russian television news came in the form of external diversity – each channel had its own political agenda. Beyond that, some news is actually bought and paid for or planted by interested parties. The payments may be made for attention being drawn to something advantageous (covering the opening of a commercial plant or a press conference during an electoral campaign) or spinning an event in favor of the sponsor, or to something disadvantageous, such as killing a story. Sergei Yushenkov, first in television administration and then in the Defense Committee of the State Duma, told me that no television station (including state TV) would carry his press conference without being paid; later Yushenkov was assassinated. During election campaigns there are even rate sheets describing the prices for the various media outlets, not just for ads but for news coverage as well.[18]

Speech protections are included in Russia's laws governing the press. However, they exist in a nascent, uneven legal culture in which enforcement is neither predictable nor uniform, and interpretation is far more variable than desirable. The media sector can thus depend neither on the weak judiciary nor on effective governmental regulatory

---

[17] Yablovkova, "Newspapers."

[18] Y. Vlasova, "All Quiet on the Mass Media Front," *Rossiyskaya Gazeta*, May 15, 2005. Reprinted in *Johnson's Russia List*, 9150, May 16, 2005, 8.

structures, and the media market is left without rules that are applied impartially across the country. This weakness affects the granting of broadcast licenses,[19] reporters' access to information, war reporters' access to war zones, slander and libel cases, and protection of investigative journalists and their work.

Russia is one of the most dangerous places for journalists to work. The killing fields of Chechnya have taken many lives. Death threats and murders of Russian journalists have served as warnings to desist, or to drop their investigative reporting. Dmitry Kholodov, an investigative newspaper journalist, was sitting at his desk opening a package when the parcel blew up, killing him instantly; it was rumored that he had been investigating corruption in the military. Vladimir Listyev was one of a quartet of young men who started a late-night talk-cum-news show in the Gorbachev period. It was something entirely new in Soviet television and Listyev rose in the industry so that in the new Russia he was charged with leading the largest television network. His agenda began with overhauling the advertising system. A lot of advertising money flowed around the television market and into private hands. Advertising was the key to television power and much of it was carried on in the shadows; shortly after his appointment, Listyev was shot dead at his apartment building. Paul Klebnikov (an American of Russian extraction) went to Moscow to open a bureau of *Forbes* magazine. He had been working in the main US *Forbes* offices as an investigative reporter, publishing an article on Boris Berezovsky, virtually accusing him of ordering Listyev's death. Berezovsky sued in London, and *Forbes* lost, and full-page ads apologized to Berezovsky, as ordered by the settlement: Berezovsky did not ask for money. Klebnikov wrote a book on the same subject and then went to Moscow to continue his work there; not long after his arrival, he was shot dead. In the regions, more journalists and editors have been killed. Anna Politkovskaya was killed, execution-style, in her apartment building in Moscow, in 2006, a contract killing. Politkovskaya was one of the bravest of investigative journalists, very well known, outspoken, forthright, and she was on the trail of what was happening in Chechnya.

---

[19] ITAR-TASS, "Putin, Mass Media Top Positive Rating List – Poll," May 23, 2006. Reprinted in *Johnson's Russia List*, 121, May 24, 2006, 4.

It seems to some Russian journalists that solidarity should go far toward constraining the violence and coercion and curb the ease with which local officials have pressured regional media organizations. There are two unions: the long-established Journalists' Union of Russia and the Media Union. The former, which has remade itself since Soviet days, publishes valuable information about the national scene and helps regional journalists. The Media Union was begun with the sponsorship of President Putin and the leadership of producer, actor, and director Alexander Liubimov to drive a wedge into the old Union. The expected clash may not take place and the old Union remains just as vigorous, if not well endowed. However, that still does not mean that there is a strong protective and aggressive defense for all journalists and for principles of diversity and the free press at every level.

In July 2005, Vladimir Putin decreed the formation of the Public Chamber, a body of 126 people, appointed in various ways but easily kept from genuine power by the President. One part of the Chamber was to take up issues relating to advice about the media. The appearance of the Chamber may be thought of as another occasion on which to co-opt some media figures who believed that slow steady oversight, even without political power, might still influence the press. Others in the Chamber came from very different political persuasions. As in much of the story of the media in Russia, collective action is overwhelmingly difficult to achieve: journalists are not a professional body with a sense of a common mission and common standards. There have been letters signed by a number of famous journalists decrying conditions, but they have been very few.

Television, negotiating messages, and control

Does the individual or family have enough disposable income to access the Internet at home and go out to plays and movies? Judging by the contributions of many in the focus groups, income severely limits choices, even the choice to subscribe to a newspaper. This paragraph should perhaps have begun by stating what we all know, but often forget: television is free, although there may be subscription costs or taxes in the future, and the vast majority of viewers cannot afford satellite broadcasting. The Internet is extremely important for those who use it, and it is accessed for the most part at the place of work.

In the course of learning about preferred daily activities, a picture emerges of the ordinary life of ordinary people, and because it is focus groups that have been used a good deal of explanation and emotion can help us to interpret the picture. We preferred to do it this way – considering television and its "competitors" as an interrelated system adding up to "life."

Television plays an extraordinary role in people's lives. Before looking at the cognitive strategies people apply to television news, chapter 2 explores a unique skill that Russian audiences have, essential to aid their viewing power – I created the term "viewing power" to indicate a particularly effortful engagement with the news in order to extract the maximum amount of data in an environment of limited information. In a sense, all of the cognitive choices throughout this study are at least partially oriented to broadening this difficult environment, but chapter 2 begins with the most basic: the degree to which publics are able to distinguish one channel from another. Russian viewers have very different skills in "reading" news than do Americans, for the former, especially in Soviet times, had to squeeze out of very meager information the cues that might affect their lives. One of these skills is the ability to know a channel by its content, tone, or approach: it is important in post-Soviet Russia to arm oneself beforehand against the agendas of owners and to be ready to apply mental correctives. Viewers know well that "news stories" may be bought to support an economic venture or product; they also know that individuals buy news stories to make themselves into more visible players, or to back allies. Infomercials and VNRs are slotted into the news and treated by the correspondent or anchor as news. Purchased stories can also accomplish the opposite purpose: Defaming individuals and their ambitions.[20] The purchase of "news" is not confined to television; almost all media organizations want a cut of the revenue out there, nor is this form of corruption in the form of planted news something new:[21] biased news began with the first days of the new Russia. The price lists differ for each media organization, and for each

---

[20] E. Mickiewicz, *Changing Channels: Television and the Struggle for Power in Russia*, rev. and expand. edn. Durham, NC, Duke University Press, 1999.
[21] T. Tsyba, "'Cherny Yashchik' TV, ili chto mozhno uvidet za dengi," *Argumenty i Fakti*, 6: 30; Oleg Dobrodeyev, "Otkrytoe pismo Olega Dobrodeyeva Evgeniu Kiselevu," *Izvestia* September 4, 2001: 1.

time slot.[22] At a higher level of influence, each of the big Moscow-based networks is monitored by the government.

At the end of this chapter is a bar graph (figure 1.2) showing the penetration of each of the channels available at the time of our focus groups. ORT is Channel One and RTR (Russian Television and Radio) is Channel Two, both government-controlled or government-owned. NTV was the first private network with a substantial news operation. TV-6 started as a youth-oriented channel with little news. TV Center is a channel belonging to the mayor of Moscow. REN TV will be analyzed in chapter 7; it also was a private network. Figure 1.3 shows the ratings of each channel's news programs. It is fascinating that in Nizhny Novgorod a privately owned local news program is by a long margin the overall ratings winner. The program in question, *K Stati (By the Way)*, is a roughly put together digest of "stuff that happens." It covers a fire somewhere, then jump cuts to a lost dog; then perhaps something about a school, a car accident, etc. Though the production values are extremely low, and there is no narrative flow whatever or attempt at analysis, it is recognizably "our town," gossip and all.

Chapter 3 digs into that central event on television: the electoral campaign story. The Putin administration has been loath to permit television stations to disseminate views disagreeing with his policies. He and his associates in the natural resources fields – primarily energy – have closed down every important privately owned media organization that has opposed him. Election time is the most critical time: the wrong move, it is thought – a channel that disagrees – could presumably sink the entire administration and cause its defeat. It is at this time that the mass-media organizations, especially television with its huge audiences, cannot withstand the pressure applied to them and crack. When the station is shut down, the best journalists leave, the ratings plummet, and the revenue with them. It is an expensive operation buying all these networks, but business is not the primary motive. Once again, the viewer's reactions go unheard. Although it is sometimes done, it really is not accurate to assume that every vote is the result of a viewer persuaded by

---

[22] ABC's *Nightline* program spent a week in Moscow and broadcast pictures of rate sheets and both producer Jay Lamonica and the show found evidence of the practice. The same information came from the author's conversation with the head of public relations for the Yabloko political party, a "Western-style" liberal party.

a television campaign. There is every likelihood that the viewers' reactions are *antithetical* to presidential strategies. Chapter 3 asks: if the people in power are able to get their message across without fear of contradiction, how is it received on the other side of the screen? Isn't that the point of it all? Political consultants and candidates alike would be very surprised by the viewers' comments on their highly paid work.

In chapter 3, each of the focus groups looks at real news stories of an election that had national significance and coverage, but was distant from them. This prevents partisanship "drowning out" an examination of the processing path and instead permits us to see how the "election story" as such is received. Each clip of a naturally occurring news story is a different treatment from a different station of the election and the candidate. Because we were lucky enough to have been in the field both before and after TV-6 closed down, we could include a clip from that station as well, and thus introduce the effects of diversity of viewpoint. Since, as chapter 2 shows, Russian viewers have a singular capacity to identify television stations and their views, we made sure that for these election stories there was no trace of the name of the station: we covered up the logo; did not show well-known reporters; and the clips excluded the studio anchor. In this way, focus group participants could not use station identification to illuminate station content.

The same method for a different policy domain was used in chapter 4; the focus groups were shown clips of a major economic and technological success associated with the completion of an oil pipeline. The international ceremony of congratulation held near the end of the pipeline in Novorossisk, in southern Russia, plus information about the pipeline itself and the international consortium (including the United States) that paid for it, was featured on the national news. Again, without any identification of the channel, these clips were shown to the focus groups to help us to understand the theoretical question we had set ourselves about tradeoffs. Tradeoffs in any area of life are difficult to communicate and to think about. They involve the conflict between two or more core values and are thus unpleasant to contemplate. They challenge the kind of "you can have it all" attitude we have grown used to. Campaigning on clarifying tradeoffs in policy is not exactly a politically winning platform; one learns what must be sacrificed to achieve the other goal, and although that is surely more honest it is also politically debilitating. Americans live in a media environment in which information about tradeoffs is scarce; Russians live in a media news environment where tradeoffs can be so totally absent as to leave not the slightest hint of their presence behind. We used the different treatments of the oil pipeline opening to test the cognitive response to the tradeoff issue, even when it was absent in the story.

We "want it all": we do not want to face a choice between competing core values, and so we don't. No politician who wants to be re-elected will run on a platform of what we need to give up, and voters prefer not to think about the necessary sacrifices. In our pipeline study, the first three treatments of the event have some differences. All of them suppress any possible note of sacrifice, tradeoff, and discomfort. All three are stations toeing the government line. So far, for the focus groups, this is the world of television without diversity of viewpoint; the world they would soon face in a week or so. We can thus analyze what happens to the notion of tradeoffs – never brought up as such by the facilitator – absent opposition ideas. This is not an unfamiliar situation for most of our participants; however, in this exercise we can look at both discourse with no diversity and, thanks to the timing of the project, discourse with diversity. TV-6 was on its last legs but as long as it was on screen it was as feisty as ever and it, too, covered the opening of the pipeline at Novorossisk. The discourse reveals a number of individual strategies for processing news; their very breadth is unexpected.

Many mass-opinion surveys ask Russian respondents which television channel they trust most: the answer is usually Channel One. It is not uncommon to take this expression of trust and convert it into an independent variable to be tested for the degree of association with other factors, including the usual demographic ones (i.e. what has the highest degree of association with trust?). Equally, it could be placed among the dependent variables in which trust in Channel One is analyzed among other variables to explain variation in the independent variable, such as voting behavior. Chapter 5 includes a look at what Russians *mean* when they see a story on Channel One and then tell pollsters or our facilitator that they "trust" this story. Here, again, we use a story from the most highly watched channel (Channel One) which is also the one people give on surveys as being that they trust most. It turns out, as chapter 5 demonstrates, that in these cases – of evaluating a television story just seen – "trust" means something quite different. It turns out to be a form of trust, if that is the correct word, that has virtually no power to help the brain to generalize, to distinguish categories of information and give them meaning.

From trust it is a short distance to the use of the word "objectivity." The journalistic profession everywhere and all the time deals with this recurring dilemma. Today's Russians, since they know the source of the story and have the watching habits described earlier, also have their own understanding of objectivity, something I would call "functional objectivity" under difficult circumstances and demanding considerable effort from the viewer.

During the early years of the transition to a different political system, at times, life was very difficult: food was in short supply; elderly people could not live on their fixed pensions even before inflation made them trivial. When, earlier in this chapter, people spoke of work and television as the sum of life, they depicted a hard life. One heard about the Soviet period when, though many products were in short supply and poorly made, at least the allotment was regular. To get some purchase on the innovations of the present – the collapse of the Soviet Union and all it implies – it is helpful to see how a Soviet institution is thought of at present. Naturally, the Soviet institution we are interested in is one that has a counterpart today: television. The Soviet leadership, as chapter 1 points out, was attuned to television, not just to spread their own personal ambitions but also as a leading source of news for the population. Soviet television operated without having to watch the bottom line; it was a "*biudjetny*" organization – all its support came from the government budget, and they could always ask for more: no rubles were spared in the grand recreations of classic books and plays. By the same token, talking heads were frequently on, often discussing factories and agriculture. The new Russia brought in a television of fast-talking anchors; products from abroad, often of low quality and cheap, featuring sex and violence; advertising, music shows of gyrating rock bands and clones of "Wheel of Fortune" and "Larry King Live" (hosted by Listyev). This was one institution in two very different periods, so we asked our focus groups to write down three things that came to mind about pre-Gorbachev television, and then they were later discussed. This was in some ways a trip down memory lane, and it taught us about memory, its mutability under certain circumstances, and its connection with an age of childhood. At the end of this discussion, the facilitator asked if they wanted to replace today's television with that of the Soviet era. Another insight into how words are used and need interpretation in today's Russia is most starkly posed by a man who uses the word "censorship" three times in his brief comments, and, every time, it means a totally different thing. Examples like this – and there are very many – support the methods I used here of working always from the words people spoke in the focus groups, not translations. Going over the texts time after time, always retaining the context, always catching the coloration of black humor or sarcasm, has made it possible to catch the real meanings and dynamics in the group.

Chapter 6 of the book concerns endings. First, steadily failing TV-6 sought with increasing desperation for a way out of its legal and financial morass – and association with the President's enemy, Boris Berezovsky. Some participants said that the Kremlin could not shut down a television station: it's different now; it would be against public opinion. TV-6, the only station providing a different and opposing take on presidential policies, closed its doors one day and the next was replaced by a sports channel. Some in the focus groups remarked that the exercise of state power had forced the last remaining non-state station off the air. There was comment in the focus groups both before and after the event, a window on the reaction to the exercise of state power "in their face sold her minority share and left."

The second ending dragged on much longer. REN TV was owned by Irena Lesnevskaya, a highly principled woman who, with her son, Dmitry, ran the only national news television station not receiving money from the government. Her newscasts were commended by liberals and viewership in Moscow rose. Her largest investor then told her he would have to sell his shares (70 percent of the whole). Institutions close to the state purchased the 70 percent; Bertelsmann bought the remaining 30 percent. Lesnevskaya sold her minority share and left.

Figure 1.2 and 1.3 explain the differences in penetration for each channel or network in 2002. Channels One and Two blanketed the country, just as they did in Soviet times. NTV was well over the halfway point and heading towards 70 percent. TV-6 was a problem: due to obsolete transmission methods it was very difficult to get certain signals unless special equipment was available. When the focus groups discussed the imminent closure of TV-6, a number of people, especially from Volgograd, had never seen any programs on the station. REN TV was even more isolated. Less than a third of the country could receive its signals and instead used it for news capsules, with regional programming filling in most of the time. The emphasis in the book is on the big Moscow news networks, from where Russians take their news. REN-TV surfaces in chapter 6 because,

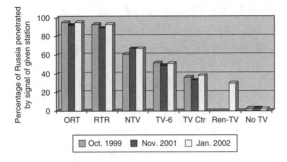

Figure 1.2 What channels can be received: survey of the Russian Federation, October 1999–January 2002, percentage of Russian Federation receiving news channels
Source: Public Opinion Foundation, Moscow

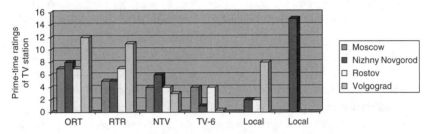

Figure 1.3 Prime-time ratings of news programs in focus group markets
Notes: In general, sports programs replaced TV-6 on its frequency after TV-6 was taken off the air. Some local stations used the frequency for part of the day for their own local government-controlled news.

The most popular Nizhny Novgorod local channel is *K Stati* (*By the Way*) on Seti NN, a commercial channel. It is purely local – featuring mainly human-interest stories, crime, accidents, and fires; hand-held cameras are used. *K Stati* also features "lost and found" features and includes a 5-minute, not very informative, news capsule from REN-TV in Moscow.
Source: TNS Gallup.

as the last of the commercial channels left standing, it, too failed in its desperate attempt to surface.

APPENDIX: FURTHER INFORMATION ON METHODOLOGY

The Public Opinion Foundation recruited focus group participants in two stages. The first – and basic one – was from the "respondent pool" constructed in cities in which the Foundation carried out its mass-surveys. As part of a regular, representative survey, information was collected on the respondents' socio-demographic profiles (age, sex, education, occupation, and others). This is necessary for the quality control of interviewers and validation studies. When there is a request for a focus group, respondents from this pool are given a supplementary questionnaire (by an interviewer or by telephone) and are told the time and date of the group meeting. When numbers are insufficient, the numbers are supplemented by "snowball" methods (participants recruit other participants and the numbers grow). Participants in a focus group are not eligible to participate in another until a year has passed, and are given a small payment.

In all but one of the focus groups ten people participated; one had eight. They came to a comfortable small room where they were offered tea and cookies. When they watched stories, they would often nibble on cookies, almost absentmindedly, as they would at home. Each person was given a first-name name tag (not their real name) and after a welcoming introduction by the Russian facilitator, the conversation began. The same facilitator traveled to all four cities and conducted all sixteen groups. She is the most experienced and successful facilitator in the organization, and someone with whom I have worked for over fifteen years.

Many mass-public opinion surveys and focus groups in Russia and the West have had to deal with hackneyed responses to questions that cued predictable and not very informative answers. For example, many Russian focus group and mass-opinion surveys include a question that asks something like: What role should television play in our society? As soon as the respondent hears it, Soviet official values come to mind. For Soviet citizens, as the doctrine went, every institution – family, school, court, job, and so on – should be enlisted in the mission of socializing society in the goals of collectivism over individualism and Soviet values over bourgeois ones. As this practice was doctrine, many times repeated, it was widely known. So, asking a respondent about the norms television ought to have in society often results in answers coming out fully formed from a previous time: the formation of the person with Soviet values; the betterment of society; inculcating worthy habits of selflessness and putting the Party first; forming better citizens to adopt collective character traits and eliminate greed and selfishness. I do not exclude the possibility that these might have been genuinely held beliefs among numbers of consumers of the media but, interestingly, they are absent from the discourse of most of the participants in the focus groups when we avoided these cues.

2 | Detecting channels

In the United States, for many years after television was introduced, the individual channel had little meaning for the audience: it was the program that was branded. Viewers would be unlikely to say, "let's watch NBC," or "let's tune in to CBS." Later, niche television was both a response to and a source for fragmenting the public by precisely targeting preferences with cable, satellite, and the Internet. The palette of the news among the "Big Three" networks (CBS, NBC, ABC) when they dominated the television scene – especially the news – differed little in choice and positioning of stories.[1] Perhaps it was only in the lightweight last story, presented as an audience-pleaser to keep viewers from changing the channel, that there might be some trivial difference. The original "Big Three" networks were sold and folded into large conglomerates where news was a very minor part of the product mix. Yet viewers' choices were still based on the program and not on the owners. Did viewers express their preferences when choosing Disney, General Electric (GE), Time-Warner, or other owners? Programs, music, films, and the rest could emerge from any platform and be transmitted by a range of people from seasoned journalists to bloggers.

Russian viewers follow a decidedly different strategy, in which knowledge of a station and a station's owners may be vital in deciphering what is meant to be a persuasive agenda. The Russian viewer comes equipped with a larger tool box of instruments for processing news than would the average American viewer, even though the rise of highly partisan and aggressive talk radio and cable talk shows presents a different model. It is an essential part of living defensively and squeezing out from limited information something they can call "objective." Russian and American

---

[1] P. Beck, R. Dalton, S. Greene, and R. Huckfeldt, "The Social Calculus of Voting: Interpersonal, Media, and Organizational Influences on Presidential Choices," *American Political Science Review*, 96(1), March 2002: 61.

definitions of commonly used words, like "objectivity," and the practices that follow from them, are very different.

President Putin, as head of government, consolidated as many media organizations as possible under his ultimate control and to serve his political interests. Before Putin came on the political scene and after Gorbachev had left it, the rich and politically ambitious first bought a media organization. Boris Berezovsky, the so-called "oligarch," currently in exile in the West to avoid jail at home, bought the controlling shares in Channel One; the mayor of Moscow bought himself a station and called it Center TV (see chapter 1). These are only two of numerous examples. Every day, the owner was shown repeatedly; he was, in effect, the "star" of the news. Because of the long-held official Russian belief in the power of television to imprint its message onto the entire viewership, the owner was thought to be in an excellent position to move into the Kremlin.

Viewers are not shy about characterizing individual networks on a wide range of dimensions. What they turned out not to know, according to a post-parliamentary elections national public opinion national survey I conducted in Russia in 1993, was the figure of the owner or boss of the channel. I was surprised by this finding, because at that time Boris Berezovsky was using Channel One daily to project himself and gain personal visibility for a possible run for the presidency. The strategy was one of constant visuals of the oracular owner – it seemed his face was everywhere on that pervasive network. In the survey, the interviewers asked respondents who was the head or owner of three channels: Channel One, RTR (Channel Two), and NTV. We made it as easy as possible: a name would do, but if it might be too difficult to recall specific names, a group of pictures was laid on the table (the "lineup" included television owners, entertainers, and others in public life), and the respondent was asked to pick the right picture; naming it was, of course, fine, too. Fourteen percent picked Berezovsky as in control at Channel One. For Channel Two, the directly state-owned channel, the correct answer (the Russian government or a variation of that answer) drew 7 percent of the responses. For NTV, 3 percent identified Gusinsky (the real owner) and 1 percent, Evgeny Kiselev, one of the founding partners and on-screen personality. No one got the network's President and third partner, Igor Malashenko. These responses were minuscule compared to the "Don't know" answers: for Channel One, 70 percent, for Channel Two, 86 percent, and for

NTV 86 percent could not answer.[2] Most of the small number of correct answers came from college-educated respondents in Moscow and St. Petersburg. Normally, there is no incentive for viewers to know who a channel's owners are. Under conditions of media consolidation in the United States, there are frequent references to owners, when media watchdogs (other media or nonprofit monitors) watch for correlations between content (or killed content) and owners' interests. In the case of Russia, when there was still a small diversity of owners, it was the path to the top that interested the owners; but for all their self-advertising, viewers were still not inclined to commit any of it to memory.

Choice and advocacy

In the Russian political environment, it does make sense for viewers to have a sense of which network they are watching, not just which program. During the Soviet era, they had got used to a total of two national channels, both loudspeakers for the government. After the dissolution of the Soviet Union, for the first time two private television stations with news-gathering capacity were awarded licenses. NTV's self-declared brand was news; TV-6 showed some news but was mainly a youth-oriented station.

In 1993, NTV was running some programs from St. Petersburg and by the end of that year had moved into prime-time slots in Moscow. Russians viewers now saw viewpoint diversity, even if it was often tied to competing economic and political interests. Viewers now had the chance to figure out for themselves how this setup would skew the news, so that they, in turn, could apply their own correctives. Instead of asking how channels differed in their treatment of news, a much more active and original strategy was to ask the participants to imagine news of a well-known topic. I did not want to solicit a description or evaluation of the stations in the abstract – people can be very free with attributing adjectives to generalities. Rather, I wanted to call for more work and more candid thought about these channels and their characteristics. We therefore chose two subjects and asked how each of the four channels might cover them. The subjects had to be ones that

---

[2] *Issledovanie, "Informatsionnye i analiticheskie teleprogrammy,"* Fond "Obshchestvennoe mnenie," Moscow, July 1998. This was a survey prepared by the author in collaboration with the Foundation.

had been in the national news for a reasonable length of time; the themes were chosen so that they did not evoke a particular partisanship. Just as we did not want to conduct this research before or after an election to try to have as "normal" a time as possible, uncontaminated by the ideology of partisanship, so we did not want to choose a subject that triggered polarizing political ideology, but still represented a topic of importance. Our purpose was to determine the instruments by which ordinary viewers processed the news; we did not want campaign and election passions in the mix.

Coverage of HIV/AIDS

The state channels

What Russian viewers expect from the news is part of the process of making sense of it, storing it, or ignoring and forgetting it. Members of the focus groups were asked to describe how the four channels would cover HIV/AIDS. In each of the cities, among post-Soviets, and for people with high-school and college education, there was across-the-board agreement that a line could be drawn; as Igor (26, college-educated analyst, Moscow) says: "for me there's RTR [Channel 2] and ORT [Channel 1] and on the other side NTV and TV-6." Most also said that ORT and RTR were "identical in presentation"; Andrei (23, economist, post-Soviet group, Rostov): "ORT and RTR give out Sovietism"; Maxim (53, high-school-educated bookkeeper, Moscow): "both stations are similar to the state position"; Viktor (46, college-educated merchant marine captain, based in Moscow when not on the high seas): "ORT and RTR are about the same"; Katya (59, college-educated, employed in the education system, Moscow): "I think ORT and RTR are the same"; Viktor (60, college-educated, pensioner, Volgograd): "I think RTR and ORT are close in information; these are old channels. They were government and that's how they've stayed." To a young person, such as Vera (25, teacher, post-Soviet group, Rostov), the two largest channels in Russia are dinosaurs: "ORT would be very traditional and banal; RTR, the same. This is all just echoes."

Everyone who spoke in the groups agreed that the two state stations were much more like each other than like any other station. AIDS is inherently a story of pain and suffering. Even hopeful signs are embedded in a much larger universe of dismaying and depressing growth in the numbers afflicted with the disease. It is particularly challenging to the state stations, because as high-school-educated Alexander (63, pensioner, Volgograd) says: "ORT and RTR are generally government channels and they do not like to go deeply and [squarely] into an unpleasant theme." The participants' discourse brought up the techniques that state stations use to minimize or camouflage the "bad news" and declared that none was an adequate approach to a very serious problem. They mentioned: shifting from coverage of human beings to lists of numbers; diluting the Russian situation by emphasizing the disease's global dimensions; concentrating on bureaucratic measures taken and nostrums for improvement; providing "naked" facts without context and short on meaning; low-key, calming and slow presentation; avoiding perturbing the viewers by softening the story.

Shifting coverage into numbers

Among the college-educated from Nizhny Novgorod, Marina (43, employee) says that a story would be covered: "with numbers and statistics"; Olga (47, bookkeeper): "on ORT"; Marina [on Channel 2]: "other numbers."

In Volgograd, Anatoly (56, College-educated, employee) says: "ORT and RTR are more official. They would have statistics and a speech by a minister." Almost all the participants in all the cities speak of coverage by the state stations as drier, and the endless and, for these viewers, unenlightening statistics.

Global dimensions of HIV/AIDS as an avoidance strategy

In our focus groups, Russians spoke of the state channels as reducing real and necessary news about HIV/AIDS in Russia by blending it in with HIV/AIDS as a global problem. Alexei (63, pensioner, high-school-educated) spoke of the nonstate channels examining the social dimensions of the disease, which matter more to him. Instead: "ORT and RTR are more on a world scale." Or consider Svetlana (39, high-school-educated, unemployed, Nizhny Novgorod): "ORT and RTR would have shown naked facts, nothing humane, naked facts." The diversionary use of numbers, lack of emotion, and remoteness from everyday Russian life help the state stations to carry out their chief mandate, according to our viewers: fidelity to and support of state policy and, relatedly, tamping down or, better yet, preventing mass fear and lack of faith in government policy.

Bureaucratic solutions

Focus group viewers expect the state stations to refer to bureaucratic policies in order to conceal real news. According to post-Soviet viewers in Moscow, the state stations would certainly not leave the impression that "it's alarming; we'll die." Rather, they would say "a committee has been created; everything is under control; there's nothing to worry about." On ORT, says Vladimir (59, college-educated, unemployed, Nizhny Novgorod): "On ORT, they'd say that the highest percent of AIDS infection is in Chechnya and the Caucasus. And do a survey right away." He adds sarcastically: "on ORT it's required to say what percent is infected in Belarus."[3] But a calming note is also there: for Andrei (35, engineer/programmer, from the same Nizhny Novgorod group) the story on RTR would show "how successfully we struggle ... I can simply really summarize: really on state television it would be the successes of our medicine and on the rest, let us say independent, channels there would still be really horrible facts." Masha (22, college-educated, unemployed, Rostov) says that ORT rushes through the story so fast "as though it's simply not there." Aleksei (college-educated, Volgograd) predicts that ORT and RTR "[lessened] some of the speed of the spread of AIDS ... they gave the impression that it was declining, so that general maximum outrage would be avoided." And as Anatoly (56, college-educated, employee, Volgograd) notes, ORT and RTR, being more official, present the statistics and can also trot out a member of government to give a "speech by a minister." Andrei (42, college-educated, entrepreneur, Volgograd) makes the trenchant observation – a weakness of journalism in many places – that on "ORT probably some political or social figure not connected with the problem of AIDS would declaim and questions would be posed to him. The program, 'Good Morning,' for example, they'd ask some musician

---

[3] This sarcastic comment refers to the virtual union between Belarus and Russia. Lukashenka, Europe's last dictator, is not a popular partner with the Russians, possibly even the government, which moves at a snail's pace to do anything significant to strengthen the union.

about AIDS." The state stations clearly have advantages not only in their size and penetration, but also in the people they can call on to appear on their news stories. The surprising conclusion from our focus group members is that they don't do it to maximum, or even minimal, effect. The ministers are boring; the words of celebrities are of no use in imparting information – this is, after all, a life and death issue. A rock star's blather doesn't seem to convince these viewers.

"Softening" the story

Another Andrei (35, our engineer/programmer, Nizhny Novgorod) contrasted the state stations' emphasis on success and victory over the disease, while the nonstate stations presented "some really horrible facts." The state stations wanted to reduce concern and reduce the likelihood of any anti-government backlash or collective action initiative. Yet, the state stations are caught in a paradox: they have to cover HIV/AIDS (though they are doing it less often, in the view of focus group members) – an epidemic which is by definition a story of dispiriting and sad images, the incidence of which is growing in Russia – and at the same time make it obscure through numbers, and less threatening by merging with world figures and by words of hollow confidence from a gamut of ministers down to entertainers. There is another strategy the focus group members frequently brought up: the state stations "smooth over the edges." These are their words, and suggest that in their judgment, at least with regard to coverage of HIV/AIDS, the state channels actually alter what they know to be true to give a false impression of security.

The nonstate channels

When the focus groups were being conducted, NTV had been taken over by Gazprom, the natural resources giant allied to the President. It had gone from a feisty, fearless, professional channel – the one that uncovered the first Chechen War, attracted the best reporters, and continually held up the government's weaknesses and false steps to the viewers. In fact, it was often at war with the government. It was a shock to many that the owner, Vladimir Gusinsky, offered the government a deal: postpone or cancel debts and stories would be pro-government. This severe violation of journalistic norms, this form of blackmail, had had its antecedents when NTV joined government Channels One and Two in a consortium to prevent the Communist Party from returning to power in the election of 1996. Gazprom (and probably the Kremlin) soon foreclosed on the debt and forcibly removed anyone who was working at the station the morning before Easter. Most of the team were invited by Boris Berezovsky to settle in at TV-6. In the past, TV-6, the first nonstate channel, had targeted a young audience with entertainment to build brand loyalty for the future; it had very little news. Berezovsky acquired the controlling shares in the economic meltdown of the summer of 1998 and was in a position to install the famous faces from NTV: Evgeny Kiselev, Mikhail Osokin, and others; pay their salaries; help provide the equipment (everything they had was left behind at NTV). Now there was one national channel of opposition to the government. TV-6 did not have the national penetration of NTV (see Chapter 1), not to mention the state channels, but as usual throughout Soviet and post-Soviet Russian history it was Moscow that desperately mattered to the government. In the summer of 2001, TV-6's news ratings in Moscow rose to the top, really quite remarkable from a newly created crew in cramped offices and short on equipment. From uneasy disapproval, the dissatisfaction in the Kremlin now turned to open threats to TV-6 (presumably on the basis of the station's economic troubles). It was precisely during our focus group discussions that TV-6 was fighting its last fight and then disappeared, replaced, as we saw in chapter 1, by a sports channel.[4]

Sensationalism

Modernity has increased the tempo of life. Members of the focus groups noted the considerable difference in tempo between the non-state and state stations. TV-6 was "gripping" and "more lively." It was more "today." Perhaps equally contemporary was the sense among focus group participants that TV-6 and, to a lesser degree, NTV specialized in sensationalism. I should say at this point that it is very

---

[4] TV-6 then managed to assemble some investors and became TVS. However, there were soon predictable differences among investors, and TVS ended, as well. It is important to keep in mind that every move – from NTV to TV-6 to TVS – resulted in a reduction of technical resources and, therefore, in the penetration of the station. Fewer eyes meant a drop in advertising; more limited penetration meant that the vast majority of Russians could not get TV-6 on their sets.

difficult to define what "sensationalism" is in covering a world epidemic with such wasting and painful consequences. Is it close attention to HIV/AIDS itself that shocks the viewers in their armchairs? In the discourse of the focus groups the nature of the disease itself frightens the audience and anchor Evgeny Kiselev was also prone to drama. In Nizhny Novgorod, Olya (the young translator) says of the original NTV: "I can say that NTV as it was earlier ... Kiselev would have had a lot of alarm. By showing this information, they already began a panic. And now we are rather calm about it." Andrei (studying neurosurgery): "I think that TV-6 and NTV would have a panic ... probably even more with TV-6." Lena (young math teacher) added "They would have dug something up, TV-6, some horrible statistic. Some frightening, events. Something 'red hot' [sensational], I'd say"; In Rostov, Ira (university student): "TV-6 shows someone ill with AIDS, that is, it would go more for the sensational with a living example. NTV would take one point of view and contrast it with another, say, maybe two hospitals, how they treat AIDS, or how two medicines work."

Nonstate stations better reflect reality

Even if viewers had never seen an HIV/AIDS victim, they recognize what is real and what is not. They suspect the state channels of presenting a prettified reality (at least "smoothed over," as they say,) so as not to mobilize the audience. Evgeny (from Volgograd) says: "In principle NTV can give a sharper program because in principle AIDS is a very big problem, ... But ORT and RTR would keep off quite a bit more, so as not to frighten the viewer." Olga (from Nizhny Novgorod) observes that: "I think that only TV-6 would differ ... [the rest would be] almost the same ... [TV-6] could show more disasters ... the others would have it more smoothed over."

Maxim is startling. He believes that the powerful are beginning to be disoriented by their own unreal presentations; he says: "There [TV-6] for sure it would approach our reality ... and then they'd prod our state a little, a government which doesn't fight; which keeps quiet about the numbers and so forth." Lena, Oksana, and Olga agree.

Andrei (42, college-educated, entrepreneur) remarks in a Volgograd group that: "NTV would cover it, more broadly even from the heartland of the country." The Moscow-centric prominence of correspondents for state stations, according to at least some of the viewers, prefer their comfort and wrapping up the story quickly. Sometimes they will treat even the *suburbs* of the capital as examples of coverage from the heartland. It stands to reason that these focus group viewers almost all say that the nonstate stations provide a "deeper" account of the issues. As Volodya (college graduate, Moscow) put it: "Yes, they'd show something more real, there, something that if you looked at it, my God!"

Weaknesses and divisions

Up to this point, there was general agreement on what the nonstate stations might be expected to do, and on some dimensions there is no argument. The viewers see clearly that TV-6 tilts its stories toward political opposition. Maxim takes the issue very seriously: "And finally, TV-6 is now the only channel which permits itself to be in the opposition." This is the same person who objected to the Russian government's passivity and underestimation of the problem. The members of the groups are certainly aware that a story on TV-6, even one as apparently remote from politics as HIV/AIDS, would be morphed into an anti-government political issue. Here is a discussion of TV-6's policy among college graduates from Rostov:

Lilia: I think they'd [TV-6] show sick young people.
Sasha: I think somehow that TV-6 will tie this to politics.
Alexei: Everything will tie this to politics.
Gena: TV-6 will differ from all the others most of all. Sasha said it's political there, that is, it's always tied everything to politics.

The nonstate stations, NTV and TV-6, are not equal, nor equally admired. NTV had been bought by Gazprom, even though the station was debt-ridden. It was not about money. It was about depriving the television market of a station that criticized the government. Even though NTV did not have the penetration the government channels did, just about everyone in our groups mentioned it at some point.

That is not true of TV-6. This station's signals could not be received by a very large part of the Russian population. Then, too, the dramatic, rapid tempo of the news on TV-6 is not to everyone's taste. Julia (from Rostov) prefers NTV and finds it the most interesting, in large part because she objects to the formulaic hysteria of TV-6: "I think that NTV would be the most interesting of all ... because there it would always keep up the interest. On TV-6, there would be a lot of yelling . . . I don't know on account of what. Probably a lot of yelling, there will be noise, but maybe behind the noise a little bit would get in."

The once-daring NTV has been brought to heel, according to the observations of the groups. Anatoly (college-educated, Rostov): "NTV shows the traces of the bad side of ORT. I think it would show the measures taken by the minister of health against spread of this disease . . . by the government." In a different Rostov group, Vika says: "The current NTV in my view has already drawn close to ORT, even though Mitkova is there."[5] Another Anatoly (56, college-educated employee, Volgograd) told the group: "NTV has now begun to hang noodles on your ears [make up stories for the naïve]. Oh well, but they are freer; they are simpler, because really they are unofficial after all . . . NTV would say a lot more that's not true. But this is the stuff of tragedy." In Nizhny Novgorod, Zoya told the group that she thought the three channels provided similar coverage from one side and TV-6 from the other. Slava said in response: "I also think, I agree with Olya, because on TV-6 – this channel already is more free and it's very sad that they closed it."

Some observed that news on NTV has been changing (see chapter 1). Oksana in Nizhny Novgorod says: "NTV somehow would be in the middle. It's now somehow changed from what it was before. As for NTV [now], I still don't have a clear and comprehensive image of it." NTV rapidly passed the interim state of transition. In a 2006 content-analytic study, two Russian associations found an overwhelming amount of prime time news devoted to Vladimir Putin on the state stations. "The survey produced almost identical results for the Gazprom-owned NTV,

---

[5] Tatyana Mitkova, a strikingly attractive young woman, had been an anchor for a short time on Soviet television. When, at the beginning of the year that ended with the collapse of the country, Soviet anti-riot troops took over the headquarters of Vilnius Television in the capital of Lithuania, for secessionist behavior. Mitkova in Moscow was told to read what most people present in the studio at the time called gibberish about an invitation. Mitkova refused to read it. Instead she said the headline about Soviet forces in Vilnius and then said that a different newsreader would read. At the end, Mitkova came on again and said that that's all they were allowed to say. She was fired. When NTV began to broadcast, it was Mitkova who was the face of the news. When NTV was taken over, the decision was difficult; Mitkova finally chose to stay with NTV and became news director, to try to keep some honesty in the news.

thus confirming the station's transformation into little more than a junior clone of the state channels."[6]

Approaches to coverage of corruption

HIV/AIDS proved to be a good topic by which to gauge viewers' sense of the differences among the channels offered to them. It did not invoke skewed, partisan, or regional attitudes, and it was a subject everyone knew about. It was not yet known, at that time, what had been declared at the international conference on HIV/AIDS in Moscow in 2006 – that Russia and its neighbors actually led the world in the rate of new HIV/AIDS infection. Still, the members of our focus groups were aware of the growing pall that AIDS was casting over life and were thoroughly pessimistic about what patients would experience. For these viewers, the majority, it was a death sentence.

The second topic we used to gauge how viewers decided how channels might differ because of ownership was corruption, well known to be pervasive at all levels of the economy. According to Transparency International (TI), Russia ranked 79th in governmental corruption, slightly more corrupt than Kazakhstan and Uzbekistan and slightly less than Ukraine and Azerbaijan.[7] The focus group facilitator did not suggest that corruption touched one political ideology or party more than another, or that some regions were practically lawless. It was, like the HIV/AIDS issue, excoriated by all the parties and officials and attributed to officials and private businesspersons at every level of the region. Veteran Oleg Poptsov, once head of Russian television and then of Moscow City's Center Television, did a television program as a long imaginary dialogue with an absent President Putin. After the show, Poptsov handed in his resignation. In the show, he warned about the spreading and quite open corruption. He said that ministerial and parliamentary positions were for sale. "'Don't you know how much an MP's seat costs? Come on, Vladimir Vladimirovich, you must do. You should ask bureaucrats to give you a price list'." He noted that corruption had moved down the ladder of administration, so that "parties in the

---

[6] BBC Monitoring, "Analysis: Survey Highlights Pro-Putin Bias on Russian News," May 3, 2006. Reprinted in *Johnson's Russia List*, 104, May 4, 2006, 10.
[7] *RFE/Rl Newsline*, 5(124), part 1, June 29, 2001; RFE/RL List Manager, listmanager@list.rferl.org, June 29, 2001.

region [were] no different than officials at the federal level."[8] The most primitive form of corruption – the bribe – has been on the rise and involving more citizens. The national average for a bribe is about $18–$36, but prices increase the closer one comes to Moscow. Bribery is quite open, especially on the roads, where cars and trucks are stopped by traffic police, documents checked, an infraction cited (its relationship to the truth tenuous) and then a bribe makes the whole thing go away.[9] That is the smallest-scale bribe; corruption can include money launder- ing, buying political or other offices, winning ownership not with the highest tender. Many more transactions have been accompanied by some form of add-on corruption, including threats – serious ones – backed up by the use of assassins, called "killery." Or it could be the threat of investigation by the tax police, sure to find some infraction, or opening up the conversion of state into private property in the early 1990s. An excellent description of the lower levels of corruption, and how much more systematic and "ordinary" it, too, has become is given below. It demonstrates rather well the frightening series of hurdles from which none is spared:

Observers tell stories of how corruption reaches down to the very existence of ordinary people. There is the "dilemma of Lena N., a young actress who says she can't afford to pay the bribe to get her children into a state-run kinder- garten, or Sergey Odinartsev, a businessman who found his warehouse confiscated by thugs he said were sent by the local secret police … These days, any transaction of value from getting your kid into university, to arranging visits to doctors, to starting a business depends upon the [overlords of corruption]."

The mechanism is simple, explains Gennady Gudkov, a former KGB major-general and afterwards head of the State Duma's security committee. A would-be raider "finds an influential cover, either a bureaucrat or someone in State Security," he says. After a fee has been agreed, the bureaucrat "goes to the owner of the business you want to steal and says: sell your business for five rubles or you go to jail."

---

[8] BBC Monitoring, "TV Presenter holds Monologue with Putin to Air Concern for Russia's Future," Center TV, Moscow, in Russian, 1825 GMT, December 12, December 13, and December 14, 2005. Reprinted in *Johnson's Russia List*, 16, January 18, 2006, 16.

[9] Agence France Presse, "More than a Quarter of Russians Pay Bribes: Poll," Reprinted in *Johnson's Russia List*, 95, April 24, 2006, 8.

The only defense is to have more powerful patrons than your opponent. Moscow businessman Vladimir Moiseyev learned that rule when he tried to make a successful takeover bid for a large Moscow hairdressing salon. He had money, already owned 30 percent of the shares in the company, and, most important, had good friends in the Interior Ministry's Organized Crime Unit. Unfortunately for Moiseyev, there was another bidder, someone connected, he says, to the presidential administration. As in a card game, Moiseyev was trumped by his rival's superior connections.[10]

Post-Soviet groups everywhere but Moscow have little to say on this. They speak in broad generalities about the coverage of corruption by television, but nothing concrete, nothing original, and nothing that displays any knowledge. Participants with only high-school education also seem to be unable – or unwilling – to speak of corruption and television coverage in any detail. Talking about it seems very remote from their worlds, even if corruption is not. For example, in Nizhny Novgorod, Natasha says: "I don't know, corruption, ... they talk and nothing changes." Or Zoya, who offers: "Well also that probably TV-6 and NTV could be sharper." In Rostov, Olya says, about appraising the coverage of corruption: "I can't answer." Misha: "I don't have any thoughts."

It has not been lost on Russians that looking into corruption could easily result in murder. In chapter 1, we gave examples of investigative reporting that came too close to what was tolerated and the journalists were assassinated. Many have probably bribed their way out of police sanctions or into a position to get a telephone. Higher levels of corruption among ministers and heads of huge resources companies are so remote and walled off that there is often, literally, nothing to add and nothing to say, except what the media have already reported. There is so much corruption and the media make so little sense of it when they do give it anemic coverage, that Galya (college-educated, Moscow) observes: "You know, I, for example, think this: what they show us on the channels about corruption in principle it is such a little bit that they show us. And it's simply necessary once or twice, crudely speaking, to pass [something about it] on to the people." Sveta responds: "It's

[10] O. Matthews and A. Nemsova, "The New Feudalism: Forget Corruption. In Putin's Russia, the Nexus of Payoffs and Patronage is almost Medieval, Touching every Aspect of Life," *Newsweek International*, 8, October 23, 2006. Reprinted in *Johnson's Russia List*, 232, October 16, 2006.

the very tip of the iceberg." Galya does not expect much truth-telling on television about this topic: "On any channel, because television, I think, so much money flows around there, that it's not simple." This is a subject of unquestioned importance that *all* channels successfully keep from their viewers because, as some participants say, the media properties are businesses, too, and the question of corruption touches them as well.

In the post-Soviet group in Rostov, Maxim says: "Whoever pays more, they talk better about him." Andrei responds: "It will depend on whose channel it is. They will praise depending on whose horse it is." Dima: "I already said that depending on whose corruption will be unmasked, if it's the boss, then none. But if he's not our man, if he's hiding already for the fourth year [with laundered money] on some [offshore] island, they hunt for him." Ivan: "What a view! Here is the power, all the same there are four channels, but all of them are under the power . . . of course under one power. We live in one country. And nobody moves against the chief boss." Andrei: "Nobody will move against Putin." Maxim: "Nobody would sling mud so openly and crudely. Maybe somebody very close to him can squeal and everything." In Rostov, in a college-educated group, they discussed the dismissal of a minister for building himself a lavish summer home with state funds. Vika: "But if such a dacha exists, it's criminal theft, nasty. Why is it necessary to keep quiet about it? So it's not pleasing to the government . . . Why is it necessary to keep quiet?" Mark: "It's impossible for the first [channel], second, and NTV. It's impossible to speak about it. Impossible. They don't allow it, otherwise searches will begin there." Not only is the topic impossibly large, and there is little coverage on the media, the national channels are themselves permeated by corruption and, moreover, covering corruption, the viewers believe, could easily result in the unleashing of the tax police or another governmental armed unit to search what they please with no prior warning. While they search, as we have seen in the example at NTV, the station is thrown into chaos and makes carrying on nearly impossible.

The viewers simply lack so much of the story (thanks to inadequate coverage and, with reason, fearful investigators) and have so few tools for making associations and bringing memories and strategies to bear (the tip of the iceberg is not a very spacious workplace), that they often concede defeat – that is, they do not even try to squeeze meaning about corruption from a resistant media source. To access at least some form of information, there must be a point of entry – something that permits them to see unintended connections – and these viewers find that there is not, and that the size of the corruption issue would make meaningless any small extract of hidden meaning, even had they been able to access it.

Are there differences among the channels, since each has at least one dominant bank-roller who calls the tune? It depends. HIV/AIDS, in our participants' views, would definitely have different coverage by state and nonstate channels. But corruption is something else. It is tough, patient investigative reporting that uncovers the pieces of the corruption puzzle and since so many are interconnected – both within Russia and beyond to havens for laundered money – the topic could at some point reach essential levels of government. That possibility, in turn, would trigger an overwhelming backlash, change of the channel leadership and financial foundation, and possibly worse. These viewers do not mention the fact that many of the anti-corruption campaigns started in American, Swiss, or Italian banks, not to mention what happens in Grand Cayman and Cyprus. This foreign aspect to the battle against corruption is either not known in any detail, or presented in a way that viewers have a difficult time recalling it.

Some in our focus groups pointed to the special role of TV-6 and NTV. NTV was the station that broke the story of the first Chechen War, acted independently and often in an opposition mode – opposition, that is, to the government in power. When its much-respected founder – news director, Oleg Dobrodeyev – went over to run Channel Two, he published an open letter to the new head of NTV and long-time associate, Yevgeny Kiselev. In it, Dobrodeyev accused NTV of in effect pressuring the government with a form of extortion – threatening to broadcast anti-government stories if its loan was not extended. If this political game with financial benefits went on in the background, what appeared on the screen was still the independent, feisty, unafraid NTV. In 2001, when the tax police broke into NTV's offices, that was the end, it was bought by Gazprom. What the energy giant wanted with a television station is unclear but it is clear that President Putin did not want a station of opposition. Television networks are expensive desk ornaments.

It is curious to see what the viewers made of this change. Some college-educated Moscow participants talked about where they would see information on corruption:

Natasha: I think that ... NTV is such a channel that it differs from the rest, I
   think, and there would be more information ... They'd tell [that] here
   there exists some kind of up-to-the-minuteness; they know that this theme
   is interesting ...
Maxim: I think that generally on Channel 6 it would be more interesting ...
   Not on NTV. Before, it would be NTV; now ...
Ira: Well, yes, of course.
   [*Facilitator: what do you think about corruption and NTV?*]
Ira: You mean the NTV that was before?
   [*Facilitator: the one that's now.*]
Ira: Now it hardly differs from the old-fashioned ones.
Lena: It differs a little.
Volodya: They put a brave face on a sorry business, and probably they no
   longer differ on anything. More statistics, that's for sure.
   [*Facilitator: and TV-6?*]
Ira: Heroic, risking their life.
   [*Facilitator: who?*]
Volodya: Their journalists.
Lena: Kiselev.
Volodya: Yes, absolutely, they carried it out with desperate agony ...
Igor: Again, TV-6 can show some really individual examples in the quality of
   Gazprom.

He goes on to say that there's a taboo where Gazprom is concerned
and no one "wants very much to stir it up [too] deeply." The participants did discuss the impending or extremely recent closure of TV-6;
the sources helping the discourse to make sense of that news will
be examined in chapter 7. Before ending this chapter, I turn to the
rise and fall of the embodiment of the anti-corruption hero, Alexander
Nevzorov. When he came to power, still in Soviet days, Gorbachev
wanted to accomplish a reform that would end corruption and usher in
transparency – at least at the lower levels of the economy. Convinced
that the mass-media were persuasive in ways that other forms of communication could not be, he was determined to use television, which
had the advantage of pictures, an emotional content, and a huge
heterogenous national audience. His equivalent of the "caped crusa-
der" for this job, the personification of the hero rooting out crime and
corruption, was Alexander Nevzorov. He had done many jobs: ridden
horses in the circus, worked in hospitals, had ties with the KGB, he said.
He started a news program unlike any yet seen in Russia: called "600
seconds," it was fast-paced (unheard of in Soviet television) and vividly

displayed corruption, crime, and corpses. Sometimes he would burst in on a local government meeting to accuse the members of malfeasance and incompetence. The viewer could see it on the screen; the unease of the bureaucrats facing the photographers and their blinding lights; the dead language of committee-talk in the world of the fast-talking, graphic discourse of the television professional – or maybe it would be more accurate to say television star with a megalomaniac ego. Along with this outsized self-regard was the figure of the man: tall, good-looking, dressed in black leather, dominating the scene in speech and image and reducing everyone else to pygmies. After all, it was his show and he determined the camera angles. In 1990, he was shot and spun a mysterious, but not especially enlightening story about it, and remarkably was not hurt. With increasing national recognition, Nevzorov commanded more time and attention. At the beginning of 1991, he did a faked "documentary" on the Lithuanian takeover of the center of Soviet television in Vilnius and the ensuing violent backlash as Soviet troops took over, full of faked montages and interviews. His extremism grew; for a while he was a supreme monarch. Inevitably, with his extravagant Wagnerian pose, he became increasingly extreme politically and was eclipsed by a different Russia. He merits attention as the spearhead of Gorbachev's anticorruption campaign, and how superficial and ultimately ill-conceived, unco-ordinated, and unplanned it was.

The college-educated group in Moscow recalled Nevzorov when the subject of corruption came up:

Volodya: No, if you speak about corruption then right away you recall Nevzorov's show … although it was shown some time ago, but there wasn't any, that is, they showed, how to say it, mother truth. In several programs, in part with Nevzorov.
Sveta: He reminded me of a kamikaze.
Volodya: How they didn't kill him.
Katya: Kamikaze or not, he did have an attempted assassination. The only thing that saved him was [his] leather jacket. The bullet bounced off [it].

Nevzorov was a self-promoter and liked nothing better than to provoke a scandal. Most people recalled the mysterious assassination attempt and the miraculous jacket. I was, apparently, on his agenda for another scandal. He was looking for one in St. Petersburg, when the International NGO, the Commission on Radio and Television Policy (of which I was the Director) met, a meeting chaired by former President

Jimmy Carter and Eduard Sagalaev, the founder of TV-6. Over fifty media decision-makers from all over the former Soviet Union were there, as well as the "opinion-makers" of St. Petersburg and the city's director of foreign relations, Vladimir Putin. Mayor Anatoly Sobchak, who had been a professor of law, was to give the welcoming remarks. Sobchak's office permitted only journalists with official press passes to enter the meeting room. I was told that Alexander Nevzorov was outside, but did not have a permit. He was waiting in an anteroom determined to get in. When I came out to talk to him, there he was, impossibly tall, clothed in black, black pants, shirt, dark hair and penetrating eyes, black leather jacket (was this the one the bullet just "bounced" off?). With him were his crew: a couple of cameramen, and perhaps two or three others. Cameras were rolling. Nevzorov glowered and in a bullying, aggressive posture lectured me on the freedom of the press and denying him that freedom. I agreed on the absolute importance of freedom of the press and invited them all in. I walked into the conference room and turned around to see if they were following. They were not. Nevzorov first and then the whole crew went down the stairs and left the building: he had to strike this unconsummated scandal from his lineup of stories.

When Ira, Volodya, and Lena, college-educated group participants in Moscow, talked about TV-6, they spoke of heroism and "desperate agony." When Moscow youth talked about TV-6, Katya said: "NTV tried to go beyond the boundary separating the legal from the illegal. That is, all the same they go up to the boundary, closer to the boundary. TV-6 tried also to jump over it." TV-6 was closed down in 2002. All the groups experienced either the last hopeless days of TV-6 or the first days of television without TV-6. Later in this book, the participants talk specifically about the closure of this station.

In chapter 6 "Endings," we shall examine how the viewers in the focus groups went about decoding or making sense of two events: the closure of TV-6, which happened after eleven groups had been assembled, but before the remaining five had been. It is an unusual and fascinating time: with remarkably different tones, atmospheres, and discourse on either side of the TV-6 lifeline. We also examine REN-TV, a channel with very low penetration (see chapter 1), that did not take state funding, and developed a Moscow following for its news – the best of what was left after the forced closure of station after station. Praise by Moscow's intellectuals for its professional newscasting was its undoing.

3 | Election news and angry viewers

The myth of Vladimir Putin's victory in 2000 tells of a man from nowhere made President solely by television. This myth easily took root in Russia, because it fused with the Soviet belief in the extraordinary power television exercised over its viewers. During Soviet times, the head of the Communist Party was often on television, when he was, he was always featured in the first story, and if he met with his fellow Politburo members or greeted them on arrival from a foreign trip, or was seen off by them, with a three-kiss protocol, all the members had to be named, each time in order of status. The newsreader carefully read through the list of over a dozen names, being quite sure never to stumble. Sometimes the group might be seen more than once in a news show, and, according to the rules, each one was named again in the same order. It was during the partially more liberalized time of Mikhail Gorbachev that the head of news tried out an experiment: he named them all only during their first appearance and then referred to them collectively. The Politburo acted immediately and forbade the innovation.

Just being on television was assumed to have a powerful impact on viewers. By the time Gorbachev became a prominent member of the Party's top circle, many of his colleagues were old, some were visibly weak, and some were sick. None of those weaknesses mattered; the power was in the projection. That is how they saw themselves and it was axiomatic (with them) that this grand impression was conveyed to and appreciated exactly the same way by the viewers.

Surely the most unforgettable example of this way of thinking was the determination of the Politburo to uphold the tradition of showing

This chapter first appeared as "The Election News Story on Russian Television: A World Apart from Viewers," *Slavic Review*, 66(1), Spring 2007: 1–23, published by the American Association for the Advancement of Slavic Studies and is reprinted with the permission of the publisher.

the leader casting his ballot at election time. This time, the leader was Konstantin Chernenko, Mikhail Gorbachev's predecessor. Chernenko was ill from the time he was named General Secretary; his wheezing voice and unsteady gait were very apparent. When he awarded medals to Soviet cosmonauts, he had to hold on to his desk with one hand while he stood before the healthy heroes and spoke unintelligibly. As Chernenko secretly lay dying, his colleagues determined that the tradition could not be broken and during the coming election he still had to be seen casting his ballot on television. Television professionals tricked out a room in the hospital to resemble a polling booth and dressed him. They held him upright while leading him to the "polling place." When his trembling hand could not put the ballot in the box, his arm was guided by someone out of camera range. With street clothes over his hospital gown, Chernenko performed – however unconsciously – the rite of casting the first vote and exhibiting the power of the Kremlin.

No one working in television at that time could have asked what seems the quintessentially commonsense question: what would viewers think? Boris Yeltsin's election campaign of 1996 had a similarly thoroughgoing focus on the media. To combat single-digit approval numbers and a candidate sidelined for much of the time by serious illness, the Yeltsin strategy team worked on designing an approach to overcome a huge ratings lag behind the Communist Party candidate, Gennady Ziuganov.

The Yeltsin campaign modeled its strategy on the critically important Referendum campaign of 1993. At that time, Ben Goddard (an American consultant, who pioneered issue advertising in the United States with compelling short spots criticizing the Clinton health care plan) devised, on a napkin in a hotel in Moscow, an innovative television advertising campaign for Yeltsin. Television did not observe parity of time or let critics have their say. As a strategy analysis for a later campaign said, it was "the best expression of the model – which is carrying out elections from the top down with advertising propaganda accompanied by the central channels of TV." They intended to achieve "domination of the information space."[1] By the time Vladimir Putin won the Presidency, Moscow elites were disposed to grant the medium of television sole influence over the victory.

[1] M. Meier, "Prezident v 1996 godu: Stsenarii i tekhnologii pobedy," Fond effektivnoi politiki, Lecture 1, March 1996: and "Epilogue," July 1996: 44.

Although the influence of television may be seductive as a unique explanation for Putin's victory in 2000, there are many other factors that should be included in a properly complex election model. The media were certainly crucial to the rapid development of name-and-face recognition; they were an invaluable conduit through which a political nobody assumed the trappings of a political player seeking high office. On August 6 President Yeltsin appointed Putin Prime Minister (and, later, acting President). Shortly after his appointment, the newcomer's ratings stood at 2 percent. Television helped mightily to change Vladimir Putin into a household word. However, it was far from the only asset. A number of critical events occurred so quickly afterwards that they would have to be included in any model of the election. After a period of disengagement, the Chechen question arose again in a surprise strike at neighboring Dagestan, and the Chechen call for a "greater Ichkeria" (the Chechen name for their land). Russian troops sent to the Caucasus pushed the invaders out. Only days later, the unthinkable happened: terror came to Moscow on a huge scale. In September 1999, two apartment buildings in Moscow were blown up and bombs were set off in other apartment buildings in two other cities.

Putin immediately blamed the Chechens and launched a large-scale attack, not only as retaliation but also to finish off the Chechen problem for good. His earthy language made it clear: Putin was propelled forward as a decisive warrior; how different a stance from images of the bloated, sick, and remote President. Voters' decisions were prompted by retrospective factors – comparing the Putin who would be President with his predecessor (as opposed to comparing candidates' plans and future strategies which, though it is the more thoughtful and rational thing to do, is actually much less rarely done).

Finally, there is the question of political parties. Henry Hale's market approach to the presence and absence of real political parties provides insights of value.[2] He notes that:

[w]hether parties successfully dominate a political system, ... hinges critically on factors that affect the balance between parties and party substitutes in a country. Some important such factors are found to be historical legacies and transition paths that influence the relative quality and volume of political

[2] H. E. Hale, *Why Not Parties in Russia? Democracy, Federalism, and the State.* New York, Cambridge University Press, 2006: 235.

capital available to parties and substitutes. They are also found to be broad institutional contexts that set rules of competition and, even more importantly, that define major actors with the power to alter election rules and otherwise strategically intervene in electoral markets.

These factors function not only at the center, among the top leadership, but at the numerous levels of local government and stretch across a landmass so vast, that it is almost impossible to organize campaigns. (Hale 2006)

As noted above, the variables required to model the election of Putin, the man from nowhere, are multiple, partly path-dependent, and partly a reaction to the unprecedented terrorist strike at the heart of Moscow, Putin's response, and the inertness of his predecessor. That he was mightily helped by his domination of television is unquestioned; that television was the *only* variable in the model is not the case.

Even in the United States – with a competitive party structure and huge campaign expenditures on television advertising, and some less well-known candidates seeking to spread their image and identity as quickly as possible, no matter what the cost, as did Steve Forbes, Ross Perot, and Michael Huffington – the model is far more complex than "the ads did it." As Kenneth Goldstein wrote: "candidates and their advisors know that [television] ad campaigns do not win the presidency by themselves and that they must play with the cards they are dealt – past voting patterns, the partisan composition of the electorate, the state of the economy, and America's place in the world."[3]

It is not the study of elections I consider here, but rather the dominant pattern of overblown confidence in the medium and the consequent undervaluing of an invisible audience. How *do* viewers actually process the news – especially about elections, the most important event for the government and the reason it shuts down media companies, even if these strong-arm tactics incur sizable debts and attract international opprobrium? To what extent are viewers' frames congruent with those of broadcasters (and owners), or is there a significant gulf between the two? We do not know enough about *why* people think as they do and *how* they talk among themselves about what they have seen on the news.

---

[3] K. M. Goldstein, "Political Advertising and Political Persuasion in the 1996 Presidential Campaign," Paper prepared for presentation at the 1997 annual meeting of the American Political Science Association, Washington, DC, August 28–31: 15.

Taking the problem apart

Parties and politicians use a variety of forms in the hope of convincing the voter to vote their way in an election. They use outdoor billboards, political advertising in print and electronic sources, free time allotted randomly by the Election Commission, leaflets, and opportunities to open hospitals and tour schools, and trumpet economic achievements. Of all of these forms, research has determined that in Russian elections viewers are most attentive to television news coverage, rather than to paid candidate spots or debates, or the time given randomly to all registered parties or candidates. Colton (2000) has observed that news broadcasts are watched more often than ads or public-service broadcasts.[4] Analysis of the Russian elections of 1999 and 2000 found that "campaign commercials of partisan rivals were of secondary importance" to news and analysis programs, and subsequent ratings appear to bear this out.[5]

In contrast, many Russian media elites believe that audiences are tired of news. They say that people just want to relax, that television news and political discussions have become unpopular. The ratings still show otherwise: no matter how much this *idée reçue* has been repeated by pundit after pundit, it is not, and has never been, true. Channel One's news program *Vremya* is usually in the top ten for at least two editions per week, and Channel Two's *Vesti* editions rank seventh, nineteenth, and twenty-second in the top 100 programs of *all* genres of programs for *all* of Russia.[6] This is a ranking of the entire market: in competition with all categories of programs: sports, movies, variety shows, pop music, sitcoms, gangster and police serials – all of these going on at the same time, but still surpassed by the news on several occasions, even far from Moscow. It is not especially productive to compare Russian and American news stories. US election stories on evening broadcast news programs follow a markedly similar formula on each network; network news coverage, as Beck *et al.* (2002) note,

---

[4] T. J. Colton, *Transitional Citizens: Voters and What Influences Them in the New Russia.* Cambridge, MA, Harvard University Press, 2000: 19.

[5] T. J. Colton and M. McFaul, *Popular Choice and Managed Democracy: The Russian Elections of 1999 and 2000.* Washington, DC, Brookings Institution Press, 2003: 100–101.

[6] For these ratings, see www.tns-global.ru/rus/data/ratings/tv/russia/top_100/ _20051010_20051016/index.wbp, last consulted November 11, 2005.

may be configured as a "horse race" to the finishing post or action and controversy in news bites of diminishing size: "These tendencies have profound consequences, but they are only indirectly partisan and are ignored in our study."[7] Russian election news stories, in contrast, are propelled by the advocacy of a candidate and the denigration of the opponents.

It is important to note that, structurally, news, debates, and political advertisements play rather different roles in Russia and the United States. They also have rather different organization and priority of content, editorial autonomy, and templates to guide the format. In Russia, it is this template in particular that has perverse consequences for those conceiving and transmitting the message.

We focus on the discourse of Russians in Rostov, Volgograd, Nizhny Novgorod, and Moscow who were asked to watch videotaped, naturally occurring treatments by three national channels of news stories about the gubernatorial election in the huge, diamond-rich republic of Yakutia (also called Sakha). We chose a contest that was significant nationally, had been in the national news, but where our participants had few if any political ties and loyalties. Like the scholars of American elections Neuman *et al.* (1992), we also deliberately chose a "normal" time for this project, without national elections either coming up or just completed, and an election about which the discourse would not be skewed by personal partisanship. To get a better fix on audience processing, they choose to study the phenomena in a "normal" time, so that the contortions of the crisis mode were minimized and the discourse of the participants as far as possible "uncontaminated."[8] We were especially fortunate to be in the field during the last days of TV-6, the last oppositionist channel with significant national penetration (see chapter 2). These were the last days of viewpoint diversity.

In chapter 4 I analyze the discourse prompted by a quite different kind of news story – a story, in its way, no less difficult for viewers to penetrate or on which to bring to bear their own frames and their own experience. In that study, viewers watched four channels' treatments of

---

[7] P. Beck, R. Dalton, S. Greene, and R. Huckfeldt, "The Social Calculus of Voting: Interpersonal, Media, and Organizational Influences on Presidential Choices," *American Political Science Review*, 96(1), March 2002: 61.

[8] W. R. Neuman, M. R. Just, and A. N. Crigler, *Common Knowledge: News and the Construction of Political Meaning*. Chicago, University of Chicago Press, 1992: 88–89.

the opening of the Novorossisk oil pipeline. The research centered on how, or if, or under what conditions viewers thought in terms of tradeoffs, current or potential, even when the slightest reference or cue to tradeoffs was wholly absent from the first three treatments and plentifully and emotionally (in a single direction only) presented by the oppositionist TV-6 in the fourth story.[9] In their discourse, viewers challenged the notion that any policy would not entail tradeoffs: they expected them. They lived their lives – no matter what their age, or level of education, or place of residence – as though they had internalized two proverbs: "There's no free lunch" and "you can't have it all." They know that in their bones and are prepared for explanations that try to conceal it. Discourse about these tradeoff-free news stories, as we might expect from the theories elaborated above, was heavily dependent on elements of the publics' personal experiences, observations, and assumptions, which were pervasive and cognitively available to apply to these stories. They used heuristics to get beneath the message, with the accessibility heuristic perhaps the most powerful organizing or learning shortcut at their disposal.[10] This will be discussed at greater length in chapter 4. What is remarkable, though, is what happens when the story turns to election campaigns.

When the news story is about election campaigns the pattern changes drastically. How do audiences in the focus groups in our four different Russian cities process three treatments of an election story from three different channels (TV-6, RTR, and NTV)? What tools or heuristics are most important in sorting through the electoral materials? A second major question relates to the viewers' frames for the election story *as such*. Is there some media phenomenon that the audience recognizes or labels as "an election story" and, if so, what are the characteristics of this genre with respect to the broadcasters' utility or preference and the

[9] Ellen Mickiewicz, "Excavating Hidden Tradeoffs," *Political Communication*, 22, 2005: 355–80.

[10] See the extensive studies by J. A. Ferejohn and J. H. Kuklinski, *Information and Democratic Processes*. Urbana, University of Illinois Press, 1990; D. C. Mutz, P. M. Sniderman, and R. A. Brody (eds.), *Political Persuasion and Attitude Change*. Ann Arbor, University of Michigan Press, 1996; A. Lupia, M. D. McCubbins, and S. L. Popkin (eds.), *Elements of Reason: Cognition, Choice, and the Bounds of Rationality*. Cambridge, Cambridge University Press, 2000; R. McDermott, "Arms Control and the First Reagan Administration: Belief-Systems and Policy Choices," *Journal of Cold War Studies*, 4(4), Fall 2002: 29–59.

viewers' reception? Does audience reception rest on heuristics derived from personal experience, as might be expected from previous studies, or does the audience identify a *sui generis* frame for the election story – and, if so, what are the components and how might they affect the individual's understanding of his or her role in the electoral process and normative views of democracy and elections? The discourse following the airing of election news stories was radically different from the discourse concerning other stories. Why this happens is an important research puzzle.

Western research on heuristics

Viewers make sense of the flood of information around them by employing shortcuts to meaning. Iyengar *et al.*'s (1982) early experiments in New Haven, analyzed how television could affect viewers' agendas in terms of whether coverage might change what people thought important, and what they thought less important: a policy agenda would predictably change from the time before they had seen the stories to the time afterwards. As was often said: *what* one thought about might change, but agenda-setting did not answer the question of *how* one thought about it. This research also found that *priming* was important: "problems prominently positioned in television broadcasts loom large in evaluations of presidential performance."[11] Iyengar (1991) summarized the priming effect as "the ability of the news programs to affect the criteria by which individuals judge their political leaders."[12] Priming, if it lasts, and if the viewer can retrieve it, can influence evaluations in subsequent considerations of an issue or an individual.[13] It is a powerful result, but its use in cognitive strategies, of course, depends on its effective retrieval. Priming is effective when its results have been internalized and are ready to be called upon to be applied to what could be called similar situations, people, or issues.

[11] S. Iyengar, M. D. Peters, and D. R. Kinder, "Experimental Demonstrations of the 'Not-So-Minimal' Consequences of Television News Programs," *American Political Science Review*, 76(3), September 1982: 855.

[12] S. Iyengar, *Is Anyone Responsible? How Television Frames Political Issues*. Chicago, University of Chicago Press, 1991: 133.

[13] S. Iyengar and S. Ansolabehere, *Going Negative: How Attack Ads Shrink and Polarize the Electorate*. New York, Free Press, 1995.

To be effective, priming must *not* be perceived by the viewer as a deliberate attempt to prime. When viewers notice that those controlling content are attempting to prime them, the effect is undermined. A strong case can be made "for a causal relation between awareness of the priming episode and contrast effects in social judgment ... To be aware of a contextual influence allows cognitive operations that modify its impact of the judgment."[14] When it is known that the program or station has as its mission to prime the potential voter, that voter will likely resist and counter by raising other issues and, in any case, resolve to withstand the pressure of identified priming. Because of the long period during which the Soviet media and many other institutions were explicitly charged with persuasion and were unsubtle in its use, Russian audiences, as illustrated by their discourse in the focus groups, are sensitive to broadcasters' priming attempts and routinely identify them in news stories.

Similarly, Lupia and McCubbins (1998), in writing about the conditions under which speakers may be persuasive, find that the listener or viewer must believe that there is no incentive for the speaker to lie. As they put it: "if the principal [in our case, the viewer] either anticipates or discovers deception, then she has an incentive to disregard the speaker's advice." In other words: "A persuasive speaker can deceive only if she faces a principal who cannot see deceptions coming."[15] Russian viewers are especially aware of attempts to deceive them when a speaker on the news, whether a news-maker or a reporter, with ties to political or economic interests, is dictating the agenda. Russian viewers *expect* to find economic and political interests behind the agenda and presentation of news stories.[16]

The election story turns out to be *sui generis* for Russian viewers. It is for them a distinctive genre, regardless of what office is being sought by whom and where. In this, it differs substantially from other kinds of

---

[14] F. Strack, N. Schwarz, H. Bless, A. Kübler, and M. Wänke, "Awareness of Influence as a Determinant of Assimilation versus Contrast," *European Journal of Social Psychology*, 23(1), January 1993: 59.

[15] A. Lupia and M. D. McCubbins, *The Democratic Dilemma: Can Citizens Learn What They Need to Know?* Cambridge, Cambridge University Press, 1998: 74.

[16] E. Mickiewicz, "Does 'Trust' Mean Attention, Comprehension, and Acceptance? Paradoxes of Russian Viewers' News Processing," in K. Voltmer (ed.), *Mass Media and New Democracies*. London, Routledge, 2006.

news stories. The form of discourse that viewers use in talking about election stories is also strikingly different. This suggests that the elaborate maneuvering of broadcasters, their state sponsors, and other owners is based on scant knowledge of the viewers – publics who have made judgments about the institution of elections, their own roles in the process, and the norms they invoke. This distinguishes the election story from all others.

The Russian elections context

In post-Soviet Russia, editorial autonomy on the few national television news channels has been so fragile that it has repeatedly given way under the pressure of elections. Diversity or pluralism of viewpoint has fallen victim to the government's enormously exaggerated belief in the power of television to persuade. The government appears to have a strong unexamined attachment to the myth that to ensure electoral victory requires closing down one dissenting channel after another. By 2003, the number of national news stations had been reduced to three, and all adopted a position of agreement with the government's position.[17] Although this is a cross-sectional and not a longitudinal study, it is obvious in the way that viewers talk that they have come to regard the electoral campaign story as separate from other stories, a genre with distinctive properties. The pressure of electoral outcomes was so great a burden on a nascent television market unprotected by a functioning judiciary that apart from the free time guaranteed to all registered parties, and the paid advertisements some purchased, candidates from the President's preferred party had the lion's share of the supportive news while their competitors were often excluded from the news altogether.

In 2004, the outspoken remnants of the old NTV who had stayed on, such as Leonid Parfenov, the station's economically valuable ratings

---

[17] In 2004, REN-TV, a Moscow-based network with less than 50 percent penetration, drew ratings for its independent news coverage that made it number one in Moscow. That was not true of any of the other cities to which it broadcast truncated headline-type news. With Moscow always at the center of the political universe, however, this development made REN-TV especially vulnerable, and plans were developed to remove it from its owners' hands by redirecting 70 percent of its stock and warning the owner that entertainment should be substituted for news. In 2005, Irena Lesnevskaya and her son Dmitry, the founders of REN-TV, sold their shares in the station and exited the market.

king, came under scrutiny and was summarily fired for interviewing the widow of an alleged Chechen terrorist. An anchor's sarcastic remark got him fired immediately (see n. 3 of chapter 2). The editorial agenda for news on television lost the autonomy that is an essential bedrock element of a free press system.

When this study was in the field, there were still four stations most of the time, and viewers still had access to external diversity in the news – that is, although each channel might present a highly biased newscast with only one viewpoint, together all the channels provided some degree of diversity. This is not exactly the pluralism of many contesting points of view envisioned by classical democratic theory, but in the battle for the owners' opposing preferences a window for the wise opened, and comparisons and careful analysis provided a measure of diversity that was to disappear soon thereafter.

The weakness and limited penetration of the newspaper market has contributed to the mass audience's dependence on television for news and information.[18]

In the focus groups, coverage of the Yakutia gubernatorial election began with a story from the still-independent TV-6, followed by RTR (Channel Two), the government-owned station, and then NTV, which was, by that time, toeing the governmental line.[19] After each story, the facilitator typically started the discussion with a probe such as: "What do you think about this story?" or "What do you say about this? Did you get some information about what happened?" To help the reader's orientation in this nomination process, a summary of the election in Yakutia culled from the western press is given below.

On December 15, 2001, Deputy Prosecutor General Vasily Kolmogorov sent notice of his withdrawal from the race for governor to the head of Yakutia's Central Election Commission. At the same time, Yakutia's Interior Minister, Semen Nazarov, announced that he, too, was

---

[18] Mickiewicz, *Changing Channels: Television and the Struggle for Power in Russia.* Oxford, Oxford University Press, 1997; rev. and expand edn., Durham, NC: Duke University Press, 1999.

[19] Channel One did not cover the election that day. In any case, its stories were usually considerably shorter, and the government view was better developed in the Channel Two story.

withdrawing from the race and called on voters to support Vyacheslav Shtyrov, head of the hugely important diamond concern.

Mikhail Nikolaev, who had headed the vast territory since 1991, bowed out of the race on December 12 after Moscow officials and Moscow's Central Election Commission chief made it clear they wanted him to drop his bid for a third term. Nikolaev originally resisted Moscow's pressure, hitting back through the local courts. At that point, Putin invited Nikolaev and Shtyrov to the Kremlin together and gave Shtyrov, the tycoon head of the diamond monopoly Alrosa, an award for his handling of the billion-dollar diamond industry. Nikolaev finally withdrew and, under Kremlin pressure, threw his support behind Shtyrov.

After the election on December 23, the Central Election Commission announced that Shtyrov had won more than 59 percent of the gubernatorial vote, while businessman Fedor Tumusov had taken around 34 percent.

The election story as mandatory template: the merging of time and space

The first finding to emerge from the focus groups' discourse is that the conclusions the participants draw were based on longitudinal assumptions. This was a cross-sectional study, but participants volunteered an observation of the election story they had seen over time as essential to their evaluations. The participants' comments appear to be based on what they saw as an election story template that was repeated not only *over time*, but also *across the territory* of the country and *vertically* from election coverage of the highest post (the Presidency) down to the lowest-local one. It is a template they dislike and find confusing in its overheated attempts to prime. Viewers have thus "constructed" a *generic electoral campaign story*. One of its chief attributes, character assassination, comes as no surprise to viewers, who expect it as a central part of the template, though it appears to lead to confusion and a lack of trust. Viewers also note the absence of fairness and consistent and abided-by rules. Viewers recognize the template and have assigned it a place in their mental schemas that appears to be isolated from the richness of the experiences that figure so prominently in daily information processing. This has a significant effect on the related cognitive processes they use (or are unable to use) for election stories.

Here are two high-school-educated viewers from Volgograd:

Alena (23, artist and fashion designer): The scenario is always and everywhere the same ... They waste huge resources on electoral campaigns.
Valery (38, worker): Yes, crazy sums ... same with voting for president.

From Nizhny Novgorod, Natasha (high-school-educated dentist) says: "Where there are elections, it's always one and the same, everywhere." A college-educated focus group in the same city offers these views:

Sergei (28): I have a proposal. Let's not watch an election campaign story for one simple reason: Leila [*facilitator*], name for me, please, at least one objective story. There has never been in my life, ever, an objective story about electoral campaigns and there will never be one that's objective.
Alexander (48, state employee): The electoral campaign doesn't have any story in this coverage you can believe. This is two pickpockets – whichever you prefer can steal from you.

Another group of college graduates from Nizhny Novgorod:

Andrei (35, engineer/programmer): You know, the more you hear such information, each time, connected with each election, the less you want to go to vote in general.
Liuda (52, physician): I agree with what everyone said. Now it's very hard to believe these stories about electoral campaigns.
Vladimir (59, unemployed): I will say only one thing. This is my personal opinion. We have not had honest elections here in Russia yet, and there won't be any in the near future.

In Rostov, college-educated Vika (41, biologist) says: "Each candidate has his own staff of journalists. I, for example, don't watch such stories any more, because one's the same as another." When asked if she believed the story, Vika replied: "No, because another correspondent will talk about it from the other side."

Moscow's post-Soviet focus group decries the departure from norms. They know what an electoral campaign story *should* say; they know that in an election, the voter should be the principal and the elected official should be the agent. They find that the story template and the campaign have reversed the order of power:

Igor (24, engineer/geologist): In principle, nothing's clear. It's just the typical electoral campaigning that's everywhere.
Maxim (23, history teacher): I permit myself, maybe early on, to look at these two stories, although there will be a third coming. One is a big, fat lie.

Why? Because again in these stories it's about an electoral campaign, about some kind of pointless fuss over trifles between the candidates. We simply don't see and nothing is said about the programs of these candidates. About the people who – how the interest of the people is expressed in the program of these candidates. The people are simply excluded from the electoral race ... I personally did not get satisfaction from these stories. Honestly speaking, I want to turn off the television.

Oleg (25, university student who also works): Elections are when people choose between the candidates' programs. There wasn't any [choice]; this was completely taken away. Some concrete personalities were shown ... But what they will do for the people? What they propose to the people, this was missing. It wasn't there at all.

Galia (22, housewife): The usual electoral campaign.

Participants of differing backgrounds, ages, and regions use virtually the same words to characterize "the election story" as "always and everywhere" the same. It is the same for every level of government (the same for presidential elections, they say) and for every region.

Many Russians, when asked to respond to surveys, declare that no medium is helpful at election time; they rely solely on their own opinions. Rose and Munro (2002), using statistics from ten *New Russia Barometer* (NRB) surveys, cite data from the ninth survey conducted in 2000:

92 percent of those who voted in the presidential election regarded their own experience and observations as very or somewhat helpful in making their choice. By comparison, 59 percent said state television was helpful and 38 percent regarded private television as important. Discussion with friends and workmates were cited as helpful by 57 percent of voters, and newspapers by little more than a quarter of voters.[20]

This favoring of one's own personal analysis is seen in all the answers to this question over time.

Responses claiming overwhelming reliance on one's own powers of deduction do present some problems of interpretation. First, of course, many respondents like to project an image of self-reliance, as though

---

[20] R. Rose and N. Munro, *Elections without Order: Russia's Challenge to Vladimir Putin*. Cambridge, Cambridge University Press, 2002: 175–176. Private television stations have a lower penetration than state television stations. Reception for private stations can vary from 30 percent (for REN-TV) to about 64 percent (for NTV). Thus, for purposes of comparison, it is helpful to look at the choices made by viewers who have the given option available.

they have no need of any aid beyond their own insights. Others were likely not conscious of receiving stimuli and input from any social institution or circle of friends and workers. Television is like wallpaper in many homes. Wallpaper may surround us, but it becomes so familiar that we no longer notice it. Then, too, the television set makes an empty apartment alive and friendly. When one of the family comes home, she often turns on the television immediately, like a reflex. Now there is that familiar sound and one is a little less alone. The television set is always on, at least as a secondary activity. It runs its programs while something else is being done: cooking, and cleaning, for example. Full attention to turn the screen into a primary activity may not always be possible, although *some* elements of the messages may be absorbed. It is difficult to assess this quality in a survey, although it comes out in focus groups quite easily. Take Sergei (28, Nizhny Novgorod): on his pre-session questionnaire he noted that he had higher education, and to the question about where he got most of his news about the President and about Chechnya, he wrote that he relied on "his own analysis." Nonetheless, Sergei turned out to be a daily consumer of news, sampling four different national television stations. No matter how much contempt Russian viewers may have for election stories – Sergei said he never saw an objective one – these viewers do not exist in a vacuum. Sergei speaks in his group; he watches television. Still, the NRB's surveys do provide the valuable finding that the election story in particular tends not to give viewers much-needed information.

Channel and viewpoint diversity: smothered by the template

The Russian television-viewing public has relatively few choices among nationally disseminated news programs. In this study of election stories, as in the study of treatments of the Novorossisk oil pipeline in chapter 4, viewers were deprived of clues to station identity. In the Novorossisk study the focus group participants had already identified the station before the logo was uncovered. They did so on the basis of ideology and style. We know viewers are adept at distinguishing between state and commercial channels and can picture how different subjects (health, politics, the economy) would be covered differently by each of the four national channels. To my surprise, the viewers in the election study were baffled by the task of identifying the sources of these stories. They could not distinguish combative, oppositional TV-6 from any other station. They confused the commercial with the state-owned channel. For a public as sophisticated and willing to construct what is left out or to deflate what is biased, the election story is based on such a strong reliance of sameness – even if it includes *kompromat* (compromising materials) in the recipe – that all stories are lumped into one, neither trusted nor coherent. Thus, even the presence of a channel (TV-6) devoted to opposing government policy provided the viewer no benefit in thinking through the Yakutia election. So entrenched was the election story template that the benefits of diversity were buried in the welter of confusing charges, countercharges, and accusatory images of official malfeasance.

As the state and its allied energy firms pour billions of rubles into taking over stations and micromanaging content, one has to wonder whether the investment is at all realistic in terms of attracting the attention and sympathy of a public who long ago rejected the template and the distortion of the electoral process it signified.

The election story as the unrolling of the Kremlin's preferences

The voting public's sense of exclusion – noted above by viewers who demanded from candidates policies, programs, and attention to constituents' interests – rests on their perception that the Kremlin's advantage and direct intrusion, not the voters' votes, determine outcomes. Voters can choose only what is on the electoral menu; the Kremlin can alter that menu at will, in the eyes of the viewers, and can thus circumscribe their choice at any time in the process. The focus groups were unsurprised by the Kremlin's manipulation of the election in Yakutia: they expected it. Later, in 2004, this manipulation was to some degree codified in legislation mandating the Kremlin's nomination of governors, who had then to be approved or rejected by the local legislature. After two rejections, the President could appoint an acting governor for a period of six months.[21]

In the post-Soviet group, Ivan (21, law student, Moscow), once again appeals to norms. He notes that in the federal government's pressure on the election in Yakutia the Constitution has been turned on its head: the autonomy of the regional bodies has been subverted and the

---

[21] "On basic guarantees of electoral rights and the right of participation in referendums for citizens of the Russian Federation," December 11, 2004, para. 1.4.

independence of the judiciary politicized to discredit a candidate displeasing to Moscow:

Ivan: It's all clear. It's about how they carry out elections in the administrative–territorial units of the federation. Formally the power is formed by the will of the people and the state should not influence this will. But in the story it's shown that the power, in this case federal power, influences the will of the people, as the Kremlin tries to put in place its person as the head of the administrative–territorial unit and what means they use for this. In the story, they are listed. Second, the court is the basic law enforcement organ, the purpose of which is you follow the letter of the law formally in the quest for truth and justice. Here they are carrying out a political function and are subject to the power of the punitive organs which punish disobedient persons.

After viewing all three stories, Andrei (23, economist, Rostov) puts it simply: "Moscow is directly hitting up the locals for diamonds and oil." Vladimir (24, carpenter, Volgograd) says: "Here the theme is closer to Moscow, this last story. Because there's a third candidate with diamonds, and Moscow takes five percent they said." Misha (24, college student, Volgograd) interjects: "Part stays in Yakutia." But Vladimir interrupts: "Yes, and they want to cut it [Yakutia's share] back even more. And it appears that it's the candidate who is struggling for Yakutia [who wants to develop the resources]. It turns out that Moscow specially wants to put him in so that he will be in charge when [Moscow and he] agree then, so that the candidate nominates himself and the people simply don't know who he is. It's like Moscow on the contrary put in there in order to prevent him from [carrying it out]."

The election story and the limits of heuristics

There is an important anomaly in the way that Russian voters process election news on television. As noted above, the availability heuristic is one of the most powerful cognitive instruments in making sense of information. If it is difficult to store information mentally and retrieve it easily to apply to similar categories in the future, then internalization or persuasion has not taken place. Personal experience most strongly affects availability. It is not that Yakutia's distance from our four cities acted to reduce the relevance of experience.

The other study in chapter 4 also chose different channels' treatment of an event at some distance from our four cities, but there was an outpouring of analogies from personal experience. Participants told of trips that by analogy could apply to the story at hand; others recounted their everyday observation of the state of buildings in their towns or oil spills seen while looking for mushrooms. For all the heated discussion about election stories, only one person brought up personal experience. Slava (26, high-school-educated worker, Nizhny Novgorod) said about Kolmogorov: "If they wanted to keep him, he would have even had a third term. It was the same with us. We voted for Klimentev, and on the spot they removed him because he was not a person necessary for Moscow." None of the other focus group participants talked about *any* personal experience with voting, elections, their deputies, or governors; none brought up stump speeches or meetings with candidates. None alluded to a process of accountability or ties once an official had been elected. With respect to the election story, they appeared unable to build a bridge from personal experience to television narratives about elections, and conversely the weight and predictability of the template left little flexibility or variety with which to cue the voter to a relevant experience. There is little to nothing in the stories that would make the candidate more "like" something familiar. And without those heuristics, the stories remain confusing, aggressive, and jagged for most of the viewers.

Unlike the observations made by Gamson (1992), Neuman *et al.* (1992), and others about the United States, when it comes to Russian election stories there is only one alternative frame in the viewers' minds, and this principally among younger participants.[22] For the post-Soviet participants, in particular, the election news story is compared to something nonexistent but potent: to the norms by which a true democracy *ought* to be constructed. They are aware of the norms governing elections – not just the procedures but, more important, the rationale for having an election and why it underlies the democratic process. The twenty-somethings invoke normative frames with which to evaluate the election story, frames they have acquired through their education, at law school in Ivan's case, or at the university for Maxim, the young history teacher, or Oleg, who is still a student. These young students and professionals counterpose the norms they have never seen in practice to the repeated display of the typical election story.

---

[22] W. Gamson, *Talking about Politics.* Cambridge, Cambridge University Press, 1992. See also n. 8 above.

As a result of the continued violation of norms and the coarse imposition of a disliked template, viewers generally find little in their personal lives with which to compare the process. They talk about election stories *only* in terms of *other* election stories. In every focus group, regardless of education, watching an electoral campaign story stimulates negative references to other campaign stories on television, and the conversation turns into a meta-media discussion. The discussion does not extend beyond the television frame: it is stuck within a constantly repeating, largely uninformative loop. This phenomenon was observed only with respect to the election news story, not with respect to stories about other news. It explains why the focus group participants were unable to determine which channel they were watching – even when TV-6 was still an active player – when they could easily do so with other kinds of stories. It is a peculiarly hermetic world of conversation, in which television stories about real events of the most significant import – elections, presumably the keystone of democracy – are defined and discussed virtually entirely in terms of references to other news broadcasts.

The conclusion one might draw is that election stories in any region and for any post cue only other stories, since they all share the same frame and none engages the alternative frame of the daily life of the viewer. Moreover, a strong sense of criticism and disillusionment is attached to the much-used template, thus further distancing the broadcaster's frame from the viewers'.

Thinking about voting: the potent and vanishing "against-all" option

After the television clips were shown, participants either volunteered or were asked how they might have voted in this election. Although no one was eligible to vote in Yakutia, several of the participants thought about the connection between what they had seen and the act of voting. The discussion included repeated references to a type of protest vote still possible in Russia at that time: the ballot option "Against-all." As Hutcheson (2004) notes: "the provision to vote 'against all' was retained [from the Soviet era] when the fundamentals of the post-Soviet electoral system were established." The legal significance of the option in parliamentary elections, Hutcheson also notes, has changed over time in single-member districts: in 1993, against-all voters were able to invalidate a district vote for the State Duma since "against-all" won more votes than the leading candidate; in the 1995 legislative elections, the "against-all" votes were unable to nullify the leading candidate's votes; since 1997, "against-all" voters have had the ability to invalidate an election if their votes exceed the votes for the leading candidate. Although turnout has also fallen in many nonethnic regions, "against-all" shows "a clear upward trend," especially in single-member districts.[23] For parliamentary elections in post-Soviet Russia, the single-member district accounted for half of the seats and party-list candidates for the other half. Although candidates in single-member districts were nominally independent, about half were allied with parties and about half were running as independents. A 2005 electoral reform made all constituencies into party-list (see figures 3.1 and 3.2).

Alexander Khramchikhin, a noted Russian commentator, mused on the growing visibility and influence of the "against-all" option:

Russian citizens will be placed in an extremely difficult position during the upcoming elections. One would have to lack self-respect to vote for parties such as these. Refusing to vote at all is no solution; for one thing, somebody else will vote in your place; for another, not voting means not having the right to call yourself a citizen. The obvious thing to do is to vote for the "against all candidates" option, but even this is rather risky. Votes cast "against all candidates" get distributed among the winning parties anyway. Of course, if this form of protest voting turns out to be really widespread, the regime will take it into account. But what kind of conclusions will it draw? Its current behavior indicates that, at worst, it might abolish elections entirely; at best, it might remove the "against all candidates" opinion from ballot papers. No option – no problem.[24]

In the 2003 Duma elections, in all the single-mandate districts, "against-all" received more votes than all but four parties, and in almost one-third of these districts, "against-all" came in first or second.[25] This is

---

[23] D. Hutcheson, "Disengaged or Disenchanted? The Vote 'Against All' in Post-Communist Russia," *Journal of Communist Studies and Transition*, 20(1), March 2004, 99,103.

[24] A. Khramchikhin, "We the Non-Undersigned," *Profil*, August 2003, from wpsru/e_index.html and *Johnson's Russia List*, 7399, November 11, 2005, 8.

[25] See, for example, P. Armstrong, "Against All – A Popular Candidate," *Johnson's Russia List*, 7476, January 21, 2004, 13; Hutcheson, "Disengaged or Disenchanted?": 105; J. A. Corwin, "Russia Bids Farewell to Regional Elections," *RFE/RL Newsline*, 9(2), part 1, January 2005; S. White and I. McAllister, "Voting and Nonvoting in Postcommunist Europe," Paper presented to the American Political Science Association, Chicago, 2004.

a form of protest with high transaction costs, given the bone-chilling, snowy, or rainy weather conditions in December and the flaws of public transport that require a change of packed buses and subways always in pushing crowds just to get to the polling place. And then there's the return trip home.

Three years later, as national parliamentary and presidential elections came into view, Kramchikhin's words proved prescient. In a detailed article Andrei Gromov, in the highly reputed journal, *Expert*, reported on the war against the "against-all" option:

Of late, officials and lawmakers (at the federal and regional level alike) have been talking of the need to remove the "against all candidates" option from ballot-papers ... Most analysts now believe that the "against all" option won't be available in the Duma election of 2007. In response to the signals coming from the authorities, opposition activists are launching a campaign to defend this "last bastion of democracy."

All the same, it isn't just politicians and armchair politicians who are concerned about this issue; judging by the battles that occasionally break out in online discussion forums, ordinary citizens aren't indifferent about the fate of the "against all" option ...

In the latest series of regional legislature elections (the first using party lists only), the level of "against all" voting was fairly high. The highest "against all" votes in 2005 were recorded in Taimyr (20.1%), the Vladimir region (17.9%), the Kaliningrad region (16.8%), the Magadan region (15.9%), the Arkhangelsk region (15.7%), and the Chita region (15%). The lowest levels were recorded in Chechnya, Ingushetia, Tatarstan, Kabardino-Balkaria, and Karachaevo-Cherkesia ...

... it's precisely because the authorities control the process so strictly that voting "against all" does make sense, in its way. Firstly, it provides at least some restriction on administrative abuses, and acts as a counterweight to administrative interference in elections. As we noted, almost all cases of high "against all" vote levels have happened when the authorities grossly interfered with elections: disqualifying a popular candidate or being too insistent in promoting their own candidate. Moreover, voting "against all" is a reaction against the increasing regulation of politics; this option gives citizens a legal opportunity to express their dissatisfaction with the overall political situation in Russia, not just with individual politicians. If that opportunity is taken away, citizens will let off political steam via illegal actions, outside the system.[26]

---

[26] A. Gromov, "An Exclusively Russian Right: The History of the 'Against All' Option and the Case for Abolishing It," *Expert*, 21, June 5, 2006. Reprinted in *Johnson's Russia List*, 136, June 12, 2006.

In the focus group discourse there were several references to the stories having blunted the participants' intention to vote as well as their having stimulated dissatisfaction and frustration and a wish to protest by choosing the "against-all" option. In a college-educated group in Volgograd, Vera (39, engineer/programmer) says that she got only one thing out of the TV-6 story, that the candidate "really wants the post. If I voted, I would vote against all." The other focus group of college-educated Volgograders voiced similar views: Anatoly (56, white-collar employee): "Honestly speaking, if I were a local, I would vote against." Alena (26, unemployed): "I would vote against."

In the same city, the views of participants with a high-school education were comparable:

Alena (25, artist and fashion designer): What if I tell you that from the time I was 18, I haven't voted once: [If I had to make a decision here] I would choose. I would either not vote or vote against everybody.
Valentina (42, white-collar employee): I go to vote, but I never like anybody.
Valery (38, worker): I would also vote "against-all."
Valentina: I watch their programs, and I understand right away that nobody can do anything for the people.

The last Volgograd group – the post-Soviet group – discussed how little they had learned about the candidates. Vladimir (24, carpenter) says: "I wouldn't go to vote." Misha (24, university student) agrees: "Maybe it's easier to flip a coin." Denis (21, university student) concurs: "Yes, that would be the best in this case."

In Nizhny Novgorod, college-educated Vladimir (59, unemployed) adds: "I don't believe a single story about elections." Andrei (35, engineer/programmer) agrees: "You know, the more you hear such information, each time, connected with each election, the less you have the wish to go out to vote at all."

In Moscow, too, both the college-educated and the post-Soviet participants describe how their desire to vote is diminished by what they see. In the college-educated group, Natasha (60, retired) is tired of mudslinging: "I wouldn't go [to] vote, because it's negative here and negative there and in general they didn't show any positive sides. No one's interested in showing a person positively." Sveta (36, teacher) says:

I didn't get any positive information about any of the three, no, not any one of the three. It was always mentioned – bad, bad. This is as though it's objective – here he is, so everything will be done right, but the other one stands on the side and is ready to grab a piece, yes. In the end, I did not get positive information about them. It's understandable that with all this technology, they somewhere, somehow, already showed that we are already used to it, that elections proceed this way and we are beginning to doubt the results. Precisely thanks to what we just now saw ... I imagined myself at that moment in Yakutia. I wouldn't go [to] vote at all. Honestly, I wouldn't vote. Such an impression was created in me that there's nothing for me to do.

The post-Soviet group in Moscow was equally irritable and in the mood to protest:

Igor (24, geological engineer): [I'd vote] for myself.
Maxim (23, high-school history teacher): One should run away, to Canada ...
Viktor (22, tour manager): Against all ... I think, paradoxically, I'd vote "against-all," inasmuch as there are equal amounts of mud slung at Kolmogorov and Nikolaev.
Oleg (25, college student): I agree.
Igor: If a person is from Yakutsk, he'd vote for the acting president.
Lena (24, translator): Or not vote at all.
Maxim: Yes, he could not vote at all.
Oleg: Or "against-all."

The discourse of protest voting comes from the young and the middle-aged, from Muscovites and people in the heartland, from college-educated and from those who did not go beyond high school. But the young post-Soviets and the college-educated are the most vocal.

These focus group participants are not representative of all Russians. Yet their attitudes toward election campaign news may be helpful in understanding a phenomenon that deserves attention. Over the course of a decade, dramatic changes have taken place in the composition of the "against-all" vote in post-Soviet Russia as shown in figures 3.1 and 3.2. Taking the 1993 parliamentary election as an initial benchmark, national surveys find that the "against-all" vote was concentrated among low-income voters (monthly income up to 35,000 rubles), heavily weighted toward retirees and blue-collar workers, and people 35–45 and over 45.[27] This picture of the "against-all" vote as

[27] A. Oslon and E. Petrenko, *Parlamentskie vybory i voprosy obshchestvennogo mnenia v Rossii vo vtoroi polovine 1993 goda*, Moscow, 1993.

(a)

Age

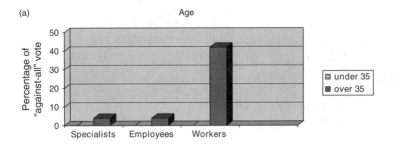

(b)

Income

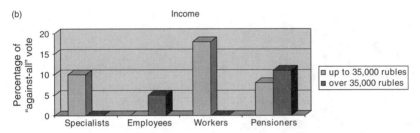

Figure 3.1 Percentage of given group among "against-all" voters, 1993 Duma elections
Source: A. Oslon and E. Petrenko, *Parlamentskie vybory i voprosy obshchestvennogo mnenia v Rossii vo vtoroi polovine 1993 goda,* Fond "Obshchestvennoe Mnenie," Moscow, 1993.

marginalized citizens is in substantial agreement with the author's survey directly after the 1993 vote.[28] Although the minimum age for voting is 18, that survey found that Russians between the ages of 16 and 24 said that they were least likely to vote "against-all" and that the "against-all" option increases with age. Voting "against-all" is found mainly among the less well educated. This picture is similar to that noted above since not having much education and being older is also related to having a blue-collar job and being a pensioner, and these groups were certainly not beneficiaries of post-Soviet life. In the 1993 survey, "against-all" and nonvoting are drawn from very similar population groups. As studies in the United States have found, nonvoters tend to be poorly educated and tend not to follow the campaign in the

---

[28] The Public Opinion Foundation Survey was fielded on December 18, 1993, with a sample of 1,593 Russian citizens, and was conducted in large, medium, and small cities and in rural areas in ten regions of Russia.

(a)   Age

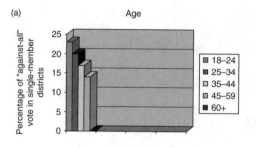

(b)   Education

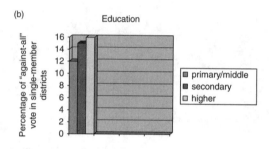

(c)   Occupation

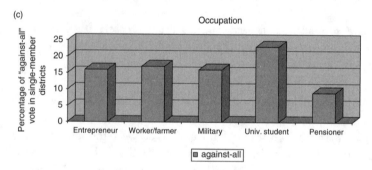

Figure 3.2 Single-mandate district voting: percentage of given group among "against-all" voters, 2003 Duma elections
Source: Moscow Times data, with thanks.

media.[29] In Russia, in the 1993 surveys, one could add that "against-all" voters were similarly marginalized.

A decade later, the composition of the protest vote had changed markedly. On December 7, 2003, the *Moscow Times* (an English-

[29] W. Crotty, "Political Participation: Mapping the Terrain," in W. Crotty (ed.), *Political Participation and American Democracy*. New York, Greenwood, 1999: 1–22.

language, foreign-owned newspaper), the Soros Foundation, and the Renaissance Capital investment bank commissioned the survey company ROMIR to conduct an exit poll. The 42,828 participants were proportionally drawn from each of the forty regions. In sharp contrast to the 1993 data, those who voted "against-all" in 2003 in the single-mandate districts were the younger voters, the more educated, and students, not pensioners. Entrepreneurs and managers scarcely differed from workers and farmers.

In 2006, the State Duma hastily took up the "against-all" ballot option, and with speedy efficiency led by the majority party – favored by the President – they took it away, getting ready for the 2007 parliamentary and 2008 presidential elections.[30]

Television consumption is always only one variable in a complex multivariate model of voting choices and media effects. Here the question is not one of voting behavior and effects: ours is an earlier question about processing messages about elections. Watching Russians process and discuss news stories about elections provides insight into how the most-watched messages about elections are received. Owners (natural resources-related firms close to the government) have repeatedly shut down dissonant channels. The discourse among ordinary Russians about an election campaign is remarkable for its overwhelming reliance on the narrow experience of watching the media in order to talk about it, not *through* its frames, but rather *using* the frames to indict *all* election story frames. Almost every reference they make is to another televised electoral story, and that includes story components such as format, narrative, action, level of emotion, and bias.

Election stories have little to do with ordinary people living their daily lives. Sometimes pedestrians are corralled outside on the sidewalk to give a "pre-cooked" comment for or against the candidate. As "vox pop" or "man-on-the-street" stories often do, they appear staged. Average people in their homes or at work – people with the ideological volume turned down to normal – are not much seen. Nor is the reverse: candidates seeking potential voters *en masse*, in halls and auditoriums. There are all sorts of elections at varied levels, but the participants of these focus groups have, it appears, never been drawn into the electoral process as a valued member of a constituency.

---

[30] "Russians Lose 'Against-all' Vote," BBC News, http://news.bbc.co.uk/2hi/europe/5133138.sstm/ June 30, 2006.

There is no reference to "ordinary elections," to visits home by their parliamentary deputies, to the work of their representatives in Moscow, to any desire or plan to *be* in politics. That a meta-media discourse about a gubernatorial contest in faraway Yakutia should be preferred and widely shared in the focus groups is worth thinking about. It is noteworthy, because that local election, in which none of the focus group participants had a personal stake, cued *all* election stories, across the country and up to the presidential campaign. It is further worth reflecting that this reaction is reserved for the election story. In other stories, viewers *expand* the story precisely because of their use of the availability heuristic.

For the younger generation – the post-Soviets – the nonobservance of norms is an attribute of the election story they find, in the end, degrading. Their normatively driven construction of the meaning of the election story may not necessarily signal a new and lasting outlook, a generational change; instead, it could reflect their stage of life and thus their views may change as the life cycle plays out. Electoral surveys conducted over the past decade in post-Soviet Russia suggest that the growing numbers of "against-all" voters, although relatively small in number, have changed from the marginal, the excluded, the under-educated, and the poor, to the young and the well-educated, indicating a true protest vote and that, in turn, suggests that we may well be looking at generational change. Once that pathway is cut off, these kinds of ballot protests may wither or, on the other hand, seek other channels.

In a 2006 analysis of the "against-all" vote using both mass-opinion surveys and focus groups, Kertman (2006) finds that the "against-all" voters divide into two groups, only one of which has protest intent and potential. Kertman finds that:

in the first case, we are looking at the discourse expressed by voters who value their votes too dearly to give them to anyone who is there [on the voting ballot]. In the second case [we are dealing] with the discourse of a participant of a political process who as a voter, harshly speaking, does not appear, as long as he's granted the same opportunity, to give his vote to whomever – at least up to this point, while he is dissatisfied with the powers and the condition of things in the country.[31]

---

[31] G. Kertman, "'Kandidat protiv vskeh': epitafia," *Sotsialnaya realnost*, Moscow, 7–8, 2006: 9–20, pp. 13, 12, 17.

These are the people who evince "not the slightest interest: in the logic of their electoral behavior comparing the advantages and disadvantages of candidates or parties in no fashion voting for them." The "against-all" voters, who have protest as a goal, are "significantly less effective" than would be the electoral support of some opposition force.

Kertman's argument is that more people who vote "against-all" probably do so because their normative goals are not met by any candidate on the ballot and that they value their vote and what can be accomplished when they vote "against-all" as a signal to the government to improve the candidates, so that their votes will be more and more meaningful. The others, who vote "against-all" to show their disapproval of the "political class" and its candidates and who disapprove of the system as such are unorganized, have no supporting group adherence, and are merely romantics – or, as Lenin dubbed them, engaged in infantile politics.

This division may be less than meets the eye. Both are, in fact, voting "against-all" and consciously holding up the electoral process by causing re-runs or substitute candidates. Further, it may be a specious argument – or, to put it more directly, a diplomatic cover – for generalized dissatisfaction to claim that the vote is such an august privilege that the voter will await the proper contender. It could be true, but in practice could also mean a behavior that does not differ from the blunter approach to "against-all" voting. Finally, the question of the "infantilism" of voting against without having organized an opposition may be asking too much at this point. But one that seeks the major overhaul and perhaps an entire change of values is not such an opposition. This is summarized by Kuran (1995), when he writes that "it is public opinion, rather than private opinion that undergirds political power. Private opinion may be highly unfavorable to a regime, policy, or institution without generating a public outcry for change."[32]

Whether collective action outcomes will follow is not the subject of this study. What we can conclude is that the Kremlin's appropriation and suppression of televised diversity has not resulted in the expected acceptance of the broadcasters' desired frame. The election story has

[32] T. Kuran, *Private Truths, Public Lies*. Cambridge, MA, Harvard University Press, 1995: 57.

become an expensive article of faith for its producers; for viewers, it is a confusing phenomenon that occurs with considerable regularity (since such stories form a single genre) and exists outside their own lives – lives from which under other circumstances they derive the cognitive shortcuts so necessary for processing information. That a protest or proto-protest having used the now defunct "against-all" option may be diffuse and reasonably private does not negate that possible motive.

Election story transcripts

The transcript of each station's broadcast shows the words heard by the viewer followed by the accompanying visual images in *italic*.

TV-6

(2 minutes, 45 seconds)
Special Correspondent Vadim Tokmenev: Despite various rumors and court hearings, texts for new flyers and street slogans were prepared in the electoral camp of Mikhail Nikolaev, current President of Yakutia. His supporters have come up with a new slogan, "Yakutia against the capital [Kremlin] conspiracy." This is probably about the long debates: would Nikolaev be allowed to be re-elected for the third time?

Establishment shot outdoors: cars, trolleys, people warmly dressed on sidewalk. Sixth floor of hotel. Voice of woman on phone and graphic of map locating Yakutsk. Second telephone interview: man giving information with graphic of map filling half screen.

The story continues. Even among the opposition nobody predicted this sudden turn of events. Today, when new propaganda flyers were about to be printed, police and public prosecutor officials arrived at the capital of Yakutia, Tygyndyrkham, where Nikolaev's electoral head-quarters are located.

Car pulls up to hotel.

They presented a search order and stated that they will spend the next hour on the sixth floor. Still it is not clear what type of documents and materials are of interest to them, and if they find something, whether they are planning to open court proceedings against the president of Yakutia. Neither side wanted to comment. Some details were revealed to a correspondent from the local television network. He said that many people saw what was carried out of the office.

Special Correspondent Konstantin Struchkov:

It just became known that the search was approved by the Attorney General. Disks, tape recorders, computers as well as other types of equipment are being confiscated from journalists. When our film crew arrived, video recording equipment was being confiscated without presentation of any document permitting confiscation. Working shots, made in the hotel, were destroyed by the public prosecutor's officials.

Special Correspondent Vadim Tokmenev:

At the same time, the republican Supreme Court tried to decide whether Nikolaev is eligible to be re-elected. However, the session did not last long. They only had time to debate the relative importance of the local constitution that does not allow the third term and the Federal law that does. Nikolaev insisted on the latter. The attorney insisted on replacing the judge. Today it became known that the husband and the son of Tatiana Antipina, the leader of the process, are employed in the public prosecutor's office. One of the candidates is a Vice Attorney General, therefore Vasily Kolmogorov could influence the court.

Court scene: lawyers, audience, journalists.

Today it was decided to replace the judge and to postpone the proceedings until Wednesday, provided the new judge has sufficient time to familiarize himself with the case. There is a little less than a month before the election, and the most complex question has to do with the names to be printed on the ballots. Tomorrow, for example, the fate of three other people is going to be decided. A new complaint was sent about three candidates: Nazarov, Slanikov, and Maximov. The authors claim that these candidates were a day late in submitting their documents and their registration is not legal. By the way, this was the same reason why the leader of the Russian Diamonds (*Almazy Rossii*) company, Vyacheslav Shtyrov, was removed. In light of these events, the closure of the presidential radio station is a minor event. Who knew that it is not profitable to support the president? This happened two days ago.

Street scenes; shot from below of looming radio towers. Man unlocks rusty lock on door and enters. Fairly small room filled with disks belonging to radio station.

Then the local newspaper "Vestnik" printed an article about the reason why the Kremlin decided to get rid of Nikolaev and to help Kolmogorov. The author was Vyacheslav Tserbakov, editor-in-chief.

Tserbakov alone interviewed on camera.

He is also the owner of the music radio station. The public prosecutor found various violations in its work. Therefore, it was closed a day later.

Shot of official document; another shot of radio station interior.

Currently the entire town is preparing for the elections in the northern dusk and silence.

Special Correspondent Vyacheslav Tserbakov: The task is simple – to paralyze Nikolaev's supporters, to keep them off balance, reminding them about what happened to Rutskoi [in another widely publicized election in another part of Russia, he was denied access to the ballot because he was too late filing for the campaign]. They should realize that there is no reason to make a fuss, since they are going to be removed anyway.

Special Correspondent Vadim Tokmenev: The editor-in-chief is going to look for justice in court. He has not yet decided which one. His colleagues note that it is senseless. It is better to wait until the end of the elections and then to see who is on your side.

RTR: *Channel Two, "Russia"*

(5 minutes, 43 seconds)
Special Correspondent Eduard Petrov:
    Yakutsk, minus 30 degrees.
Establishment shot – outside, on the street, wintry weather, automobiles, pedestrians.

The elections are scheduled to start in three weeks. The current leader of the diamond region, Mikhail Nikolaev, is not about to leave his post. He is being helped by political technologists whose task is to make him invincible. However, this group's dirty and often criminal methods no longer work in Yakutsk. Today it is cold in the streets, but hot in the candidate's headquarters. In the very center of the capital, there is an expensive hotel Tygyndyrkhan, with its good and warm suites.

Camera looking at hotel; moves inside to interior, to registration, where sign on counter says in Russian and English "No Vacant Rooms."

The least expensive is $50 per night. This modern building belongs to the Yakutsk governor's administration. They allow in only their supporters. Last Monday, public prosecutors unexpectedly arrived at the hotel. According to the information obtained, on the 6th floor, a group of so-called "black" PR representatives were preparing propaganda materials. Computers, fax machines, printers, and a lot of paper were discovered in the suites. Prepared bulletins were on the floor. Boxes with computers were loaded in the car and driven to the public prosecutor's office.

Shots of 6th floor; boxes being removed by officials dressed in parkas; computers removed. Young woman, avoiding camera, has no information to give reporter. Men looking at computer screens.

Several people involved were held as well. Tonight Larisa Vazhenova was interrogated. She introduced herself as a Moscow journalist. She was arrested while typing on the computer.

(*Larisa Vazhenova*)

No, I am not going to answer the question. I have my reasons.

Special Correspondent Eduard Petrov:

Today specialists are working with the confiscated equipment. They are trying to break into the system and to discover the hidden information. They were able to do so with one of the computers. The strategic plans of underground agitators and several versions of bulletins were printed. People who were trying to distribute them were caught red-handed.

(*Unidentified*)

We received 100 posters about Kolmogorov. I remember that they were hung on Levantov Street. I was supposed to receive 300 rubles.

Campaign flyers shown. Student interviewed but tries to block camera with large fur hat.

Special Correspondent Eduard Petrov:

A student of Yakutsk University, a future philologist, Mikhail Tolstykh, was drawing graffiti at night on the houses and monuments. He behaved arrogantly during the court proceedings and claimed that he did so because of ideological views, despite monetary compensation.

Graffiti shown – large letters on wall.

(*Sergei Nemkov*)

These posters contained libel, insults, incitement of ethnic conflict in Yakutia.

Special Correspondent Eduard Petrov:

Here are some of the confiscated documents. This is a strategy of the propaganda campaign. Its goal is to discredit the leading opponents. And this is the summary of the work completed. It noted the number and location of distributed posters and in which area the acts against Kolmogorov were organized. The search discovered contracts among the members of the underground agitation brigade. This person received $5,000 for his work. Videotapes and photographs were stored in the hotel. Here are some of the decent recordings that we can show and play. "Kolmogorov return to Moscow." "Do not stop your exit, Kolmogorov." "KPRF for Kolmogorov."

Diskettes shown. Computer shown as shell, with very little inside.

By the way, this is the first time that journalists were able to come by solid evidence of dirty, pre-election work. Prosecutors discovered a secret list of all the forty-five members of the group. They lived in three hotels. The cost of their visit was $100,000 per month. The representatives of Mikhail Nikolaev's campaign hurriedly asserted that the arrested persons had no relation to their candidate.

(Vladimir Frolov)

We are categorically against the artificial tie of Nikolaev to these people.

Frolov interviewed in hall. More shots of diskettes and computers.

Special Correspondent Eduard Petrov:

While the public prosecutor was working with the documents confiscated at the governor's hotel, the case of Mikhail Nikolaev was examined in Yakutia's Supreme Court. The head of the court claimed that the current governor can participate in the elections for the third time.

Mark Yakovlev:

Here the question is about the number of times. The governor can be elected once for five years and another time. Twice.

Special Correspondent Eduard Petrov:

According to Yakovlev, the election law is incorrectly written and has no authority over the candidate.

Mark Yakovlev:

This is not addressed to anyone, not to a person, no one, not a cat, not a mouse, not a dog, etc.

Special Correspondent Eduard Petrov:

Yakovlev just said that Nikolaev was never a governor.

Mark Yakovlev:

In practice, he was never a governor. He was not. He is only beginning to be a governor.

Special Correspondent Eduard Petrov:

The court listened to everyone and sequestered itself.

Shift to court. Door closes of cage where defendants stand. Three judges (two women and a man), prosecutor, small audience filling small courtroom.

However, Mark Yakovlev was certain. Perhaps, the court will make a right decision. And here is the verdict. The case is halted and will be sent to the Constitutional Court for clarification of certain controversial aspects of the law. This means that Mikhail Nikolaev can continue to participate in the election. Immediately after hearing the verdict, the governor's supporters went to a restaurant.

After decision to allow campaign for third term, scenes in rustic restaurant and jolly celebration. Nikolaev shown and then street scene, sense of extreme cold, young women bundled up in fur; cars move.

However, despite his tactical victory, Mikhail Nikolaev decided to insure the support of the regional administration's leaders. According to certain information, he spent a great deal of money in order to achieve this task. Some Austrian banks, where he has accounts.

Mikhail Nikolaev:

Please, search as much as you like. Here. They are searching ...

Special Correspondent Eduard Petrov:

The only real opponent is considered to be Vasily Kolmogorov. He is against the corruption and criminal acts of those in government.

Vasily Kolmogorov:

Those who enrich themselves illegally on the national budget, on the money of the people, on our governmental treasure will be tried before the law. You are afraid that once the prosecutor becomes governor, he'll put you in your place.

Kolmogorov interviewed. Scene outside.

Special Correspondent Eduard Petrov:

There is nothing to be afraid of. A few days ago the Audit Chamber of Russia finished its work in the republic. Moscow auditors discovered a large amount of violations during their work in Lensk, as well as misuse of federal funds.

Pictures of account book, where budget said to be laid out.

Who will be held responsible? We will find out soon.

NTV

(3 minutes, 37 seconds)

Special Correspondent Aleksei Veselovsky:

Three people who arrived in Yakutia to work during the elections were arrested, but it is not yet clear for whose campaign they are working. Information was received earlier that they are connected with Mikhail Nikolaev, the incumbent running for a third term. However, the public prosecutor does not have any proof. The attorney thinks the case is politically motivated.

Court with three judges, electoral commission – conference room with people milling about, surface of table covered with scattered papers.

The goal is to compromise Nikolaev. And there is nothing to prove. In Yakutia it is enough to spread the rumor.

Leonid Shemetov:

Clearly, everything is connected to politics. If there are elections, if there is a campaign, it is politics. First of all, the right of defense was violated, as well as the right to objective proceedings. Those people are sociologists and independent journalists, therefore they are neutral.

Telephone interview with lawyer for public relations group – graphic shown.

Right now, it is being decided whether they can be allowed to go free if they promise to remain in Yakutia, or whether they will be held.

Special Correspondent Aleksei Veselovsky:

The local public prosecutor has evidence that at least forty such sociologists continue to work in the republic; therefore the proceedings continue. From the UVD [Department of Internal Affairs] of Yakutsk, "The group discovered that on the wall of the building on 1 Kaladarashvili Street, at a height of 1.5 m, there was a slogan sprayed in dark red in letters of 40 cm: 'Kolmogorov, for how much did you sell Yakutia?'" On the wall of the monument "Eternal Fire" there was discovered a sign sprayed on in black with letters of 40 cm: "Chechnya for Kolmogorov." Traces of footwear were taken from the location and photographs were taken as well.

Shots of bagged material, boxes, taken out of building at night. Another telephone interview. Flyers, reporters talking to guards, kept out of room.

Similar stories take place during all kinds of elections. Therefore observers tend to consider the activity of the local public prosecutor as a desire to help Kolmogorov. The blow is against Mikhail Nikolaev. The Supreme Court of Yakutia still cannot decide whether Nikolaev has a right to run for a third term. It is not clear how the case will turn out and the public prosecutor needs a new ace. Today, the public prosecutor spent the entire day justifying his actions and denying political motivations.

Nikolai Takhvatulin:

We categorically – the public prosecutor categorically denies the claims of our opponents, who state that our actions – pogrom in their words – were motivated by the fact that there appeared to be posters against Kolmogorov, the Vice Attorney General of Russia. Nothing like that. This is not a political order. This is a legal proceeding, the result of the work we started in mid-November.

Special Correspondent Aleksei Veselovskii:

Today the Attorney General made its move in the Yakutia pre-election arena. Vyacheslav Shtyrov, the leader of the company "Alrosa" will be brought back on the list.

Shtyrov shown, huge, faceted diamond, from which a piece is cut. Court scene, press watching.

He was denied registration almost two weeks ago. The Supreme Court of the Republic made this decision given its argument that Shtyrov was too late in submitting the documents.

Court scene where Shtyrov is attempting to overturn decision that his documents entering the race for governor were received too late.

Today the Russian Federal Attorney General's Office protested this decision. The official statement was that the republican electoral committee incorrectly stated the last day for the submission of documents, thus misleading the members of the campaign. The sudden return of the director of the largest diamond mining company in Russia to the lists can mean that Moscow was able to reach an agreement with him. "Alrosa" has a profit of $15 billion a year. A fifth is retained in Yakutia, while Moscow is trying to decrease this share. Shtyrov was always against it. Now, there appears to be a reasonable question. Why is Moscow supporting him at this point?

4 | *Excavating concealed tradeoffs*

Citizens in democracies are expected to make better decisions if they understand tradeoffs involved in policy. If they know the pluses and minuses for a policy in terms of their own interests and preferences, they would be expected to vote for or against them. Scholars in the United States debate whether or not citizens are able to vote their own interests in the absence of that knowledge. However, politicians rarely have incentives to communicate tradeoffs; a campaign stump speech stressing all the desirable things voters stand to lose in pursuing a policy that is in other ways attractive would have a hard time passing the public relations phalanx. In the 1984 presidential campaign against Ronald Reagan, Walter Mondale's promise to raise taxes to achieve his goals was not a winning war cry. Why do it when, in addition, voters are made uncomfortable having to choose among valued outcomes? They would rather not face the dissonance. Even if one is prepared to take the medicine and face up to the losses to gain the better outcome, devising a common metric is difficult. How do I find equivalencies between the road I want, the parkland I want for the kids, and the medical complex everybody, including me, wants? It is not surprising that in the United States the political environment provides relatively little cuing or priming of tradeoffs in television news. Politicians don't want to alert voters to sacrifices, voters don't want to deal with the internal dissonances that conflicts of value engender, and even if the answers were positive, what should be compared to what?

Russian citizens, on the other hand, face a media environment in which tradeoff cuing is by intention thoroughly suppressed. Analysis of discourse among ordinary Russians showed that when watching news in which tradeoffs are thoroughly concealed, viewers have cognitive resources and habits identifying those that are uncued.

This chapter first appeared as "Excavating Concealed Tradeoffs," *Political Communication*, 22 (3), 2005: 355–380, published by the Taylor & Francis Group and reprinted with the permission of the publisher.

In 2003, as the United States was preparing for war, President Bush's speeches to the nation outlined an array of initiatives to improve life in America. Writing in the *New York Times*, Frank Rich pointed to a familiar problem: The "rhetoric says we can have it all – lower taxes, better schools, a war or two or three, civil defense – without pain."[1] Such encouragement of virtually cost-free solutions with no sacrifice of desires paints a world of good news and no competing claims or anguish about choice. It is a world without tradeoffs, a world that sets a low bar for what should be expected from voters. Why do they take the time to become informed about unnecessary information?

In the research literature, a tradeoff is defined most simply as a decision "among competing goals that cannot all be fully achieved."[2] Many scholars emphasize the ability of ordinary people to arrive at reasonably rational outcomes in spite of low levels of political knowledge. "Rational" means taking a position or voting in support of what is best for that individual's life. That definition suggests, as does Downs (1956),[3] that for individuals without a special need tied to economic salience or activists' special topics it makes sense to be "rationally ignorant." There is no compelling need for most people to spend their rationed time outside work in becoming expert on some place or ethnic conflict that will never touch them. For a long time before the 1979 Soviet invasion of Afghanistan, as the Foreign Editor of the *New York Times* told me, it was policy that foreign stories of little interest should be put on the Afghanistan page, consigned among the least-read parts of the paper. And then the world changed.

If ordinary American citizens score poorly on political knowledge tests, but know well their own best strategy through the use of heuristics, is that a judgment about the capacity of ordinary citizens? If we fail to have anything more than rational ignorance (which might be quite enough for most of the citizenry), is the weakness located in us – in human information processing limitations, or in an environment poor in cues? And what does it matter if individuals don't always vote in their own interests, because they are unable always to get them right? And what does it matter if, by doing so, the signals from the voters – i.e. the

---

[1] F. Rich, "Joe Millionaire for President," *New York Times* January 18, 2003: A35.

[2] J. H. Kuklinski, P. J. Quirk, J. Jerit, and R. F. Rich, "The Political Environment and Citizen Competence," *American Journal of Political Science*, 45, 2001: 410–434, p. 411.

[3] A. Downs, *An Economic Theory of Democracy*. New York, Harper, 1956.

votes – pass along to the top policy-makers a decision about valued interests that would turn out to have been quite different had the voters known more and the policy been more transparent?

Before the voting process is even on the radar, we need to know if ordinary people can recognize a tradeoff – do citizens even recognize that tradeoffs exist? Maybe we can have it all, or at least live as though we can, and think about it no further. To make the struggle between treating tradeoffs as serious elements of policy and avoiding them, our study is set in a political environment that intentionally conceals tradeoffs and avoids cues. The burden of identifying tradeoffs is thus placed entirely on citizens. This system, especially proficient in concealing tradeoffs in public policy, is today's Russia. To find out how viewers handle tradeoff-free news stories we used focus groups in four Russian cities to whom naturally occurring television news stories with different treatment of the same event were shown. The discourse of the participants is energized, sometimes passionate, and reveals not only an awareness of the tradeoffs missing from the story but also the puzzling ease with which many of the participants contribute so many tradeoffs not expressed or cued by the news. The research conditions and design, the populations, and the political environment in Russia are all significantly different from the Western research work cited.

The news story's treatment of the opening of an oil pipeline is framed as a triumph of wealth acquisition and international recognition. Many Russian focus group participants brought up likely tradeoffs between the environment and budget growth, between the pipeline placement and national security, between collective/societal benefits and harm to individuals at the site, and many others.

The relevant Western literature uses new understandings of cognition in new ways to explore such questions. The political and media context of the Russian focus groups address the following question: Based on the discourse of ordinary Russian viewers as they watch news stories, to what degree (if at all), with what strategies, and according to what sources are tradeoffs perceived, absent cues in the broadcast? Further, given the difficulty of dealing with tradeoffs in general, if Russians do so under particularly unfavorable conditions why do they expend effort effectively to create additional potential options, when the political environment makes it so difficult? It is not enlightening to compare findings about Russians and Americans: methods, polities, and populations are vastly different. The tool box Russians use to make sense of their news is adapted to particular conditions, it is true; it is certainly an asset where the provenance and reliability of information is obscure and advocacy without tradeoff cues is the norm.

To make the project even more challenging, what if the television properties of owners opposing government policies were taken away and viewpoint diversity across channels removed to eliminate opposing views? In that scenario, is it even conceivable that citizens could be aware of tradeoffs? The question is posed to stretch our notions of citizens' strategies in an especially harsh and taxing information environment. At the time of this study, Russia's media environment included a degree of external viewpoint diversity and permitted us to compare tradeoff identification both with and without diversity.[4]

Information processing and assimilating the news

The framing of a news story is critical to its assimilation by the viewer. Perhaps the most concise and comprehensive definition of framing, as used in this study, is Entman's (2004):[5] "selecting and highlighting some facets of events or issues, and making connections among them so as to promote a particular interpretation, evaluation and/or solution." Framing choices often inhibits understanding the news. Graber (2001) finds that "in the vast majority of political news stories, framing does not match the manner in which ordinary Americans tend to store such information, making matching difficult or impossible."[6] How a story is framed can have an impact on how viewers assign responsibility for the event, as Iyengar (1991)[7] found in experiments designed to look at the differences between episodic frames, "focusing on specific events

---

[4] The newspaper market is quite different from the television market in the range of views available. However, since circulation is relatively low, national reach so circumscribed, and since most people rely for their news primarily on Moscow-based television networks, a concentration on television is warranted. This is not to deny the importance, especially for the Moscow and St. Petersburg elites, of the views and long-form stories found in trusted newspapers. Use of the Internet is growing rapidly, but is still a mid- to large-size-city activity.

[5] R. M. Entman, *Projections of Power: Framing News, Public Opinion, and US Foreign Policy*. Chicago, University of Chicago Press, 2004: 5.

[6] D. Graber, *Processing Politics: Learning from Television in the Internet Age*. Chicago, University of Chicago Press, 2001: 26.

[7] S. Iyengar, *Is Anyone Responsible? How Television Frames Political Issues*. Chicago, University of Chicago Press, 1991: 2.

or particular cases" and putting an individual in the foreground, and "thematic" frames, that place "political issues and events in some general context" and may feature government or officials as main actors. Media frame news stories, but so do viewers. The research that follows also considers viewers' reactions to the framing of news stories by Russian television.

Finally, the importance of priming is a major element in the way people process the news. As chapter 3 showed, Iyengar *et al.*'s (1982) early experiments in New Haven and their continuing work, in addition to analyzing the agenda-setting effects of television, have findings also related to evidence of priming: as "the ability of the news programs to affect the criteria by which individuals judge their political leaders."[8] Priming, if it lasts, can cue evaluations in subsequent considerations of an issue or individual.

The success of priming depends on viewers being unaware that they are being primed. "Directing subjects' attention to the source of influence [i.e. of the priming] led to a correction of their judgment ... If subjects were reminded of the priming event, no assimilation effect was obtained."[9] In other words, if the deliberate insertion of the cue was pointed out, the information was simply not accepted. Official discourse in Russia during the Soviet era considered the function of the media to engage in priming and television, as the most pervasive medium, was also the most carefully managed for this purpose. Neither broadcasters nor viewers were ignorant of this stated public policy. Coupled with the importance of source credibility in the literature referred to below, there are likely to be important differences in the Russian and American public's awareness of uncued tradeoffs.

Cues in the political environment, heuristics, and low-information rationality

Cognitive processing is also part of the research on political heuristics and collective opinion from the perspective of citizens acting to advance

---

[8] S. Iyengar, M. D. Peters, and D. Kinder, "Experimental Demonstrations of the Not-so-Minimal Consequences of Television News Programs," *American Political Science Review*, 76, 1982: 183.

[9] F. Strack, N. Schwarz, H. Bless, A. Kubler, and M. Wänke, "Awareness of Influence as a Determinant of Assimilation versus Contrast," *European Journal of Social Psychology*, 23, 1993: 53–62, p. 59.

their preferences. How much political information should American citizens have to make rational decisions? Or, to put it more broadly, how much of what kind of information should Americans know to vote in their own interests and to signal to their elected representatives their views about public policy issues that will affect them? Just how much they do *not* know has been a painful subject when, time after time, tests are given to assess how many know a number of facts presumably necessary for competent citizens: questions about elected officials, the judicial system, percentage of the budget that goes to foreign aid, and so forth. But are these the relevant questions? Much of the literature says that they are not, because these questions matter little to people in their everyday lives; most ordinary people arrive at rational conclusions by employing heuristics. Some students of voting argue that low-information voters use compensatory practices to advance their preferences. Arguments for "low-information rationality" maintain that citizens develop shortcuts that generally represent their interests, and that they do not wish, or need, to engage in learning more.[10] However, the optimism of these studies relies on the view that "the environment gives people simple judgment tasks to perform and generally provides reliable cues to help citizens perform them."[11]

A second strand about positive views of citizen judgment under conditions of low information is collective opinion, which argues that the errors of individually ill-informed citizens tend to be random, not additive, and will cancel each other out. This is a position to which Kuklinski and Quirk (2000) take exception, arguing that empirical findings "do not rule out even major distortions in public opinion."[12] Collective inadequacy and misunderstanding is in no way impossible.

As is obvious from these research disagreements, much depends on whether or not ordinary Americans, with their limited fund of political knowledge, can actually find in their political environment the necessary

---

[10] A. Lupia and M. D. McCubbins, *The Democratic Dilemma: Can Citizens Learn What They Need to Know?* Cambridge, Cambridge University Press, 1998; S. L. Popkin, *The Reasoning Voter: Communication and Persuasion in Presidential Campaigns*, 2nd edn. Chicago, University of Chicago Press, 1994. See also Downs, *An Economic Theory of Democracy*.

[11] J. H. Kuklinski and P. J. Quirk, "Reconsidering the Rational Public: Cognition, Heuristics, and Mass Opinion," in A. Lupia, M. D. McCubbins, and S. Popkin, eds., *Elements of Reason: Cognition, Choice, and the Bounds of Rationality*. Cambridge, Cambridge University Press, 2000: 410.

[12] Kuklinski and Quirk, "Reconsidering the Rational Public": 161.

cues by which they can then activate the heuristics that enable them to
reach a genuinely preferred outcome. Several studies have shown that
the political environment in the United States may not provide the
information or cues with which to trigger the necessary reasoning.[13] In
other words, that larger political environment in which we all live may
not give us much to go on, or remind us of similar experiences and
similar conditions. We have to do all this basically for ourselves. Nor
are critics optimistic about outcomes of low-information rationality.
With meager information about public affairs, distracted and declining
news-consuming publics send skewed signals to policy-makers that,
ultimately, distort the democratic process.[14] They may send signals
based on an incorrect understanding, or actual ignorance, of what
policy issues are in play, and the consequences betray the premise of
democracy.

Tradeoffs as tests for citizens

Our study of Russian television viewers is designed, through their
discourse in focus groups, to see how they talk about assimilating –
or rejecting – the information they see and, as a higher-level observation, to examine the degree to which in the absence of cues they
actually identify tradeoffs. What kinds of heuristics do they employ,
and why? The case of tradeoffs is particularly difficult, because both
voters and politicians have disincentives to reveal them. The hesitation
of politicians to cue the "bad news" of tradeoffs is complemented by
people's discomfort with the unpleasantness of hard choices. "Rather
than deal with relevant tradeoffs, citizens will normally be inclined
to ignore them or to rationalize them away. It is much easier to over-
look tradeoffs through a form of wishful thinking than to confront
them directly."[15] Then, too, tradeoffs may be difficult to subject to a

---

[13] L. Bartels, "Uninformed Votes: Information Effects in Presidential Elections,"
American Political Science Review, 40, 1996: 194–230; Kuklinski and Quirk,
"Reconsidering the Rational Public."

[14] J. L. Hochschild, "Where you Stand Depends on what you See," in
J. H. Kuklinski, ed., *Citizens and Politics: Perspectives from Political
Psychology*. Cambridge, Cambridge University Press, 2001: 313–340;
M. Carpini, *What Americans Know about Politics and Why It Matters*.
New Haven: Yale University Press, 1996.

[15] Kuklinski *et al.*, "The Political Environment": 415.

common metric: apples versus oranges or electric power versus cultural–
aesthetic pleasure.[16]

On the other hand, ordinary people must be pretty good "cognitive
managers"; they face tradeoffs continuously, when they shop, plan
outings, buy a house, and vote. Should leaders of democracies, then,
seek popular support by advancing their proposals as though they
entailed no tradeoffs? Or, rather, is it the statesman-like leader who
benefits from expressing the complexities of tradeoffs in his or her
proposals? Tetlock (2000)[17] concludes:

> Many people believe that their core values do not conflict and they need to be
> prodded, sometimes poked pretty hard, into acknowledging that these values
> do conflict. But once primed to believe that trade-offs are a pervasive feature
> of political life, they become quite skeptical of rhetorical claims to have
> identified a dominant solution, often dismissing them as implausible, shrill,
> manipulative, and even demagogic.

Yet, Tetlock also points "to the high frequency with which people
deny even obvious tradeoffs [and] to the far more enthusiastic response
most people have to simple rhetoric that denies trade-offs than to
complex . . . rhetoric that acknowledges [them]."

Priming, poking, cuing – all of these prodding impulses have to come
from somewhere to help people recognize a tradeoff in a scenario.
Kuklinski and Quirk (2000)[18] note that, in America, "usable cues are
not regularly available. Statements by leading officials endorsing or
opposing proposals in Congress appear infrequently on network news
programs. If cues do not appear, citizens cannot use them." This need
not be taken as an indictment of the citizen, however. When citizens do
get the relevant information from the environment, they can deal with
tradeoffs more competently.

It is logical to assume that if cuing is so important in recognizing
tradeoffs, if it comes to a considerable degree from the television news
environment, and if there is so little of it in America, then Russian
citizens must be hopelessly vulnerable. Burdened by over seventy years

---

[16] P. E. Tetlock, "Coping with Trade-offs: Psychological Constraints and Political
Implications," in Lupia, McCubbins, and Popkin, eds., *Elements of Reason:
Cognition, Choice, and the Bounds of Rationality*. Cambridge, Cambridge
University Press, 2000: 239–263.

[17] Tetlock, "Coping with Trade-offs": 262–263.

[18] Kuklinski and Quirk, "Reconsidering the Rational Public": 156–157.

of information control and a post-Soviet television environment of limited choice and heavy-handed governmental intrusiveness, how could they recognize tradeoffs when so much of what they see is devoted to concealing them? Perhaps we can learn something meaningful about citizens' inherent limitations or, on the contrary, endowments by examining their capacity to recognize policy tradeoffs under exceptionally unfavorable conditions.

As the findings below display, although the Soviet legacy of media-processing is still in use, viewers tend to be skeptical, not cynical, for their way of processing the news requires them to work hard. Were it merely a cynical exercise we would not see the repeated pattern of engaging with the news story, dredging the memory, and using life experiences to amplify the meager ration of real news. The Soviet legacy has indeed taught skepticism which, in turn, has shaped the repertoire of methods of extraction of news unintended and uncued from broadcasts. This is a process that is sophisticated and varied among viewers, and can hardly be reduced to that old saw: "reading between the lines." Of course viewers do, but that conclusion simply obscures the difficult job of analysis of how and why given groups and individuals use certain cognitive mechanisms. Many in the focus groups did refer to their patterns of information reception during the Soviet period; not a few saw parallels between that time and the present. These habits continue, as do expectations at work and at home that one is up-to-date with the news. There is a good deal of social pressure to keep up with the news. Some focus groups described these pressures from spouses (usually husbands) and co-workers as social norms of considerable weight.

This is another argument for examining the reception of television news in a focus group – and, therefore, in a social setting. The view from the top – of political leaders and media managers – is of a citizenry limited in its ability to understand the complexities of the modern world, think in terms of tradeoffs, or critically assess the policy issues in play. Owners, including the government, display an outsized confidence in what they believe to be their mastery of compelling people to absorb their news agendas.[19]

[19] E. Mickiewicz, *Changing Channels: Television and the Struggle for Power in Russia*, rev. and expand. edn. Durham, NC: Duke University Press, 1999.

How the focus groups worked

The sequencing of the four news excerpts in the appendix was determined by ratings popularity (highest to lowest), beginning with the two heavily state-dominated stations, Channel One and then Channel Two. Next, stories were shown from the commercial station NTV, which accommodated state framing preferences, and finally the oppositionist TV-6. This sequencing served another purpose as well: after watching the first three examples of coverage, our focus group viewers were essentially in the position Russian viewers would be in later (after the spring of 2003) – without the external diversity of TV-6 or its milder, less accessible, short-lived successor, TVS. It was possible, therefore, to examine the discourse both with and without external diversity.

This definition of tradeoffs required specificity about competing nontrivial goals, not generalized dissatisfaction with the comprehensiveness of a story or ill-defined complaints about tone, aesthetics of presentation, or salience. After each story, there was a discussion, and participants provided their reactions. Discussion of a particular story would typically start with a probe by the facilitator, such as: "What do you think about this story?" or "What do you say about this? Did you get some information about what happened?" After watching the stories, the participants were asked which network they thought they had just watched. The answers were varied, especially because stories about events outside Moscow were at first said to be "local television" by at least some of the viewers in each group. However, in virtually every case, the reasoning upon which the identification was based was the style and ideology of the station, and not any familiar faces. Because we were so acutely aware that knowledge of the station during the showing could affect the resulting judgment of its ideology, we were extremely careful to keep any station logo or recognizable station "faces" out of the frame.

The subject of all the stories was the opening of the massive pipeline bringing oil from Kazakhstan to the Black Sea port city of Novorossisk in Russia. Why this story? First, stories like this, about economic achievement, are very frequent on television news, not only on channels supporting government policy, and this was a very big event with international and domestic dimensions. Second, given the meager choices for viewers, whether they like them or not, these are stories they encounter repeatedly. Finally, and most important, this kind of story is a prime example of broadcasters' assumptions about their publics: that the message of upbeat, tradeoff-free activity will be welcomed and assimilated. It was not until the fourth story – when there was still independent television available – that the downsides of the pipeline were covered.[20]

In the discussion after each of the first three stories, the participants talked about the upbeat, smoothly positive stories. There were, as the texts in the appendix show, no problematic or ambivalent moments in the transmitted messages, yet increasing numbers of people in the focus groups – with and without a college education – offered their own tradeoffs. In fact, the list of tradeoffs was quite long, came from rather diverse policy domains, and represented a range of cognitive strategies, some of which were considerably more abstract than others and linked their observations (together with what they were able to extract from the stories) into complex reasoning outcomes. When the fourth story arrived on the scene, bringing with it a thoroughly negative outlook on the same event, the participants were still unwilling to be satisfied with this mode of tradeoff-free news and, again, supplied their own.

After the first positive story

By far the most stringent test of the capacity to identify tradeoffs was the first story, with its dense recital of achievements. After the first story was shown, 27 percent of the participants introduced tradeoffs that were not cued by the story. By the end of the discussion about the first story, every focus group except one in Volgograd had at least one participant who had identified at least one tradeoff.

---

[20] Eighty percent of the focus group participants accessed the news at least three–four times a week (and 50 percent did so daily), and over 80 percent depended solely on Moscow-based networks for news. Among the Moscow-based networks, Channel One was listed by a wide margin as the first or only source. Eighty-four percent of the participants listed multiple sources for news. Of the twenty-six individuals who put down a single source, only one named the unorthodox TV-6; most of the rest cited Channel One. Those who listed newspapers among their sources of news did not name the newspaper. That most of the participants were tuned in mainly to government-influenced or government-run stations squares with the ratings data.

After three positive stories, no external viewpoint diversity
When participants had seen the first three examples of coverage, they had experienced three channels with no real diversity of viewpoint, a condition they were to find themselves in when TV-6 was shut down in 2002. Russian audiences were left without diversity of viewpoints on national channels, a situation analogous to the stage reached by our focus groups when they had seen three versions of the same celebratory viewpoint on the first three tapes. By the end of the third version of the pipeline story, 50 percent of all the focus group participants had brought up tradeoffs, and in every focus group in every city tradeoffs were discussed.

Content of tradeoffs after stories without viewpoint diversity
The number of tradeoff topics is large, even though cues are suppressed, because Russian viewers are very likely, in the normal course of life, either to bring up tradeoffs themselves or to hear people around them doing so. Tradeoffs are accepted as a necessary part of life, and viewers are predisposed to approach a news story with the assumption that tradeoffs will occur. Many viewers define objectivity as the provision of tradeoffs in a story. The elements of discourse about tradeoffs summarized below progress from simpler tradeoff definitions to those representing a more abstract navigation of the story and linkage of several components. It is impressive that tradeoffs were offered even after the first story which, as seen in the appendix, was a sterile, fact-laden set of assertions: 27 percent of the focus group viewers identified tradeoffs well beyond the frame of the story and its limited visuals. In the entire group of stories without viewpoint diversity (the first three), there were no visuals or texts (again, see the appendix) that sparked a tradeoff recognition, with one exception: the first and second stories explicitly played up the American presence as investor and international partner. These frames did cue reactions among several viewers, but not those intended by the broadcaster.

Security tradeoffs
Because the pipeline terminates at the city of Novorossisk, not far from Chechnya, some thought that security was being traded for cost savings and efficiency of transport: Gennady (31, programmer, Rostov) said that "it [the pipeline] runs through Krasnodar region or Rostov region; the Chechens will run around there and blow it up."

Direct damage to the environment

By far the most frequently identified tradeoff was oil versus damage to the environment. Viktor and Zoya (60s, pensioners, high-school education, Nizhny Novgorod) engaged in the following exchange:

Viktor: There could be an ecological catastrophe.
Zoya: In our country, of course, there will be – this pipeline.
Viktor: And they didn't say anything about it.

College-educated Viktor, 60 and retired, from Volgograd, offered this bleak scenario: "If we speak about oil, then it's something that we'll talk about – such a catastrophe for nature that at any moment, there could be an irreversible catastrophe."

Other warnings linked the pipeline to the string of resorts and children's summer camps in the area. A young teacher in Rostov said that "it might not be possible to go to university camp near here," and a photographer (31) noted that "other resorts might be hurt."

Social class and corruption

News of a major project promising revenue for Russia set off conversations about the likely beneficiaries. At issue was the cost of the project (for which the many pay) and the benefits (which may go to a few). The discourse on this tradeoff was centered on feelings of marginality and powerlessness. Some of the conversation came from people with high-school educations, such as Valentina (42, white-collar employee, volgograd) and Valery (38, blue-collar worker, Volgograd):

Valentina: For us, really the most important thing to understand is where the money's going, who is getting rich from this.
Valery: Where are our dividends? After all, they're our resources
Valentina: In the first and this story, you can understand, someone here is really getting rich.

Some of the conversation linked oil, Russia's primary source of revenue, to criminal arrangements. It was impossible to imagine that corrupt businessmen and officials would not divert a good part of what was promised. As Maxim (28, college-educated entrepreneur, Moscow) said: "The project itself is very interesting, what we just heard about, but it is a very criminal story. There was a lot that was puzzling there." Irina agreed: "Maxim said it right – it's such a criminal theme." College-educated Andrei (42, entrepreneur, Volgograd) named only tycoons as beneficiaries: "how much Vyakhirev and Alikperov [energy industry magnates] will get."

Viktor (ship captain, based in Moscow) claimed that "someone in this will pocket more money than we've ever dreamed of." In Rostov, Lilia said: "I personally doubt that there will be profits, because they're always saying in our country there's a big profit; we're doing something there. And no one gets this profit." Alexei asked sarcastically: "What, you don't get any?," to general laughter. Whether or not the participants thought that there should be strict regulation of income differences (Lilia, Alexei, Valentina, Galina) or believed that the market would sort them out (the others), all talked as though they would be denied the promised benefits, that in the face of large-scale corruption, the individual is powerless, a mood familiar from chapter 2.

Budgetary consequences

At a somewhat more complex level, some viewers tied the opening of the pipeline to the probability of higher taxes and higher oil prices. Mark (computer engineer, Rostov) asked "How much [tax] do I have to pay for this?" Natasha (50, tax inspector, Moscow) did not feel like celebrating the opening: "You feel indifference, already [there is] the thought that taxes will go up." Katya warned: "I think that they are preparing the people that, guys, you need money, and they'll raise taxes. That's the subtext of this material." Others were worried that the price of oil would go up, such as Maxim, the Moscow bookkeeper. Alena, (high-school-educated artist and fashion designer, Volgograd) asked:

What do our country's ordinary mortals get from this agreement, and how does the oil pipeline help them, that prices won't jump? We have the Volga GES [hydroelectric station], but we don't have energy. The mechanism is so complicated that they first give it to somebody and then that person sells it to us – our own Volga energy – and as a result instead of paying several times less, it's just the opposite, we pay more. So why do we have to sell it to somebody somewhere?

Opportunity costs

A still more complicated and abstract sequence weighed the opportunity costs of routing the pipeline through Novorossisk. Vladimir (30, teacher, Moscow) offered alternatives:

They could also have given us information such as why they constructed this pipeline; why did they reject other projects but began to build it ... in this story, there's no comparative information – why we built this pipeline and why it's more profitable. Although actually it is profitable for us, why is it less profitable to go through Ukraine, [or] through the Baltics? They didn't convey everything, all the pluses and minuses.

The same tradeoff was named by Sergei in Nizhny Novgorod, who asked: "Why do this when it could all be done at [the new terminal in] Petersburg?" Merchant marine captain Viktor knew that you "don't have to have tankers go right through the Caspian; [you] could do it another way."

The price of joining the club: domestic costs of international linkages

The news stories celebrated Russia's new status in the international community. In the first story (on Channel One), although the reporter referred to an international group of investors, he named only Kazakhstan and Oman, and representatives of those countries had no airtime. However, it was not until the second story (on Channel Two, directly owned by the Russian government) that the list of investors was made comprehensive. On the dais at the opening ceremony were a group of VIPs, including local politicians, Russian ministerial officials, Russian oil magnates, and foreign visitors. In the first story, only Russians spoke, but in the second and third stories, there was an emphasis on the pride of "belonging" and the fact that Americans had come with praise and investments. These stories showed America as a central participant. In the second story, it was an assistant secretary of the Department of Energy who read a short speech in English about mutual trust and cooperation. The third story similarly stressed the government's positive accent on American participation. This time, it was US Ambassador Vershbow, speaking in Russian about improving mutual relations.

But the network's preferred emphasis on having gained respectful recognition by the powerful former enemy was not that most commonly absorbed in the focus groups. Both characterizations of Americans in these two stories created for many viewers their own evaluations, in which arrogance, wealth, and exploitation (rather than investment) was the burden of the story. Many viewers worked out a different balance sheet: they, Russia, would have to pay too much for American political favor, because the Russian government had paid with domestic well-being for political advantage in the international arena. In Rostov, Igor (high-school-educated) noted: "From this [third] story, it's clearer why it [the pipeline] was done; it was done to support relations with America." Irina, a housewife in the same group, said: "I agree with Igor that it is done for Russian/American relations." From Nizhny Novgorod, after the second story, college-educated Vladimir complained: "Well, I think that all this in principle is that they built the pipeline for some plainly political reasons, that's it. I don't see any special economic achievements for Russia in it." Nikolai said: "The pipeline from the purely technical side isn't much. But the thought that now we are beginning to collaborate specifically with America, with them. And in principle it's all being done for them."

In another college-educated Nizhny Novgorod group, Sergei (28) stated after the second story: "I think it's a betrayal of national interests. Maybe I'm so emotional because my father fought in military battles. But I think that it's absolutely ingratiating ourselves with the Americans." According to Vladimir (43, college-educated, salesman, Moscow), referring to the American presence at the pipeline celebration in the second story: "Everything's normal, the boss came and you keep quiet." And Ira (53, housewife) observed that: "the visual is convincing that foreigners are already in charge here." When the discussion was about environmental protection, the image of Americans changed radically. [These viewers compartmentalize different policy domains. American collaboration on preservation was discussed as more valuable than anything the Russian government provided.]

Reversing the tradeoff direction: after the fourth story, negative views

If viewers really do have the capacity to identify tradeoffs, they should be able to do so even when the story is framed in a radically different way: eschewing officialese, highly emotional, personalized, and warning of the very tradeoffs so much of the focus group discussion had already brought up. The fourth story (on TV-6), presented an array of drawbacks. The pipeline achievement, it argued, was scarcely that: it was an ecological catastrophe in the making, sure to leak; it was vulnerable to earthquake activity; it was constructed on land fraudulently appropriated by the state from impoverished elderly people; the victimized, weeping peasants could not defend their rights and had nowhere to go. The story was also radically different in tone and angle of vision; it was about individual lives, despair, and disclosure of exploitation. Every focus group had participants who faulted the story for its failure to provide tradeoffs and contributed tradeoffs showing that the story depicted the threat inaccurately, that the advantages of the project were downplayed to nonexistence, and that both societal and individual costs and benefits, though often in conflict, should be portrayed.

The fourth story was entirely about the pipeline's negative impact, framed as an emotionally powerful story of impending disaster and exploitation of the helpless. To qualify as a tradeoff, discourse about this story would have to bring up positive options to set against the unmitigated pessimism. But, as the appendix shows, the story itself used a framing perspective far different from the first three: it was heavily emotional, concentrating on the plight of individuals, most of whom were elderly, without resources, expelled from their homes by a government that had requisitioned land for the pipeline. It had visuals of unspoiled mountain ranges and warned dramatically of ecological disaster.

The personalization of the story introduced the opportunity for compassion for the plight of others because of the emotional presentation. This side was perhaps best articulated by the group with secondary education in Volgograd. Here, the personal dimension was so powerful that it overrode other parts but, even more important, the framing of the story as about individuals and their fates made it the most gripping of all the four. The previous three, many in this group believed, were intended for "economists"; this one was for them, ordinary viewers, ordinary people:

Andrei: It touched more on the problem of people.
Alena: In principle, when Dima said that all these news, they're not for us, it's necessary for economists to know, but here they've really touched our interests.
Alexander: They touched the human factor.
Alena: This one was interesting to watch ...
Dima: Why is it necessary if it has a negative impact on ecology, if people, if they show a granny to whom they say if you don't sign this document we'll take this piece of land away anyway. That's our state which should care about the welfare of the person and its acts against [them].

Yet, in spite of the close-ups of grieving elderly women and the unfairness conveyed by the partisan reporter, focus group participants, even when evidently sympathetic to the personal dimensions conveyed so emotionally and dramatically, did identify the tradeoffs that this story concealed.

Downsizing the ecological threat: tradeoffs countering the message

The fourth story was so negative that, as some of the conversation went, it was impossible to figure out why the pipeline had been built at all. Post-Soviet Maxim (history teacher) said that this story "is only about the consequences. But we didn't hear anything about the reasons, the reasons." Maxim (the Moscow bookkeeper) noted: "If you watch only the last story, then why did they build the pipeline? Why did they cut down the grove, take away people's land, pollute the sea, why? It's incomprehensible if you watch just this story."

In much of the discourse, participants reassessed the risks asserted in the coverage. For example, according to Muscovites Viktor (the merchant marine captain) and Natasha:.

Viktor: You understand that the thing is that Novorossisk from time immemorial was an oil terminal even without this pipeline. That's the first thing. Secondly, it's not such a resort; it's an industrial city, because there's a big cement factory there.
Natasha: There it's all gray; I've been there.

Other elements of discourse faulted the story for failing to report on safety measures:

Yury (63, retired, college education, Rostov): You see, it would seem that if you give this information then you should say that such-and-such was foreseen in the project. And in the case of a rupture how it will be localized and so forth. They were obliged [by law] to examine them [risks] and there are whole volumes.

Dmitry Valerevich (33, high-school education, unemployed, Volgograd): What problem? Where? There isn't any yet, right? There's no ecological problem ... Right away, when they put in these pipelines ... they take into account that there are mountains, that it goes through mountainous terrain. It can't be that they didn't consider this; they simply don't do it that way. They have to invest money and they're [concerned] that there be no accidents.

Assessing ecological expertise, what really mattered in the discourse was the participation of the Americans who, unlike the Russian state, care about the environment and use the most modern equipment. Even though there were no American ecologists shown or named in the story, a very different dimension of America is emphasized:

Viktor (the ship's captain, Moscow): Since the Americans were also involved in the construction, they pay a great deal of attention to ecology. If a bomb doesn't fall on the oil pipeline, it's very unlikely [to rupture] or burst or be torn, because the pipe is 2 m in diameter.

Andrei (43, college-educated, working in construction and design, Rostov): The thing is that I have to confront protection of the environment in my work. I know these demands, but I know that this question is well analyzed. International expertise was in it and they watch out for ecology.

Individual and collective interests: revenue versus trees

The fourth story, in contrast to the preceding ones, focused on the pipeline as a personal issue: the plight of individuals crushed by a state. Many in the focus groups agreed with this point of view, lamenting the powerlessness and exploitation of individuals. However, they offered tradeoffs to right the balance and favored the larger entity – the national economy:

Oksana (45, college education, dispatcher, Moscow): The interests of the state there are a lot higher than the old woman crying for her piece of land.

Viktor (22, college education, tour manager, Moscow): I repeat again – the numbers and especially the details don't interest me. But this is clear that yes there is an oil pipeline, that yes it's bad for people, and that Russia can get something good from it.

Antonina (24, graduate student, Nizhny Novgorod): On the other hand . . . there should be people who can get work there. If they take away a little piece of land from the old woman, still someone there will also get work.

The focus groups were not asked to propose solutions or to take positions on preferred policy outcomes. Still, the discourse revealed integrative reasoning in that compromise solutions were offered that recognized the legitimacy of tradeoffs while placing them within a society-wide context.[21] Svetlana (36, college-educated teacher, Moscow) remarked: "Really, it's necessary to try to avoid these difficulties, that is, to find

---

[21] G. Baker-Brown, E. Ballard, S. Bluck, B. De Vries, P. Suedfeld, and P. Tetlock, "The Conceptual/Integrative Complexity Scoring Manual," in C. Smith, ed., *Motivation and Personality: Handbook of Thematic Content Analysis.* Cambridge, Cambridge University Press, 1992.

ways so the economy develops and that old women in our country do not suffer." Bogdan (22, high-school education, Rostov) argued that even if the elderly people in Novorossisk are disadvantaged, revenue from the pipeline can help Russians elsewhere who are even worse off. Viktor (46, Moscow) proposed contractual solutions: "The only thing, the green ecologists should declare their demands that in the case of pollution, leak, and so forth, the company pays for all the losses."

Sources of tradeoffs

When tradeoffs were offered by viewers, how did they identify what brought them to mind? Tradeoffs, especially about the environment – the most frequently invoked – drew heavily on personal experience and were often expressed emotionally. The accessibility heuristic is one – perhaps the most – powerful organizing or learning shortcut that citizens use,[22] and for viewers, particularly from cities outside Moscow, it was obvious that these images were readily available and could be easily accessed.

In Rostov, Sergei (23, unemployed) remembered the Black Sea as a favorite vacation spot and imagined a changed scene:

And when I see this, I vacationed on the Black Sea, at that very same place, and when I recognized that there'll be a pipeline, that you'll see towers, I understood with horror that the next time I go there, if I go swimming, maybe I'll come out of the water [covered] with oil.

In the northern city of Nizhny Novgorod, Liuda (52, physician) recalls her shock at how a Black Sea vacation was transformed by sights of rotting fish:

How much our Russian regions have endured! After all the Black Sea is a resort area. It makes you prick up your ears because, you understand, when you're there in these places and when a tour guide leads a tour, he emphasizes how many fish are dying, how this oil, [for] which they [had pipelines] even before this big one, there was always oil there . . . and there were leaks several

[22] J. Ferejohn and J. H. Kuklinski, *Information and the Democratic Process.* Urbana, University of Illinois Press, 1990; D. Mutz, P. Sniderman, and R. Brody, eds., *Political Persuasion and Attitude Change.* Ann Arbor, University of Michigan Press, 1996; R. McDermott, "Arms Control and the First Reagan Administration: Belief Systems and Policy Choices," *Journal of Cold War Studies,* 4, 2002: 29–59.

times. And they always show that lots of fish died, how the flora and fauna of this shore suffered. And in fact this threat is increasing.

In another Rostov group, Irina (49, white-collar employee) explains why she thought about tradeoffs when she saw news of the pipeline:

Because we have a building, you know, they were building it here for years . . . That means everything got worn out, all the materials and so forth. And now it's being used some, and it's beginning to break down, like we have every-where in any situation. That's how our people, how we build, you know.

Julia (24, high-school-educated) said her Volgograd region has its own candidate for comparison; it's "just like in Volgodonsk; there was an oil leak there too . . . there were many cases." Nikolai (45, company general director, Nizhny Novgorod) claimed:

A bunch of pipelines are right here, going through Nizhny Novgorod, gas, oil, and so forth. So we are practically living on an oil pipeline . . . for me, in principle, this oil pipeline just isn't there. I simply go looking for mushrooms and you go practically right through oil and gas pipelines. That is, for me, it's become already a familiar event . . . around our countryside it's the second year they are digging the pipeline. I go close by them and look at what's going on. And there's gas there; there's oil there. I imagine what will happen if they break. They've also rotted; they've been lying there for 15 years.

In a Nizhny Novgorod group with secondary education, Slava com-pared the pipeline story to local disasters:

With us, in the Volga region, they built a hydroelectric station, they built a dam. Now we have no fish in the river; there's nothing. They also thought, of course, there would be advantages for everybody. Of course there are bene-fits, but it also destroyed the ecology, destroyed everything.

Post-Soviet groups and Moscow groups differed from the rest: Moscow groups tended not to bring up those searing personal exam-ples, and post-Soviet young people lacked the breadth to see tradeoffs in areas other than the environment. In the post-Soviet groups, virtually every tradeoff mentioned about the first three stories was only about ecology. Groups in Moscow, as a rule, were limited in linking personal experience to problems in the environment. Moscow's detached beha-vior also figured in a study conducted in 2003 by a respected group of Russian social scientists. They looked at issues of all kinds of participa-tion, political among them, across the country. The authors estimated that about 3–7 percent of the general population fell into the category of "activist," engaging in participation more active than voting. Nina Andreyenkova, director of the (Moscow) Institute of Comparative Social Studies, remarked:

> We expected to find activists in major cities, but it has turned out that most of them come from regional centers. Some of them stay there, some move to the capital. People from the capital seem complacent, they already have every-thing, but those from the provinces try to make further careers: having accomplished something at their level, they want more.[23]

The opposite also can be true; lack of personal experience may exaggerate psychological distance from others. Some spoke of Russia as a jumble of parts, only some of which belong to "their" Russia. Some comments, tellingly from a Moscow group and two post-Soviet groups in other cities, concluded that the story was remote. The following exchange occurred in the Moscow college-educated group:

Volodya: I have the impression that it was shot by a local studio . . .
Lena: Even if it's a local study, why not believe it? They're not so profes-sional; it has a local character . . .
Oksana: This is certainly a local story – out there in Vladivostok. But in Russia as a whole very few will be upset.
Lena: [*correcting Oksana*] In Novorossisk.
Oksana: In Novorossisk [*with the intonation of "whatever"*] some old gran-nies suffered.

The comments from the post-Soviet group in Nizhny Novgorod (all with some or completed college education) were as follows:

Nikolai (college student): From my side? Personally for me, it doesn't affect me at all.
Alena (mathematics teacher): It's not my backyard.
Nikolai: I don't live there and I have no connection with this money.

The post-Soviet and Moscow indifference may change over time as they age, or it may eventually represent a generational inclination toward greater alienation. In elections, youth lag in turnout, as they do in most democracies: "This ordinariness is something of a disappointment: the young adults who suffered the least from Soviet repression are the

---

[23] Press conference with a group of experts regarding the results of social research on democracy in Russia (November 4, 2003), retrieved from www.cdi.org.

most lethargic about taking advantage of the democratic suffrage."[24] One fascinating note to the contrary is the radical change in the "against-all" vote (see chapter 3), in which more youth took part than ever in the past until that choice was removed.

Personal experiences appear to be much less involved in detecting economic tradeoffs. Identifying tradeoffs as economic issues tends to be a more abstract process of reasoning and comes from the groups in Moscow more than anywhere else. In this capital city, with the highest percentage of college-educated citizens, we would expect the information-rich to be more numerous than in other cities. Moscow led the other cities in this study in volunteering the types of tradeoffs that put more demands on the capacity for abstract thinking, and these participants' understanding of economics appeared to be more nuanced.

"Commissioned" but objective: Russian viewers and Western research on tradeoff behavior

Notwithstanding the formidable obstacles to detecting tradeoffs, a large number of participants in the focus groups turned out to be capable of filling in missing tradeoffs in the three thoroughly positive stories, as well as in the fourth story that challenged the positive view with unremittingly negative coverage. More important, the types of tradeoffs they brought up revealed a broad range of issues and considerable sophistication. Even before the oppositional newscast was shown – when there were still no negative cues – tradeoffs were identified in areas of national security (e.g. the war in Chechnya), ecology (e.g. the environmental hazards of oil transport), economics (e.g. the opportunity costs of routing options), budgetary consequences (e.g. the effects on taxes and oil prices), international relations (e.g. political advantage versus domestic welfare benefits and control of natural resources), and society/equity (e.g. social class, corruption, and distributional inequities). The tradeoff-conscious Russian viewers accepted the transaction costs of making sense of the news. They were likely to expend effort when tradeoff cues were absent, since many defined the objectivity of a

[24] T. Colton, *Transitional Citizens: Voters and What Influences Them in the New Russia*. Cambridge, MA, Harvard University Press, 2000: 40–41.

news story precisely in terms of the presence of tradeoffs. As college-educated Igor said in his Moscow group: "Whenever it is one-sided, that's when it jumps out at you that this is ordered up."

In fact, Russians in the focus groups in effect defined objectivity as the presence of opposing views even if those views represented the clash of special interests. This working definition departs from the Western notion of objectivity as the absence of bias and is implicitly, as noted above, an acknowledgment that whatever degree of "objectivity" is achieved results from the effortful construct the viewer makes. Take, for example Sasha and Denis, both in the post-Soviet Volgograd group:

Sasha: When a person is presented with objective information, they talk about both pluses and minuses.
Denis: Then in principle you can say about any story that it is not objective, because in those stories they said pluses, and in this one minuses.

Objectivity is of two kinds: the weighing of advantages and disadvantages in a single communication produces the rarely encountered internal diversity. The other form of objectivity comes from comparing multiple self-interested and biased (but differently biased) sources. While TV-6 still operated, it was the only source of this kind of pluralism on the national television networks. According to Oksana (high-school-educated property surveyor, Moscow): "They say what is the best channel to watch. You have to watch them all from different points of view and then there'll be the whole picture." Mark (computer engineer, Rostov) said: "At the very beginning of our discussion I said that it is my principle to watch all the channels and they lie everywhere. I understand this, I seek the middle."

Such contests supply the space – between the clashing views – into which individual powers of observation and integration can be activated and therefore become socially relevant. As Ivan (student, Rostov) noted after the fourth story: "Now you can say that there is simply a full discussion of the given issue. In principle, now it is a complete change. And it's possible now to discuss this theme with someone." The opposite of objectivity is, according to the focus group participants, "manipulation," "prejudice," and "lies," and all of them are regarded as attempts to reduce the human capacity to exercise judgment. They are recognized as priming attempts and resented as displays of contempt for them by the powerful. This suggests that the power of the media assumed by Russian political and economic elites is far less than they are paying for and that controlling the message of television news to exclude tradeoffs is likely to stimulate among viewers a larger universe of tradeoffs than a Western-style "balanced" story with only two sides might normally produce.

Russians detect tradeoffs in news stories under two difficult conditions: one is the absence of viewpoint diversity in a story, and the other is the possibility – likelihood, rather – that an owner's pressure or a patron's money has had a part in directing the agenda of the story. They expect commercial and governmental involvement in shaping the news. They believe it is the viewer's responsibility to extract significance and correct for bias. Multiple sourcing, comparisons with experience, observations from friends and relatives closer to the scene – the burden is on the viewer to expend time and energy sifting out the truth among differing accounts.[25]

Why do Russian news viewers expend the effort and actually find the trail of tradeoffs they have had to uncover without a road map of cues? The complexities of processing the news in Russia are probably closest to one of the theoretical environments posited by Kuklinski *et al.* (2001), when these authors considered two limiting cases bracketing the space in which lies a range of realistic possibilities for the American subjects of tradeoff research:

At one extreme is the environment that not only states the need to make tradeoffs, in general terms, but also indicates what those tradeoffs are in the given decision ... At the other extreme is the environment that provides literally no cues about tradeoffs. It neither explicates what tradeoffs are nor even reminds citizens that they need to make them; it might even tell them, misleadingly, that no tradeoffs are necessary. If people mentally make tradeoffs as they strive to reach a decision, it is because they (probably unconsciously) infer the need to do so from general knowledge and not because the political environment tells them about it.[26]

It is the latter that describes best the Russian political environment, and Kuklinski *et al.* are partially right to advance the notion that if tradeoffs are made at all under these circumstances, they come from general knowledge (which in this case includes the legacy of Soviet information policy). Added to that are personal experiences that are readily available

---

[25] Mickiewicz, *Changing Channels*.
[26] Kuklinski *et al.*, "The Political Environment": 412.

among Russian viewers to apply to cases lacking cues. Further, the identification of tradeoffs, at least in the social situation of these Russian focus groups, is not unconscious at all. Focus group participants were aware of the tradeoffs they offered and often were able quickly and emotionally to trace their reasoning back to what had sparked the analogy or association.

Some truth can be extracted from any story, but it needs to be completed. That is what viewers do when they offer tradeoffs to flesh out a story they know to be planted. That is why they repeatedly concluded, as did Andrei (budding neurosurgeon, Nizhny Novgorod) that: "I think this story is commissioned – objective but commissioned." And Maxim (our 53-year-old bookkeeper, Moscow) found the story: "truthful, yes, but commissioned."

A "commissioned objective" news story is not an oxymoron for Russian viewers. Nor does the term imply that the process of persuasion has taken place as broadcasters had intended. Without focus group research exploring if and how Russian viewers detect tradeoffs, it would be difficult to interpret as logically related mental categories a "yes" response to a survey question asking if the respondent believes that interests shape or commission news stories and a "yes" response to a question about the objectivity of the story. With heavy dependence on the limited choices of national television news, viewers extract meaningful information from obviously biased sources.

The effort contributed by Russian viewers and their sophistication about information are impressive, and confound the assumptions of those who determine the news agenda. Yet it may be precisely because mass-viewers are habituated to tradeoff-free framing, and because they have learned to cope fairly well with it, that their dissatisfaction remains in conversations in local social settings and fails to surface as activism at the policy level. They expect to see stories without tradeoffs; it is, as they say, "normal." Ultimately, of course, it is part of the larger problem of activism, participation, and civil society. As a study of grass-roots activism made by Russian social scientists noted, there is as yet relatively little evidence of organized activists in Russia whose focus is on grass-roots participation. In terms of protest, three national surveys taken by the Public Opinion Foundation in January, February, and March 2006 found the same distribution of answers to the question: "Let's talk about protest rallies that take place from time to time in the various regions of our country. Have you taken part in any rallies over the past month?": 2 percent said "yes"; 97 percent said "no," and 1 percent found it hard to answer.[27]

Russians' dissatisfaction with how officials frame television news, as with so many other phenomena in their lives, runs the gamut from indifference to annoyance to anger at what they know to be planted stories, and still remains localized. Masha (college-educated, Moscow) explained the logic of keeping the peace in a crowded household:

I have a complicated situation at home. My brother-in-law lives with us and he's very interested in politics and when something of this sort [of obvious bias or manipulation on television news] begins, it's better for me to leave and close the door. Because when obvious manipulation goes on, he says, "All of you keep quiet and this is going on here; we have to do something ... We have to go out on the street, and you just sit here and keep quiet. That's why the wrong people are in power. We don't have the right television, precisely because we behave this way." [and Masha explains] That's why it's better to keep quiet; you notice [manipulation] and keep quiet.[28]

APPENDIX: TEXTS OF THE FOUR NEWS STORIES

Channel One

(2 minutes, 14 seconds)
Correspondent:
    A few hours before the ceremonial opening of the new export route of Caspian oil, the weather forecasters announced a prediction of a storm in the region of Novorossisk. The weather began to deteriorate swiftly.
Waves breaking against rocks, tankers, guests arriving, guests in tent for ceremony.
    Because of the strong, cold wind, the organizers of the ceremony even postponed the planned press conference. The Caspian pipeline consortium is one of the largest and costly investment projects in the whole territory of the former USSR. But the profit from exploiting the

---

[27] "Protest Potential and Protest Activity:Monitoring," National population poll; margin of error, 3.6 percent. Reported on January 14, February 9, and March 9, 2006. Public Opinion Foundation, http:/bd.english.fom.ru/report/cat/societas/ market_economy/finances/before-tax_contributions_/protest_action/ protest_potent_...3/223/2006.

[28] Mickiewicz, *Changing Channels*: 292.

KTK [Caspian pipeline consortium] should be twice as much as covering the expenses on the construction. The KTK pipeline joins the Tengiz oilfield in Kazakhstan via specially built sea terminals in the region of the Novorossisk port.

Map of region, line moves from Tengiz oilfields in Kazakhstan to Novorossisk.

The length of the pipe is 1,510 km; it takes a million tons of oil just to fill it. From the shore the oil goes through a flexible pipeline to floating berths to which tankers are moored. This way, they can continue shipping even in a huge storm. The pipeline can now transport 28 million tons a year.

Metal pipelines; tanker at sea; pipeline and sea; guests visiting coast and pipeline.

Twenty-four percent of the consortium shares belong to Russia, 19 to Kazakhstan, another 7 to the Sultanate of Oman, and the rest to Russian and foreign oil companies. According to specialists in the next forty years the Russian budget will get more than $20 billion. A sizable part of it will go to the budgets of the regions the pipeline crosses. Sergei Gnatchenko, director of pipeline consortium: "The KTK pipeline clearly showed the investment attractions and investment opportunities in the Russian market. It will undoubtedly encourage other investments."

Consortium director interviewed, guests, pipelines.

Correspondent:

The pipeline will be fully functioning by summer of next year. At that time its flow capacity will be about 70 million tons of oil a year.

RTR: Channel Two, "Russia"

(2 minutes)

Correspondent:

Never has the small Black Sea village of South Ozereevka met so many highly placed guests at the same time. It is here on the outskirts of Novorossisk that the Caspian pipeline consortium is gathered. The pipeline was built over a period of ten years by the governments of three states: Russia, Kazakhstan, and the Sultanate of Oman and large oil companies. To fill it, with its length of over 1,500 km, it takes a million tons of oil. Of all who were invited only the Secretary of the Department of Energy of the United States, Spencer Abraham, didn't come. In keeping with the new special demands of security, the secretary has to fly on a military plane and the pilots thought the weather in Novorossisk now is dangerous for the flight. Instead Vicky Bailey, his assistant [Assistant Secretary for policy and international affairs] has come; she said that now Americans will know more about the Caspian than simply as a sea surrounded by dry land.

Tanker at sea, pipelines, tribune in tent, press, US assistant secretary reads greeting, translated, press, guests look at sea.

Vicky Bailey:

Today our peoples opened a new chapter in the book of their inter-relations. We celebrate not only the opening of this new pipeline, thanks to it we have mutual trust.

Correspondent:

After the ceremony, the guests view the system. The host is the general director of the pipeline consortium, Sergei Gnatchenko, who told about the benefits Russia will get.

Gnatchenko:

According to our accounting, the Russian Federation will get about $20 billion in taxes from the dividends.

Consortium director reads remarks.

Correspondent:

Last part of the ceremony: the guests, outfitted in hard hats and goggles for safety reasons. A symbolic opening of the spigot and oil flows.

Guests go out to pipeline, turn wheel, rocks and sea.

NTV

(2 minutes, 13 seconds)

Correspondent:

The official ceremony of the opening of the terminal for the Caspian pipeline consortium means for Russia how much its [the consortium's] partners insist on the opening of a new route for the export of oil.

Rocky coves and sea, tanker at horizon, construction, roads under construction.

The biggest American oil companies took part in the construction of the pipeline, and this happened as a result of a warming in Russian–American relations. Now Russia *de facto* has another powerful trump in the battle over the transport of large volumes of Caspian oil. The pipeline goes 1,500 km. It cost about $3 billion. Kazakhstan has a 19 percent share; Russia a 20 percent share, ... Oman, 7 percent, and Chevron–Texaco, Exxon–Mobil, British Petroleum, and Lukoil also have shares.

Vagit Alekperov (President of Lukoil):

We are not increasing the delivery of oil beyond Russia and Kazakhstan this year and next. We are optimizing and rationalizing through the KTK system.

Alekperov speaks, trucks, guests.

Ivan Matlashov (First Deputy Minister of Energy):

This event significantly changes the structure of energy delivery of Russia and Kazakhstan. Above all it changes the structure of transit delivery in Russia. It will reach 50 million tons a year.

Matlashov speaks.

Correspondent:

The directors of the consortium hoped very much that the presidents of Russia and Kazakhstan would come, but it didn't work out. Today there was no shortage of honored guests.

Alexander Vershbow (Ambassador of US, speaking in Russian):

A week ago I was present at the meeting of presidents Bush and Putin. This meeting confirmed that our mutual relations have reached an historic level.

Vershbow, construction, pipeline.

Correspondent:

So, after today's event it appears that at a minimum the first round of the competition for Caspian oil was won by Russia over its competitors Azerbaidzhan, Georgia, and Turkey. And the active involvement of the large American oil companies played a role that was very far from remote.

TV-6

(2 minutes, 49 seconds)

Correspondent:

The opening of the Caspian pipeline consortium finally took place, although this event was designated for the month of September, but then everything was postponed because of the explosions in the USA. At the opening, city, rural, and federal politicians took the microphone to talk about profits and goals – to bring Russian and Kazakh oil to the Black Sea.

Police, tribune in tent, sea, tankers, tankers at sea, pipelines.

Practically none of the people present talked about the dangers for which not only the people of Novorossisk are on the watch. In the case of a leak, even a thousandth of the oil, it would be catastrophic for the ecological zone, the entire 300 km Black Sea coast. In the city of the chief Cossack port, people were proud of South Ozereevka – a village where the KTK is now. The ecology of the mountains was considered unique; they have been part of the Opravovsk reserve up until now, until the Novorossisk mayor removes the status of reserve from the construction area.

Picturesque rural village, geese, cows. Stills of mountains, earth-moving equipment tearing up ground.

They gave away a Russian Switzerland for indefinite use and about the former beauty one can judge from earlier color photographs. The Greens are planning to take tough measures after many letters to the officials [about the] construction of the pipeline in Russia, proving that the work is illegal, that it must be stopped. And they're prepared to go to the International Court.

Correspondent:

Meanwhile, women who are suffering because of this construction gather at the house of Tamara Shevchenko. They bought her house, or more precisely, took a hectare. It was given to the women when the collective farms fell apart. There's even a document proving this.

Tamara Shevchenko:

They said that if you don't sign these papers here, we'll take your land away anyway.

Galkina speaks – lined, weathered face, glasses, wispy hair, close-up of hands toying with glasses.

Correspondent:

Tamara Shevchenko thinks they cheated her . . . but most important is that there are quite a few people in the village like her.

Peasant women (kerchief on head) enter small, rural, poor house. Women are elderly. Woman complains to camera about appropriation of her land and helplessness.

Novorossisk has a seismic rating of 8; the city is in a zone where mountain-forming processes are ongoing and under Novorossisk, according to specialists, dozens of earthquakes are registered annually. And more often in the sea.

Sea, shore, with waves breaking on rocks.

Hydrology technician Vladimir Dyachenko did all the work building the sea harbor and he says that specialists provided for the threat of an earthquake.

Office building, specialist interviewed in his office.

Vladimir Dyachenko:

In the larger picture nobody is insured against anything. It happens that a tanker is thrown against the shore. It seems that nothing can foresee disasters; they happen anyway.

Correspondent:

The opening of the Caspian pipeline consortium continues. They are still saying the same words into the microphone that they did at the beginning.

Guests in tent at ceremony and then shots of green hills.

Some junipers are still standing there, but the fight for part of the watershed of the reserve is lost.

5 | Soviet television: Russian memories

Post-Soviet television viewers

Young Russians today would likely not have watched most of the programs – political analysis, news, speeches of Politburo leaders, the high culture of opera, poetry readings, theater – on television in the Soviet era. Today's twenty-somethings were toddlers or babies at the time. Yet, for the most part, they have strong opinions about it. The research questions addressed here are twofold: First, what memories of Soviet television might have survived in the attitudes that these young post-Soviets stored in their memories? Second, what can we say about all those other emotionally charged attitudes that post-Soviets attribute to Soviet television, which they could not have seen, much less understood?

Soviet-era media discourse was largely abstract, bureaucratic, and filled with evasive euphemisms, such as "internationalist duty of a limited contingent" which stood for "war in Afghanistan." This opaque abstract world, plus their very young age, would have inhibited understanding at the time.

Theories of childhood and memory

Some memories erode and decay; others can remain stable and durable. This study focuses on two types of memory: possible memories (the object could have been experienced by the child) and something the young adult now believes are childhood memories but at the time could *not* have been discerned. For years, public opinion surveys have asked Russians about their confidence in the current government,

Elements of this chapter are taken from E. Mickiewicz, "The Conundrum of Memory," in B. Beumers, S. Hutchings, and N. Rulyova (eds.), *The Post-Soviet Russian Media: Power, Change and Conflicting Messages*. London, Routledge, 2008 and reproduced with the permission of the Taylor & Francis Group.

their expectations for the future, and their evaluation of the past. For example, the *New Russia Barometer* (NRB) national survey showed a fairly steady rise from 1992 to 1998 in respondents' evaluations of the Soviet regime, reaching a 72 percent positive score for pre-Gorbachev Russia.[1] This finding is often used as evidence of a wish to return to that era, or to substitute that era for the present one. This is a weighty claim. Is it valid across all policy domains? Indeed, from the material that follows, it is clear that Russians, given the chance to talk about it, tend to separate those domains and the value they accord them. Our methodology does not permit generalization to the political ideology of a population representative of Russia as a whole, but the discourse of the focus groups can go more deeply into why they respond as they do about the policy domain of television.

Young people in today's Russian Federation were asked what they thought of when they heard the words "Soviet television." What associations were brought to mind? About midway through the focus group session (sessions usually lasted for two hours of non-stop conversation), the facilitator asked the participants to write down a snap impression of Soviet television before Gorbachev, before 1985, when Mikhail Gorbachev began identifying television as a major instrument of his policy of change.[2] They were asked to write down two or three thoughts, put the paper away, and then toward the end of two hours of discussion, mainly about other aspects of television, they pulled out their lists and the group discussed the subject.

It is worthwhile to pay special attention to recollections of childhood. Research establishes that youth is the most impressionable time – the time when identity is formed and memories are stored. Those who work in areas of memory and identity from the perspective of cognitive science, refer to "long-term memory" and "short-term memory." As the descriptors imply, long-term memory functions as the storage area that is virtually without limits on capacity and from which can be drawn past experiences and impressions and learning. Without storage, it is unlikely that earlier elements of learning can be retrieved to make sense of new categories and new information. The

[1] R. Rose and N. Munro, *Elections Without Order: Russia's Challenge to Vladimir Putin*. Cambridge, Cambridge University Press, 2002: 63.
[2] E. Mickiewicz, *Changing Channels: Television and the Struggle for Power in Russia*, rev. and expand. edn. Durham, NC, Duke University Press, 1999.

vivid and most meaningful short-term memory holds far less information, but it is vibrant and less sensitive to content than reliant on affect.

Researchers regard childhood as the period during which the stuff
of memories and identities are most abundantly formed and durably
stored. What exactly defines "childhood" varies. Rubin *et al.* (1998)
regard adolescence and "early adulthood" as "special times for memory
encoding."[3] Graber goes further back, arguing that "children between
the ages of four and ten have a much richer web of neural information"
and that "human brains privilege childhood learning."[4] "Evidence
shows that autobiographical memories from early adulthood are
remembered the best," which Rubin *et al.* place fairly early.[5] "Events
or activities that occur between the ages of 10 and 30 are recalled more
often and judged to be more important or better than events or activities from other age periods."[6]

So far, the discussion has been about the formation and retention of
childhood memories. But that is far being from the whole story: the
process is not rigid and static. We can, and do, change our memories all
the time. Our casual understanding of the word "memory" suggests a
unidirectional process: from our mental memory storehouse to delivery
of recall. That is not the way cognitive scientists understand memory.
Throughout the life cycle, we are, as it were, rewriting the scripts of
our memories. That is, the emotions and informational content of
memories we recall may not have taken place at all; we are not, in
fact, recalling any actual memory at all, even though the memory we
see in our minds may be very convincing, and we can virtually see the
events and feel the emotions of that constructed memory. They seem to
us to have the flavor and immediacy of memory; we can recall the
context clearly. But we have *created* a memory – without conscious
motive or design to deceive – in fact, a memory that fits well into what
we are today. This is not about recovered memory or suppressed
memory, but rather a continuous pattern of adjustment, reshaping,
and creating memories:

---

[3] D. C. Rubin, T. Rahhal, and L. Poon, "Things Learned in Early Adulthood are
Remembered Best," *Memory and Cognition*, 26 (1), 1998: 3–19, p. 3.
[4] D. A. Graber, *Processing Politics: Learning from Television in the Internet Age.*
Chicago, University of Chicago Press, 2001: 19.
[5] Rubin, Rahhal, and Poon, "Things Learned": 4.
[6] Rubin, Rahhal, and Poon, "Things Learned": 3.

An interesting aspect of autobiographic memory is that it is intimately tied to conceptions of *self* – of who and what we are. Many studies have found that memories are reconstructed to satisfy self-serving motives, and that people remember themselves in a more favorable light than is warranted ... People also tend to distort their memory of how they used to behave (or their former opinions) to be more consistent with their opinion of today ... These and other tendencies suggest that social, motivational, and personality factors play a significant role in the way memories are altered over time.[7] (Emphasis in the original)

Rewriting the script of one's memory helps to impose a continuity: "Adolescence and early childhood are special in other ways in our culture, it is when people *come of age*, when their place in society is formed. It is a time of *identity formation* ..., [in] their era things were better then or at least more vivid and exciting (emphasis in the original)."[8]

One of the most interesting models of this process is that based on a study of on-line (OL) processing. In their work with OL models of information-processing, Alwin and Krosnik (1991) refer to symbolic attitudes as having more stability over time and being formed "through conditioning processes in which attitudes develop a strong *affective* basis, with little informational or cognitive content (italics mine)."[9] The OL model of information processing has political import, because "OL tallies attached to memory representations of political candidates, parties, important issues, and events serve as *affective* cues for subsequent information processing (italics mine)."[10] "Affect" is italicized to indicate that emotion plays a strong part in creating durable attitudes. Emotionally infused attitudes are both more stable and more powerful, though less related to specific content or information. "OL tallies attached to memory representations of political candidates, parties, important issues, and events serve as *affective cues* for subsequent

---

[7] G. H. Bower, "A Brief History of Memory Research," in E. Tulving and F. I. M. Craik (eds.), *The Oxford Handbook of Memory*. Oxford, Oxford University Press, 2000: 3–31, p. 27.

[8] Rubin, Rahhal, and Poon, "Things Learned": 3.

[9] D. F. Alwin and J. A. Krosnik, "Aging, Cohorts, and the Stability of Sociopolitical Orientations over the Life Span," *American Journal of Sociology*, 97 (1), 1991: 169–195, p. 172.

[10] C. Taber, M. Lodge, and J. Glathar, "The Motivated Construction of Political Judgments," in J. H. Kuklinski, (ed.), *Citizens and Politics: Perspectives from Political Psychology*. Cambridge, Cambridge University Press, 2001: 202.

information processing."[11] Yet it is often assumed that survey respondents who do OL-processing are less endowed with civic intelligence. It is assumed that if a person gives an opinion, but has forgotten the data on which the opinion was based, then the survey analyst considers "his opinion a snap judgment, devoid of informational basis." OL processing results usually in retention of the end-point opinion, but sloughing off the information that went into achieving it. We should keep this in mind as we examine the evaluations of past television by our post-Soviet participants and then by other, older groups.

The process of constructing meaning in information-processing is an issue partially of message production and partially of message reception. The latter is distinctly more variable than the former, derived as it is from as many different experiences, values, and memory stocks as there are viewers. What is the best way to access this process of constructing meaning? "More open-ended approaches may be the solution because they encourage respondents to think about issues from multiple perspectives, which may then trigger appropriate memories ... Stored opinions may then surface, thanks to the additional cues."[12] Many Russian respondents will tell public opinion survey interviewers that they "trust" Channel One, the leading channel now and in Soviet times. When shown a list of all the stations, they also said that they "trusted" Channel One. Interpreting the response as unproblematic and straightforward would be a mistake. In addition to the usual problems of degradation of memory – the respondent trying to please the interviewer; retrospective answers that correct inattention to social duties (nonvoting turned into voting, for example) – there are seemingly innocuous terms and questions that do not cross borders easily. Personal experience of commonly used abstract terminology – such as the meaning of democracy, checks and balances in government, a strong leader, and categories of rights – may be experienced so differently in Russia that any interpretation for purposes of comparison with other countries should be very carefully checked. It may have little in common with ordinary Western usage.

"Trust" is a concept that has come up frequently in this study, and it deserves our attention. Russian viewers use it in various ways in

---

[11] D. A. Graber, "Government by the People, for the People – Twenty-First Century Style," *Critical Review, Special Volume, Is Democratic Competence Possible?*, 18 (1–3), 2006: 171, italics mine.
[12] Graber, *Processing Politics*: 50–51.

different contexts, and Western and Russian scholars have met different findings at different times. One of the most comprehensive studies of the elusive nature of trust in the media in Russia is Sarah Oates' study, *Television, Democracy and Elections in Russia*.[13] The advantage of Oates' study is its use of both mass-surveys and focus groups to provide greater attention to the key points. She describes the continued primary status of Channel One and the trust people say they accord to it. She found that "it was particularly surprising that Russians had such a high level of trust in state television even though propaganda and the obvious manipulation of the news had increased steadily in recent years."[14] VTsIOM, a noted polling agency, found that 75 percent prefer television to all other media, especially Channels One and Two and, moreover, that "The overwhelming majority of Russian citizens – 85 percent – prefer to receive information from central television broadcasts ... In the last year television has increased its audience: the proportion of Russia's citizens who use central television to receive information rose from 76 percent to 85 percent."[15] Yet Oates sensed an "undercurrent of anger" at the few choices with which they were presented at elections.[16] The mixed reactions of Russian viewers – they stress their trust in the chief government station and yet are irritated at what they are offered – have long been known to scholars of public opinion. It is precisely for this reason that the focus group participants in this study were encouraged to speak at length about concrete analogies to trust, or about what they associated with trust, so that the *sense* of what they mean could be narrowed down.

Post-Soviet evaluations of Soviet television

What do young people, most of whom have watched only children's shows of that period associate with television of the Soviet era? All the groups were asked to do this. Box 5.1 shows their responses, the

---

[13] London, Routledge, 2006.

[14] S. Oates, *Television, Democracy and Elections in Russia*. London, Routledge, 2006: 149.

[15] Y. Yakovleva, "The Internet and the Person," *Rossiyskaya Gazeta*, October 11, 2006. Reprinted in *Johnson's Russia List*, 229, October 11, 2006, 2. davidjohnson@erols.com and davidjohnson@starpower.net JRL homepage: www.cdi.org/russia/johnson.

[16] Oates, *Television, Democracy*.

Box 5.1   *Post-Soviet focus groups: associations with Soviet television*

Words that come to mind	Age at focus group	Age in 1985
Moscow		
Olya: *no trust in information,* Vremya	24	6
Ivan: *ideology, totalitarianism, lie*	21	3
Viktor: *patriotism, lack of objectivity, old age* [i.e. archaic]	22	4
Maxim: *strictness, impressing, greyness*	23	5
Igor: *visiting fairy tales,* Vremya, *song of the year*	24	6
Oleg: Vremya, *November 7 parade, Soviet movies*	25	7
Lena: Vremya, *parade on Red Square, a ton of grain harvested*	24	6
Julia: *framing, tricks, censorship*	20	2
Katya: *lack of objectivity, covered with a veil, outward glitter – hidden lie*	23	5
Galya: *New Year's Ogonyek* [party given by magazine], *black-and-white television, communism, prohibition of many movies*	22	4
Nizhny Novgorod		
Kolya: Vremya, Good Night, Children	20	2
Andrei: Vremya, *USSR anthem*	24	6
Olya: Vremya, Good Night, Children	23	5
Boris: Vremya, Spotlight of Perestroika, 600 Seconds	25	7
Irina: *childhood, rose-colored glasses*	27	9
Masha: *information, entertainment* (Good Night, Children)	20	2
Lera: *Plan, Five-Year Plan,* Bringing in From the Fields	21	3
Sergei: *Party Congress,* Vremya, *framing*	20	2
Alena: Vremya, *Party Congresses*	24	6
Marina: *news every day at 9:00 p.m. on* Vremya *on Channel One*	24	6
Rostov-on–the-Don		
Andrei: *absence of television, no entertainment concepts, maximum influence on masses with political positions*	23	5

Irina: *Respect, loud-speaker of the Party, very, very cultural*	20	2
Natasha: *harvests in Akromakh, people preparing for holidays and very bad in foreign countries*	25	7
Sergei: *The cat's out of the bag, we exaggerate what's small and reduce what was big*	23	5
Maxim: *censorship, silence about the most important problems and what's going on*	20	2
Oksana: *propaganda, communism, "the bright future"*	20	2
Lena: *"the bright future," "beautiful life," everything will be fine, good anchors*	21	3
Dima: *joyful news that the "bright future" is coming soon*	24	6
Ivan: *censorship, sleaze, low quality*	21	3
Alexandra: *subordination to power, unemotionality, a whole lot of censorship*	20	2
Volgograd		
Volodya: Good Night, Children, *one single television, sports*	24	6
Evgeny: Vremya, Morning Post, *KVN*	25	7
Denis: *work at the direction of the party, struggle with drunkenness, CPSU[17] Congresses*	21	3
Natasha: Vremya, Good Night, Children	20	2
Katya: *Communism, criticism, censorship*	19	1
Dina: *analytical programs*	20	2
Vera: *Program* Vremya, *related moderators (don't remember their names), censorship*	24	6
Mikhail: *in the USSR there is no sex (space bridge),[18] everything is fine, agricultural hour*	24	6
Sasha: Good Night, Children, *the world and peace, TASS*	21	3
Aleksei: *KGB, Soviet Union, old television set, Brezhnev*	25	7

[17] The Communist Party of the Soviet Union.
[18] In a live television program joining a Russian and an American studio audience by satellite, a young Russian woman said these now-famous words, but she intended to continue that Soviet television did not feature sex, unlike American programs.

answers to the request to create a short list of words that come to mind about Soviet television. On the right are two columns: the first is the respondent's age at the time of the focus group; the second, their age when all there was to see was the last of the canonic Soviet model of television programming.

Attitudes toward Soviet television

Two programs appear in the overwhelming majority of the lists. One is the most famous of children's programs, *Good Night, Children*. This show left a powerful memory to which the participants responded with such excitement and freshness that it was hard to imagine that at least twenty years or so had intervened. These post-Soviet participants spoke with nostalgia about missing most of all the particular emotion they used to see in this program. Viktor (Moscow-based tour manager) who had written about Soviet TV's "lack of objectivity" recalls: "they were very good hearted, these children's programs." Words often used about these programs were "tenderness," "goodness," "sweetness." There *was* an unusual quality about them; it was not simple sentimentality. The shows did not appear to be condescending or manipulative. The environment of tenderness and kindness was very important to these young people. In Moscow Oleg (university student) called the programs and the old films "spiritual"; Viktor, "good-hearted." Sasha (university student, Volgograd) talked about his favorite, *Good Night, Children*, through the eyes of his childhood. "Everything was peaceful. I don't remember that there were any wars then or that … they broadcast [any] horrors." In Nizhny Novgorod, the participants found much to admire in the old Soviet television. When asked what they might like to take from that former time, Boris (lawyer) said: "Actually, everything was so terrific then." Olya (translator) talked about the need for more children's programs. In fact, in their comments on the emotions of the children's shows, there is more sense of personal experience than in any of the negative comments, and with reason.

The post-Soviet focus group participants, having grown into young adults, display an emotional attachment to childhood. In talking about programs or television, Ira (sales consultant, Nizhny Novgorod) says: "I have an association with childhood, with rose-colored glasses, because everything was wonderful then." Kolya (university student) said that in newscasts "they didn't recount anything bad." Masha (another university student) said: "They didn't show anything horrible. And now children watch more than we did and with such a corrupted outlook, perverted." Ira adds that there was no advertising then and Sergei (another student, Nizhny Novgorod) talks about "less violence." After this reversion to thinking about childhood with the affect of the memories of the time, the focus group participants begin to talk with distinct hostility about the present and its effect on the child, even though their written descriptions were decisively negative about the past and displayed their preference for the diversity and choice that adults enjoy now, but could not then. Within individual focus groups there began to be strong differences in references to the process of growing up and making choices or, alternatively, looking back at the disappearance of the "peaceable kingdom" of childhood, which craves not choice but a warm blanket of positive affect, exclusion of life's horrors, and joining the family gathered to watch the news.

There are also many references to the authoritative evening news program, *Vremya*, which came on right after the children's show. During the Soviet era, this was a program that moved at an almost glacial tempo. The news readers did just that: read from approved scripts. The top of the newscast featured speeches and official statements by Party officials and then agricultural or industrial stories, stories of success. The program was dictated from above and there was no room for personalized treatments of news or human interest stories, or debates and disagreements. That this program should appear on virtually everyone's list is a puzzle; much like that in chapter 4, the toddlers that the post-Soviets were then could scarcely have understood, much less stayed awake for, the bulk of the program. The evening news came on live at 9:00 p.m., in Moscow. In the Moscow studio different pairs of anchors read the news beginning in the afternoon, beaming it to the Maritime Provinces and ending with the 9:00 p.m. Moscow edition. This pattern allowed the censors to see what was in store for Moscow when the program moved west. Changes were often made between the Far Eastern version and the one about which the Kremlin was most concerned: Moscow. The news had a high viewership because of its importance to the lives of those acted upon; it could be used to parse what little political and economic information was provided. Besides, there was no competition for the authoritative news program: no matter what button you pushed, you saw it. In those days, households had one television set – black and white – and it was customary for the family to assemble in front of the set. The children's favorite, *Good Night, Children*, ended just before *Vremya* began. Going off to bed or staying with the family through the news? It was not a difficult question: children would rather be part of the family group watching the news, even if it was above their heads, than go off to bed. A "child's view of *Vremya*" still resonates – in their references to how they discovered music as a child and in their descriptions of the pictorial aspects of the program.

Many of the remaining epithets on the lists of associations could not have come from the stage of toddlerhood: lack of objectivity, censorship tricks, hidden lies, prohibition of many movies, totalitarianism, lies, maximum influence of political positions on the masses, silence about the most important problems, no trust in information, sleaze, unemotionality, Party Congresses, propaganda, no entertainment, party directs the work, KGB, outward glitter – hidden lie, analytical programs. These notions could not have come from assessing the past as they had remembered it from childhood in primary school or the crib. They could not have understood the concepts and words at that time. They might have overheard their parents use these terms and make these judgments, but parents were usually circumspect around young children during those times and the gamut of terms appears much too wide to be attributed only to home life. Of course, they have had plenty of time to learn about Soviet-era television from older friends and well-known TV officials' and stars' (rather tame) memoirs. How effective such transmission of information later in life is in lodging itself in the memory may be doubtful, especially without the important ingredient of first-hand experience and affect. On the other hand, the post-Soviet participants – in their twenties – still qualify as early adults, a propitious time for internalizing memories. Schuman and Rodgers (2004) write that "learning about the same event some years later . . . does not raise the same urgent questions and therefore the event is not likely to have the same deep emotional impact." Even learning about the events in school or having them recounted is not as strong as the direct experience. But to be more specific: "first, in most cases the crucial carriers of collective memories of an event are not all who were alive when the event occurred, but mainly those individuals who experienced the event during their critical ages of adolescence and early adulthood."[19] These post-Soviets are still in the age cohort that is deeply attuned to important events and the affect that cues them to become activated as memories. Still, the puzzle remains: the young people never saw Soviet television, but have reacted to it as though it were a strong direct experience. They *have* become memories, constructed ones.

What makes sense is the proclivity to "rewrite" and reformulate memories to make them more consistent with current identity. Some descriptions of Soviet television drip with heavy sarcasm: participants in Rostov use "the bright future" to describe Soviet television, a boast of Soviet officialdom that the new life of Communism was just around the corner. These participants are not deliberately altering their impressions of Soviet television. They strongly and emotionally believe that these *are* their impressions of Soviet television, but their constructed, current view of the past relies more on today than on the past. These characterizations of Soviet television also suggest that what they structured in altering or creating these memories is heavily negative, to be congruent with the people they have now become.

A further complexity

The participants' lists of attributes of Soviet television, negative as they are, also do not tell the whole story. It has been difficult for Russians to reassess the Soviet past, and with reason. They have few guides. They may say things that appear internally contradictory but, in my view, they are not, because they come from different aspects of memory. These other dimensions may seem dissonant, such as the thought expressed by Ivan (university student, Rostov), who thinks about Soviet television in terms of "censorship," and "sleaze," and later declares censorship to be a good thing. Does "censorship" have the same meaning for Ivan in both contexts? I rather think not, but it takes a focus group to get at it.

So many of the focus group participants included censorship in their short list of associations with Soviet television, and it was virtually always placed in a list that included nasty, unpleasant, and angry responses. There is little doubt that in these cases the participants

[19] H. Schuman and W. L. Rodgers, "Cohorts, Chronology, and Collective Memories," *Public Opinion Quarterly*, 68(2), 2004: 217–254, p. 250.

intended censorship to mean a Party-directed controlling oversight and the restricted freedom of the Soviet era. Then, however, later in the discussion, censorship assumes the meaning of sensible regulatory procedures protecting families from intrusive (and pervasive) indignities. Use of the Russian language is now termed "vulgar" (which differs from sleaze, in that "sleaze" refers to low production values, while vulgarity is intentional debasement), unlike the old-time, slow-paced Soviet news with its carefully pronounced and to-the-letter correct Russian language. As Ira (Rostov) said: "Yes, I think that TV was very cultured. The people who worked there elicited respect, served as examples. . . . There was censorship? So, there was censorship and in the language [there] was also culture. And that was the most important." Ivan (university student, Rostov, who earlier had described Soviet TV as censorship, sleaze, and low quality) responds: "I think of censorship in the positive sense of this word. There was never vulgarity at all. But the only minus, it wasn't done with a high quality." Thus the signification of the word "censorship," which carries multiple meanings from the past, is extremely context-dependent – sometimes meaning a negative straitjacket of government control, sometimes a positive meaning in which censorship actually implies a reasonable regulatory system, and sometimes a different positive sense of maintenance of cultural norms, especially in language use.

The problem of how to understand a word that is so protean and yet so commonly used for many differing important narratives is a difficult one, made even more problematic by its use as a single-word response to be integrated into world-wide studies. ROMIR, one of Moscow's leading survey facilities, does an annual survey on censorship: the choices are: "want censorship," "don't want censorship," "want to some degree," and "don't want to some degree." The combination of "want censorship" and "want to some degree" covered some three-quarters of the responses. The most obvious flaw in the survey is the failure to inquire about differences between censorship and regulation; what kind of censorship (politics, sex, violence); and the time when programs may be shown (the British "watershed" notion or the American "safe haven"). In any case, to say that this survey provides significant information would be hard to justify. Yet, it has had appeal not only in Russia, but also beyond. *Foreign Affairs* published an article by Richard Pipes in 2004 in which he used these unhelpful-to-opaque results to write: "Enhancing personal freedoms and improving civil rights do not attract much support . . . A survey conducted in the winter of 2003 by ROMIR Monitoring, a sociological research unit, found that 76 percent of Russians favor restoring censorship over the mass media."[20]

One other benefit from Soviet-era television which *was* likely to be closely related to a real childhood memory was a by-product that had a considerable effect on some of the participants – the beginning of attention and attachment to music. Several in these groups developed a fondness for the musical themes of *Vremya*. Vera (teacher, Volgograd) said that she remembers the news: "that music, then the newsreaders." Evgeny (in the military, Volgograd) reported: "And also I'd say that symphonic music is really engraved on my mind. In Soviet times, somebody from the government died, they didn't show anything; they transmitted only symphonic music." Before Gorbachev was chosen, three Soviet leaders had died in a period of four years. Each one could be seen on television lying in state; all day there were eulogies and throughout the day symphonic music, most of it Western, was played. Most thought it boring; some children apparently were happily inspired by this unusual introduction to music.

Substitute old for new? Retain the new?

After having discussed the positives and negatives of Soviet television the facilitator prompted each group with the question: Would you like to substitute that [Soviet] television for today's? The reaction is mainly energetically negative: Lera (university student, Nizhny Novgorod) said: "Absolutely not"; from the same group Kolya (university student) said: "[now] there's a choice and absence of monopoly." In Rostov, in chorus, they yell: "NO"; Andrei (economist) says: "God forbid." To the contrary, Ivan (university student, Rostov) says "yes," and Maxim (university student, Rostov) wanted to clarify the question: "Do you mean changing completely, completely?" *Facilitator*: "Yes." Ivan, "Then NO." Maxim: "It's already long overdue to introduce censorship on TV." Sergei (unemployed, Rostov) ends the discussion: "But the whole 'high' is in the variety."

[20] R. Pipes, "Flight From Freedom: What Russians Think and Want," *Foreign Affairs*, May–June 2004.

Capturing complexity

Scientists do not claim that they fully understand the brain, or can model its capacities, but they have made so much progress that fields probing the problems of cognition have changed significantly. In looking at the top-of-the-head responses toward Soviet television we deliberately confined this first part to young people who could have seen and understood some, but by no means the majority, of programs at the time. They were people in very different places: in a tough city in Southern Russia near the Northern Caucasus (Rostov), a stagnating, remnant of Communist Party loyalty still mourning the sacrifice of so many citizens when it was Stalingrad (Volgograd), a progressive, northern, investment-friendly city (Nizhny Novgorod), and Moscow, where ostentatious wealth is paraded while bodyguards and armored cars preserve it. In every city, the pattern was similar – strong views about Soviet television from the programs they *were* able to connect with and equally strong, but very differently expressed attitudes about the model Soviet program, which our group had been simply too young to understand. Their characterizations (and their emotions) fell mainly into these two streams of attitudes but, as cognitive science suggests, *for different reasons*.

We know that childhood memories are the most durable and that affect strengthens those memories. Not a single participant was critical of *Good Night, Children*, the leading children's television program. They felt its kind and generous mood and gentle music and characters. This program elicited emotional responses of affection and delight; it was central to their childhood. These are memories that appear to have some enduring heft in them, real memories that turn into reveries about childhood. In fact, one could say, that in discussing this loved program they are really looking fondly back at childhood. These comments about their favorite childhood program may be more relevant to thoughts about childhood and longing for childhood's simple choices, than about Soviet television as such.

The other strain of comments that emerges in all the cities is angry and negative. They describe Soviet programs and practices they could not possibly have consumed themselves or, even if placed in front of the set with the family, the most they could talk about were the pictures (Party Congresses, speeches) and the music. The content was not accessible to these toddlers. As the research literature tells us, long-term memory is especially linked to vivid and emotional experiences and not content, which is why the emotional and comfortingly nostalgic recollection of the children's program rings so true. There are also very different memories the participants say they recall. They are memories, but likely to be memories constructed to avoid dissonance and keep the participant congruent with what he or she has become. Into this category fall the criticisms of Soviet television as sleaze, political control, censorship, tricks, lies, totalitarianism.

Censorship has a particularly central role to play, but it depends on what "censorship" means: sometimes it refers to ripping the heart out of a work; sometimes it is meant as a kind of regulation that most countries have in place and that limits the times when sex or violence may appear, usually after children are presumed to have gone to bed. The harsh judgments undoubtedly come from any number of sources in the environment not confined to television, for many are generalizable to the Soviet system as a whole, but television has become for many the most pervasive display of vulgarity and brutality. And, finally, there is still another sense in which memory is invoked by the participants. When comparing the special memory of childhood to the present, some participants decry the changes in vocabulary, violence, and taste. Others look to the future, pleased to have choice (mainly in entertainment programs) and flitting from one to another, feeling in command of corralling all these different shows at will. It gives us some insight into the larger questions often asked – that, on the whole, very few support the replacement of current television by Soviet-era television. Yes, they complain, especially about the changes since childhood, but they will do nothing about those complaints and even give thanks that the past will not be restored.

The college-educated remember Soviet television

We had two focus groups of college-educated people in each of our four cities. The range of ages was large and although some young people fell into these groups, the post-Soviet groups had *only* young people. Earlier we looked at recollections, or what were called recollections, of participants in the post-Soviet groups, even though they had been too young to have personally consumed much of what prompted the strong and emotional judgments they offered. Now we look at the participants with higher education. The task given them was to note what came into their minds now about television before Gorbachev. Some took it as a request to take a mental inventory to see what they could summon up; others just gave the impressions of the moment.

Among the college-educated, there are, for example, housewives, bookkeepers, unemployed, pensioners, teachers, computer engineers, a merchant marine captain, and a specialist who works with children. The discourse of just about all of the participants is more matter-of-fact and less emotionally charged than that of the post-Soviets. And, unlike the post-Soviets, these participants were able to draw on a variety of Soviet programs they actually had seen.

Longing for childhood as a serene stage of life is still a feature of the discourse, though much reduced from the post-Soviet comments. College-educated Olya (24, economist, Moscow) finds that the "sense of life ... probably it was simple and you didn't need to think" – another feature of the nostalgic sense of childhood, where others made decisions for you. Antonina (college student, Nizhny Novgorod) said to her group that her memory fastened on *Good Night, Children*. As Viktor (47, computer technician) in the same group said: "when they talk about old television, it seems like something warm but far away. It's already being forgotten." The context of kindness was important to all the viewers. Participants with higher education are altogether a more critical and skeptical group, but in one respect they, like their counterparts in other groups, keep returning to the special quality of Soviet children's shows. When asked what they would like in today's television, Sergei (28) says: "yes, absolutely, goodness. I would throw out all these new games [that are] growing so much [and] are not understandable now." Angela (31, college-educated operator, Rostov), says that the news was "boring and predictable – but entertainment programs were sincere, moving and it was concrete: this is good and that is bad. Everything was clear and understandable."

In praising the children's program to which they all refer, they are mourning the loss of childhood, when the better path and the worse were clearly demarcated and the instructions to the viewers clear, where there was no risk, no multiple goods and multiple dangers. To do nothing in the new world of competition and markets is to lose out. Nothing could describe this atmosphere better than the new reality shows. To note the most popular example, *The Last Hero*, a version of the American show "*Survivor*" (itself a copy of a European show), takes place in a constant Hobbesian war, with co-operation only sporadically and instrumentally useful. It is a zero-sum game, hardly the welcome kindness and goodness of *Good Night, Children*. The new template features contestants who claw their way to the top by deception, bullying, and lying.

High-school-educated and college-educated: how similar are the viewers?

The political side of Soviet television programming was also a compelling feature of discourse, with differences among the groups. The high-school-educated were much less likely to include news and public affairs programming when asked with what they associated Soviet television. In Nizhny Novgorod, Olga (49, artist and designer) wrote down: "New Year's flame, KVN, travelers club," and Viktor (62, pensioner) wrote: "something warm but very far away." In the same group, Liudmila (52, economist) wrote: "flame, concert, good," and Natasha (55, dentist) wrote: "our Russian films, no irritating advertisements." In Volgograd, Valera (38, blue-collar worker) spoke about Soviet television: "nostalgia for the life past. We didn't live badly; just a little bit needed to be changed." When the facilitator asked if he meant nostalgia for television or about life, Valera responded: "about everything; about life" and Valentina (42, white-collar employee) said: "he means nostalgia for the past life."

Equally, there is a significant distance in discourse when high-school-educated groups are asked what, if anything, they liked in Soviet television. They name concrete, individual shows; they do not put these offerings together in an abstract evaluation of the period or what brought about change in leaders and then in structures. In one focus group, one of the weakest consumer experiments of the Soviet era was held up as an exemplar of consumer trust. They remembered the long-discredited "mark of quality" campaign as something positive. It was well known that too many Soviet-made products were of low quality, shoddy, and short-lived. Consumer goods were in short supply and quality was not a feature that was rewarded with bonuses, and in the distorted criterion of output (mainly in physical units within a given time), quality did not fit. The economy provided disincentives to improve quality. Inputs of material and labor were fixed (though there were ways to deal at the margins). Every month a production stream was required to meet the number of physical units by a deadline, and deviation was penalized. And indeed, experimenting with quality, using up raw materials, redoing a defect and squandering time – none of it made sense if there were no incentives or benefits to the factory or the worker.

A thoroughgoing reform of the economy required a massive political and economic upheaval at a time when much more modest reforms usually petered out or were simply canceled by the recalcitrant bureaucrats charged with their implementation.[21] As so often happened in the Soviet economy, exhortation was resorted to instead of incurring real costs for real resources. The decision was made to stamp a "mark of quality" on a product that was better than others. It received a good deal of television coverage, and in the beginning of the campaign the mark of distinction seemed carefully applied. It is absurd even to think of individually designating the countless products in an industrialized economy and soon, as so many times before, the mark of quality faded and disappeared into the sizable bin of failed micro-reforms. Nonetheless some of the high-school-educated viewers recalled the campaign on television. They did not, apparently, connect this doomed gimmick with so many that had preceded it. Put another way, they lacked the abstract quality of analysis that would provide an arc of logic across a history of failed temporizing measures. It was one of the positive memories of Yura (29, trainer, Moscow): "I remember there were more good products. There was a program: big, good products." And Maxim (53, bookkeeper) answers: "mark of quality. Also good."

Asking the college-educated about what was positive about Soviet television offers a much more complex and involved discussion that takes on the political dimensions much more deeply – and more analytically. Perhaps Oksana (45, dispatcher) sums up what will be thematic among the college-educated: "There's no special nostalgia. But there are individual [programs] that one remembers well." What came up

---

[21] See, for example, the economic reforms proposed by Yevsei Liberman and adopted in the Soviet Union in 1965. They were modest compared to the reforms Gorbachev initiated, but startlingly liberal at the time. Factories were to be freed of some of the many controls Moscow put on them and thus gain a measure of flexibility, a small step toward seeking profit. Though championed by Alexei Kosygin, Leonid Brezhnev's Prime Minister, the many ministries charged with implementing the reforms opposed and killed them.

frequently among the well educated was the newsreaders' devotion to a standard of Russian that has disappeared. Irina (49, white-collar employee, Rostov) says: "The newsreaders were clear and crisp, magnificent language." She is not alone. Nikolai (45, general director, Nizhny Novgorod), thinking about what he liked about Soviet television, replies: "for me, to this day, these news readers, the quality of language." Liuda (52, physician) echoes: "language." Vladimir, in the same group (59, unemployed): "Soviet TV was professional. Now the newsreaders can't speak. Tyk, dyk, dyk, you know [mocking Evgeny Kiselev's dramatic stutter]." Mikhail (52, programmer, Volgograd) talks about the "very cultured readers plus magnificent Russian language. Now that's completely gone. Very cultured newsreaders." When I spoke to the most famous of all newsreaders, Igor Kirillov, he said that he considered himself a guest entering millions of living rooms; it was his obligation to display the highest form of civility and fidelity to language.

As the Soviet regime was collapsing, the head of television news believed that the strongest signal of change he could send would be a striking difference in the presentation of the evening news. Eduard Sagalaev changed the music from the martial music of old to the modernist music of the officially shunned composer, Alfred Schnittke. He started a parallel late-night news show, in which young newscasters spoke as fast as they do in ordinary life, used street idioms, and were deliberately casual onscreen. This was the style that was to replace measured elocution.

Higher production values were also missed: in sports, movies, and theatrical productions. During Soviet times, television did not have to turn a profit or even stay within financial constraints. It was heavily subsidized by the central budget. It employed, in some outsiders' views, at least ten times the number of staff than were needed. Period dramas were lush, and Soviet sports stars, banned from moving to teams outside the country, made for exciting competitions, both domestically and internationally. All of this was recognized in all the focus groups.

When it came to news and public affairs coverage in Soviet times, there are three main views: it was bad then and bad now; it was bad then, but today, by contrast, makes the earlier way seem less bad; it was bad then and better now. Soviet television gets high marks for *not* having advertising, for not featuring gore, cruelty, terror, crimes, and punishments in movies and series about cops and criminals.[22] Some participants were sorry to see the many Soviet programs on agriculture go, leaving this sector practically without coverage.

College graduates, when invited to consider what they liked about Soviet television, delivered a host of complaints, often making comparisons to present-day offerings.

What follows in condensed form are the lists of the university graduates. In the lists of Muscovites, Soviet television was characterized by "lies, boredom, prohibitions." Maxim (28, entrepreneur) – "monotonous, politicized, with successful serials and programs"; Irina (54, housewife) – "news bad, entertainment good"; Olya (24, economist) – "little international news (capitalist countries and one-sided coverage of them)"; Volodya (34, salesman) – "sluggish journalists," but he adds "good language"; Yura (22, student) – "monotone, bureaucratic language," but he adds "literate"; and Natasha (50, tax inspector) – "unreal coverage of events (decoded), pushing its own opinion, deflecting information"; Natasha says that there were good entertainment programs and live dialogs. In Moscow, they spoke of "faked representation" in the news, "Lies with respect to the real picture on any question (absence of freedom of speech, complete dictatorship of the state on all material of state broadcasting)." In Nizhny Novgorod, it was "rotting socialism," "absence of fairness," "boring, much subjective politics"; "too politicized and commissioned news programs"; "Politicization"; "monotone, correctness"; "dryness, one-sided point of view." In Rostov, it was "Boring, stupid news about tractor drivers, milkmaids, etc.; on the struggle for independence of developing countries; musical programs with patriotic songs, generally boredom"; "propaganda, uninteresting, dry"; (28, prison personnel officer): "I don't remember well"; "information broadcasts boring and even uninteresting to watch. Entertainment, better than now. Feature movies and cartoons could not have been better; they don't date." In Volgograd, it was "100 percent manipulation of society's public opinion – everything's good; all is wonderful. We don't have anything, but we don't need anything (in the sense of the masses)." What is quite remarkable in all of the conversations about

---

[22] To summarize those who displayed these kinds of values: Moscow: Katya (59, educator); Olga (24, economist); Lena (29, housewife); Natasha (60, retired). Rostov: Irina (49, white-collar employee); Lena (31, white-collar employee); Lilia (54, blue-collar worker). Volgograd: Polina (23, housewife); Viktor (60, retired); Julia (27, specialist with children).

Soviet television is the lack of content in discussion of any of the shows. The feelings of affection for the children's programs is almost palpable but, absent that emotion, even the grim epithets many of the participants apply to Soviet TV are curiously isolated from the speaker. Bower's work on memory and the brain finds that:

Some of the [autobiographical] knowledge is in the form of personal episodic memories that are experienced in recall with imagery and often some emotion; and it has been noted that these specific memories can often be a mistaken blend of fact and fiction ... In addition to these episodic memories, large portions of people's autobiography are in narrative generalizations with no more sense of "personally being there" than they have for the knowledge that they were born on a specific date.[23]

College-educated participants were not all negative in recalling Soviet television. They missed its superior diction and literacy. Sometimes judgments were mixed. The following comments drawn from all the college-educated groups give the total range and volume of why a dozen or so college-educated participants thought of Soviet TV in positive terms. There are relatively few of them and most come from Moscow. Ira (54, housewife, Moscow), after running through several negatives, ends her comments with the observation that Soviet programs were spiritual and made "a sincere effort to interest the viewer." Oksana (45, dispatcher, Moscow) liked Soviet movies, some entertainment shows and concludes it was "generally not bad." Lena (29, housewife, Moscow) liked Soviet movies; Natasha (60, pensioner, Moscow) liked it when they showed achievements in agriculture, science, and technology and especially liked what was *not* on Soviet television: "they did not show horrors, killings; they showed films of high art." Olya (61, pensioner, Moscow) thought that Soviet television "gave accurate information on events in the country; fulfilled their goal of the correct education of youth (love of Homeland, work, and so forth), and, in general, education in patriotism in people." Finally, Svetlana (36, teacher, Moscow) lauded Soviet television for its portrayal of successes, "official information without a slant," Soviet movies, including movies for children.

Only one of the participants from Nizhny Novgorod's two groups (Tatyana, 50, teacher) praised the past with the words "USSR, grand

---

[23] Bower, "A Brief History": 3–32, p. 27.

scale, state orders, unity." In Rostov's two groups of college-educated viewers, Alexei (43, employee) wrote "quality, propaganda, culture." Alexei is positive about the past; later in the session, he sums up his view of Soviet TV as "there was quality of programs." Mark (31, computer engineer) recalls the programs he liked: "Kirillov (news reader), *Travelers' Club*, and *In the World of Animals*." Finally, in Volgograd, Vera (39, engineer/programmer) associates with the "national anthem, building, sports, harvest, cosmos, Soviet television." Sergei (41, employee) finds that overall there was more positive than negative in Soviet television and mentions the big celebratory events of Leonid Ilych [Brezhnev], plus a little on sports, but he regretted that no news was available before he had to go to work. Viktor (60, pensioner) associates with the old system: education in patriotism, labor successes, and education of youth; while Julia (27, works with children) noted there was more positive information and news about harvesting.

Two accounts: two conversions

In the groups there were two rather graphic accounts of testing the credibility of Soviet television news. Both were emotional events; both provided for the individuals who experienced them a permanent disillusionment with the news at home. Olga (64, retired, college-educated) is from Nizhny Novgorod. While her fellow participants were discussing their associations with the words "Soviet television," Olga spoke of a story from her life during the heyday of the Soviet era:

You know, I was an enthusiastic patriot before. Back then I liked all the achievements, the kind of assurance in tomorrow that everything is good with you. I didn't know very much that was bad. Then I went to Leningrad, and there somebody said that it's not good here. I thought, Oh, my God, watch out for the police, these are practically dissidents speaking. From the depth of the revolution they said such things. When, later, Gorbachev said it publicly, then we all knew this.

The other is Viktor's story. Viktor is a 46-year old, college-educated merchant marine captain and, when he is ashore, lives in Moscow. What he was a student sailor, he was a cadet on a Soviet ship:

I was a cadet on a sea voyage, a sailor. I landed in Africa in the crappy country of Sierra Leone, the size of Latvia. Stevedores were brought by cars to offload the ship. So, they were used cars and old ones, but they came with cars. I was surprised. How, then, I think do they live poorly here? All education is free there; they get a wage of four pounds a year! Not so much. You know, in a year they're paid, plus they're given free uniforms. There they study in school 12 years. You know, I thought wow! They tell us here that they live badly, but in fact it's all different ...

In 1973 we came to Cuba on the sailboat *Kruzenshtern*, and the Minister of Fisheries and Agriculture of Cuba came to us in a Volga 21, and we talked with the chauffeur. The minister's chauffeur, they give him one shirt a year – a *year*! There they go around only in shirts [because of] the heat. I think, what the hell? What's so good about this? Stores have nothing except vodka and tobacco. That's all. There's nothing. We traded there all our hats and under-shirts. Each one of us gets a pack of those pesos. We don't know where to [use] them. We bought only vodka. And here [in the Soviet Union] they show how well they live and somehow it didn't fit into the brain and I was young then, 18, 20. No way to understand what's going on. They show us from the Komsomol tribune one thing and reality shows us everything differently.

In reality, things are different Yes, there is something different. Yes, there are homeless there – those Negroes in Africa who, too lazy to work, eat a banana and don't need to work. But there are those who do work; they live as normally as we do, for example. It's exactly the same situation. There they had 100 dollars; in the States, 3,000 and now we have 100 dollar salaries, but they don't have problems with outerwear, with fur coats, with hats and so on.

In this group of well-educated people, the ability to process – in Viktor's case, to correct for what he knows – can derive from experiences and observations that have been stored in the memory. Their recollections are rich. Victor the ship captain's are especially rich, because the emotional shock of seeing the Soviet news so blatantly contradicted lent weight and staying power even though it had taken place thirty years ago. Just after Viktor's tale ends, Igor (37) remarked that he had complained about how Soviet news was restricted solely to positive information. "I did not go abroad," he says, "and I was not able to see the other side, but now we understand this."

If we encounter life stories in which the freely spoken opposition of Leningraders, and why "oppressed" countries and "socialist" countries differ so vividly from the daily news at home, then we must conclude, as some in the groups do, that at least some of the message of the news was assimilated as the broadcasters wished. It depended to a large extent on shutting off opportunities to compare treatments of events. That meant that events taking place in foreign countries were least likely to be contested by viewers, who had no leverage on contrasting views. Thus, although, during the Soviet period, these kinds of stories tended to be more accepted, they were also very much less salient to viewers.

The hypothetical substitution

The obverse was also examined. The groups were asked if they would replace current programming, about which there are so many complaints. The facilitator's prompt asks if the participants would like to substitute that [past] for this [present] system. None wants to sacrifice the variety and choice of present-day television. How tone deaf and isolated is the famous television anchor and one-time administrator of RTR (Channel Two): Nikolai Svanidze is the host of *Zerkalo* (The Mirror) a news analysis program. Although he has guests, it is all Svanidze pontificating, alas, with little sense of humor. Svanidze has very impressive name-recognition as a major television authority. Yet, how off-base he is in his understanding of the very people to whom he imparts his wisdom. From the beginning of the new Russian Federation, his stance was consistent and familiar. In 2006, Svanidze contended:

that Russian society had become "tired of all the different choices it had in the media ... Our guests from the United States and European countries may not understand what I'm talking about, but the classic Russian reader is not used to having a variety of opinion, he's used to having one opinion handed to him on a platter. It is fatiguing to have a choice because you have to think."[24]

Here is someone who has responsibility for programming, is himself a major figure on television and a "philosophically wise" judge of Russia and its future. What could be further from the viewers on the other side of the screen, for whom choice is the very central contribution of post-Soviet television and who get a "high" from the power to surf? In chapter 6, these viewers also display a complex, varied response to the loss of TV-6, encompassing both indifference and grief. How can Moscow-centric programming meet the needs and

---

[24] World Association of Newspapers: "The Russian Media: From Dictatorship to Democracy," Moscow, June 4, 2006. Translated and reprinted in *Johnson's Russia List*, 129, June 4, 2006, 25.

preferences of its audience, when it holds such denigrating stereotypes of them?

Earlier, the question of dissonance came up and, with it, of compartmentalization, so that attitudes and memories of different policy domains, could and did, co-exist. We need only to recall that while the happy memories of children's programs and the boredom of television were discussed, there was no reference to other domains, such as gulags, rural deprivation, substandard communal housing, the power of the security police, and the calls in the middle of the night. These evidently represented to the participants different policy domains. Here it was television, both Soviet and post-Soviet, close, but not the full measure of Soviet power.

No one in the focus groups wants to substitute the past television regime for the current one, and some do not believe it would be possible in any case. But almost all, across the board, urge that advertising be eliminated or heavily reduced and controlled. Andrei (43, college-educated, a member of the armed forces, Volgograd) argues that "when a film runs two hours, if of the two hours, there are a minimum of 40 minutes of advertising, that's really serious." The groups find advertising "irritating"; they want it "removed." Galya (43, college-educated, working as a supplier, Moscow) echoes Andrei: "You look at television and you don't understand: which was more, advertising or movie." Add to this the uncounted and uncontrollable covert advertising, and one sees that Andrei, Galya, and the others are not likely to experience improvement any time soon. Like American television-watchers, when asked to choose between paying for television programs or continuing to have free television, supported by advertisements, most choose the latter.[25] Many of the focus groups would prefer a compromise: add a little from the past. Increase the number of gentle children's shows and cartoons. Removing advertising altogether, or at least its most objectionable manifestations, and returning to some programs that will attempt to socialize children instead of the glorification of crime and violence that is so popular at present is quite enough for most participants.

---

[25] E. Vovk, "TV Advertising," Public Opinion Foundation, Population Poll, 4–5 March, 2006, National sample; marginal error 3.6 percent. Reported in http://bd.english.fom.ru/report/map/ed061023.

For Soviet television to displace the imperfect, often objectionable, loud, and sometimes cruel palette of today would simply be anathema to almost all of the participants. And this is where the operation of memory would have been most useful: there are almost no concrete suggestions, no details, no well argued alternatives. Though some Soviet programs, especially children's shows, are meticulously described, the rest are generalities. The tone, the boredom, the uniformity have remained, but the details are no longer available. The comments lack emotion. The obvious exceptions are the vivid comparisons sea captain Viktor drew from his travels, and the shock Olya experienced when, at a time of strict censorship and harsh punishment, she heard her Leningrad friends openly critical, sounding to her like dissidents. The power of early memories, of which emotion is a strong component, might no longer be available to very many – except as automatic generalizations or homage to their youth. Much of that past has become absorbed by its contemporary lessons or "truths," and such reactions as liking the old way and believing the output of the old way have, in a sense been converted, if they are remembered at all, into a less dissonant, more compatible current memory.

6 | *Endings*

TV-6 will be remembered for its combative style and a view opposing governmental policy – whatever the policy was and whether or not it had been thoroughly researched. Not everybody could receive it; in Volgograd, it was not easy to get the signals. The focus groups observed the death throes of TV-6. One day, after a long struggle, it just disappeared from the screen, replaced by all-day sports. With TV-6 gone, there was still REN-TV, a small Moscow-based station that could be received in some 30 percent of the country. In Moscow, it was increasingly known for independent and balanced news, but the independent leadership of the station – the founder Irena Lesnevskaya and her son Dmitry – were helpless to prevent the loss of their station after the major investor had pulled out. Seventy percent of REN-TV's shares were initially bought by Severstal, a steel company close to the President, and Bertelsmann, the German publishing and communications giant, which accounted for about a quarter of the shares.

On January 22, 2002, if a viewer sat down to watch TV-6, she would see sports. She might use a remote or push buttons on the set to find it, but it would be gone as though it had never been. The decision about what, ultimately, would be on this frequency was postponed, but one thing was sure: TV-6 was not coming back. All sixteen focus groups were convened between January 14 and January 28 of that year. The TV-6 issue was in the air and in the press; it was not nearly as clamorous as the ending of NTV, for the latter station had had far greater penetration all across the country and its takeover was effected by an armed occupation. As TV-6 hung on under increasing pressure from officials and as its tone grew more beleaguered and critical of the authorities, its survival was itself news. Eleven focus groups were conducted while TV-6 was still on air (four in Rostov, three in Moscow, and four in Volgograd). One focus group in Moscow and four in Nizhny Novgorod were convened right after the fall of the station. We should also keep in mind that TV-6, unlike NTV (see

chapter 1) had much less penetration, and fewer people could evaluate
TV-6, in contrast with the "new" NTV which followed the government
line.

REN-TV, an independent, though small station, had also come up in
the conversation: Maxim (53, high-school-educated) described how he
knew nothing about the station until he stumbled on it:

Here we are speaking now about VHF channels, but there is very interesting
news ... which we practically don't see now. I rarely turn on REN-TV. After
RAO-EES [the electricity monopoly] bought this channel, it started a very
interesting news program, but to watch it is somehow ... you rarely think
about it, but at 7:00 somehow [you can] watch very interesting news, by the
way. [He rarely gets home before 7:00] and therefore I also don't watch, but
several times I just pick it up ... after RAO-EES bought it, it got more or less
rich and can permit itself interesting news programs.

The end of TV-6: what prompts viewers' reactions?

It has often been remarked by Westerners and by some in Russia,
particularly in Moscow, that viewers passively accepted the closure
of NTV and equally passively accepted the closure, a little while later,
of TV-6. There were demonstrations in Moscow about the harsh
occupation by the tax police, forcing their way into the NTV studios,
but nothing like spontaneous national outrage. When TV-6 went
down, the public reaction was even less noticeable. Surveys found
that most people thought that the reasons for closure were economic;
some thought political. The conclusions drawn were that Russians
simply do not value viewpoint diversity and, in addition, are passive
and fatalistic, just as nineteenth-century literature portrayed them.
Given the limited penetration of TV-6, some in our focus groups
never saw it. Yet, is the perception created above, of an accepting,
immobilized population of viewers, correct? Undoubtedly it is in
some respects, and we shall see them below. But, more to the point,
this slow-motion reaction with flickering attention is contradicted by
so many people in our focus groups that perhaps we should rethink the
utility of mass-surveys when such subtle and original arguments are in
play. It is for that reason, to explore the "whys" of the positions in their
own words, that the focus groups were so helpful. It is an added benefit
that of the sixteen focus groups, eleven took place before TV-6 was
taken off the air (though it was much talked about). An additional five

were conducted within one–six days after the station's run ended. Because the discourse varies so much among cities and post-Soviet and other groups, I prefer to let the reader experience these arguments, rather than breaking them up to analyze each one. It will therefore be helpful to place before the discussions the "backbone" of the discourse, so that its many parts may be recognized as the conversation proceeds. That does not mean that each group has a homogenous argument; there is quite a lot of sarcasm, irony, and what appears to be ill-feeling among the younger and less well-educated groups. In these references to discourse, the reader will recognize the larger issue of heuristics and memory that permeates this study. We move up the ladder of cognition from the discourse bounded by self-absorbed thinking to consideration of society-wide and, further, more universal considerations.

Discourse restricted to what difference having or losing TV-6 programs make on "me"

1. Can I receive its programs ?
2. Do I find them boring ?
3. I don't understand the reasons for the closure: yes, it's politics and economics, but it is happening behind a veil of secrecy. I can't have any positions on what I know nothing about. Thus, there are no analogies that will help me to understand; no insights I can draw from party labels or positions; it is not even known who is making the decision, except that it comes from the Kremlin and the door is closed to observers. I think that there has been no information vacuum comparable with this, in large part, because it is sealed within the fortress Kremlin and therefore very difficult to take a position resting on some, even small, insight that "got away" or leaked through the walls.
4. It's all about personalities: the outsized appetites, rich living of company head Evgeny Kiselev and his moneyed sponsor Boris Berezovsky. These are internal squabbles and infighting; it has nothing to do with me.
5. When NTV was closed, the team went to TV-6. They will always "land on their feet." So, when TV-6 is closed down, they'll find someplace else.
6. Who knows? When there's an auction for the license, we may get a station that's better than TV-6.

7. We've lived through a time when there was no television at all, when the transmitters and studios were damaged by fire. And we now can live through this. The fatalism of being able to make it under any conditions is assisted by comparisons not to an ideal future, but a lived past.

All of these reactions are genuine and sensible, but they are blinkered. They have not sought to seek meaning by using ways to penetrate the mystery by the use of heuristics, and that has kept their responses somewhat thin and narrowly situated in the realm of, and within the confines of, their own personal preferences. Some minimal use has been made of the recent past: the fate of NTV and the fire in the television tower qualify as relatively fresh news. No one in this form of discourse has gone further, and the opaque minimalist comments issued by the authorities has worked as an obstacle, which has, in turn, stopped dead any inclination to enunciate a position based on evidence.

Discourse pushing beyond the personal frame and invoking overarching elements, such as human rights, foreign policy, the basis of viewpoint diversity, and the nature of precedent for society

1. There is in human beings the prior existence and inviolability of human rights, such as freedoms of speech and press.
2. The underlying value of viewpoint diversity and speech freedoms. What purpose do they serve?
3. There is a direct ratio between the closure of TV-6 and the strength of Russian Federation foreign policy.
4. This is not a trivial event. It points to the importance of precedent and the ever-present threat of authoritarianism.
5. Two focus group participants draw US foreign policy into the fray.

A range of preferences emerged, from a refusal even to speculate on what undisclosed issues lay behind the station's closure, to a more integrated consideration of thinking about society as a whole while taking into account opposing arguments.

To repeat, in order to preserve the often lively give-and-take within the groups, I have not disturbed the sections of the conversation that particularly revealed the kind of discourse invoked. First, we look at the groups that met just before TV-6 was closed down. When it had been shut and replaced by sports programs, we conducted the rest of the focus groups (five). Similarly, I divide the discussion below into before and after the event.

TV-6 still in operation

Moscow

We begin with *college-educated Muscovites* who were in the focus groups while TV-6 was still on the air. Vladimir (34, salesman): "it's already so boring that we already think the same thing. Let them close it." Both Natasha (50, tax inspector) and Maxim (28, entrepreneur) do not agree. For Natasha, it appears to violate the law and the constitution, and is happening too hastily. For much of the rest of the session, the discourse is about the costs of ending diversity of views. Igor (26, analyst) believes that diversity is so important that even direct, unconstructive opposition is better than another pro-government outlet:

I think that here it's a question of political accounts with TV-6. And whether or not you like TV-6; whether or not you like the people who work there, since they present information, I think that it comes to accounts [how much political protection can be counted on] and they are closing ... The same will happen with TV-6. It will pass into different hands and then, crudely speaking, there simply will not be an opposition. It will be all pro-government ... I think in some way it [TV-6] may not be completely constructive. Its programs, let's say, may be biased, but in any case it's some opposition ... opposition is always a good, because there are different opinions and you can put together out of pieces of mosaic a normal picture.

Maxim says: "I don't agree [with Vladimir] because it worries me, for example, that they're closing still another channel that I found interesting to watch and from which I received more honest information." Olga and Oksana do care, but are confused by possible violations of the law which do have to be prosecuted and note that it is specific people who are the targets, especially Boris Berezovsky, the owner.

Yura (22, student): "Of course it worries me, because I think that it's a certain lack of boundaries. I think simply the coverage of political accounts, the removal of competitors, well not competitors, but political, other influence and it will be totalitarian." Oksana begins to form her opinion that "there will be roughly the same coverage from the same angle on all channels of the political life of the country. And generally it's better of course to have different sides."

Vladimir is bitterly sarcastic: "And what use is it to have many opinions in our society? We have many opinions and we call miners cattle when they begin to pollute our ecology, we sit in the kitchen and discuss it only among ourselves. So for what purpose [does] a multifacetedness of opinion and freedom of choice of channel [serve]? Who needs it? So that we can meet here and express ourselves? And that's all?"

This feeling of helplessness, of the impossibility of collective action, has come up with some frequency in this study. It is not answered. It is not seen as coming together to fight for better television. It is not seen as overcoming what the viewers see as the transgressions of news programs. Elsewhere there were two interesting upheavals, both sparked, in part, by television anchors. Naturally, revolutions and uprisings are made up of many variables, and what follows is not the anatomy of those two uprisings, but the "preview," as it were, that journalists headed. It might well have been that the demonstrations and popular anger against the government in these two cases passed over the obstacle that "it couldn't happen here." In the first, in the Republic of Georgia, Akaki Gogichaishvili, anchor of the investigative program *60 Minutes* on a private station, became the face of integrity and was the most-watched journalist. When his studio was stormed by the armed men of President Shevardnadze in 2001, Akaki turned on the cameras. Thousands of Georgians came out to form a living wall of protection for him and then spilled over into the main square calling for the ouster of Shevardnadze, who promised to fire his entire cabinet. Although this was a forerunner of the "Rose Revolution" that removed Shevardnadze from office, it is not hard to see that spontaneous crowds could be formed to protect a valued "friend," and it raised the hopes of those who had more ambitious plans. Before Ukraine's "Orange Revolution," a well-known television journalist, Andriy Shevchenko, resigned from his position because he would no longer bow to censorship. He founded a group of journalists against censorship who demonstrated in the main square. It was not a large demonstration, but from there Shevchenko went on to direct the news at a small private station. This station was the only one to broadcast to the rest of the country that a revolution was in the making and participation was welcome. There was no other source to inform and mobilize the country.

In the second *college-educated Moscow group*, convened while TV-6 was still alive, the discourse of the group is mainly about legal decisions they do not question. Some in the group think of media elites as having a revolving door and that the people at TV-6 are sure to find some other alternative. These are all naïve judgments. At the end, they acknowledge that it saddens them to lose TV-6, "it's a pity"; "a channel will disappear"; "another source will disappear where we could compare, see something new." Viktor, the merchant marine captain, reacts fatalistically. Throughout the focus groups, his have been among the most telling and experienced comments, drawn from experience of ports around the world and a keen memory for history. He says: "Ostankino [the television headquarters housing studios and telecommunications equipment] burned, and we didn't die. Generally they didn't show anything, you understand? Nothing. We will also stay alive. It's just that it will be bad that there won't be TV-6." None of these comments ponders the consequences or reasons for society at large: why is diversity necessary for overarching reasons beyond the personal preferences of individuals?

The *Moscow group with high-school education* was the last one in the city convened before TV-6 was closed. Oleg (27, unemployed) says: "it's already a superfluous channel. There's generally nothing to watch there." Others disagree, saying there are good journalists, a good team, truthful coverage. Later Oleg brings up the economic factor and is answered by the others that all stations lose money. When the facilitator asks what feelings they have, the answers are: from Olya – nothing; from Katya – sad; two others predict that the TV-6 team will just go some other place and register. Oksana (24, property surveyor) rarely watches, "so more likely, no feelings." Yura (29, trainer/instructor) has no feelings. He thinks "they'll get out and solve this issue and they will exist." Maxim (53, bookkeeper) raises the point about the necessity to have an opposition:

It's needed, probably. Even the communists are needed although I don't like them and can't stand them ... There should definitely be different points of view, otherwise we are returning to the old [ways] again, to like-mindedness. We return again to not having anything to click on. The remote will not be needed. There is one program and that's all. But we lived without the remote and we survived.

Yura, Katya, and Lena close the session by saying the station won't be closed. "That can't be" (Katya); "I don't want to believe [it could happen]" (Lena).

Volgograd

In *Volgograd among the college-educated*, the conversation starts that events around TV-6 are intended to "pressure" some individuals. But from there, the discourse becomes wholly about the importance of diversity and their powerful belief that a corner has been turned. It is no longer *possible* to do such things; those days are over, they firmly believe. Mikhail (52, programmer) says that it affects him:

because although I say that there exists great psychological pressure, they all broadcast differently. There is a choice, that is, if you want the official view, then watch first channel [Channel One], and I'd not tune into it at all ... We can't witness all events, no matter what, we'll have to wait so that somebody or something gets it to us.

Polina (23, housewife): "It isn't worth closing it down. Every channel broadcasts its own way and *the individual has the right to watch all four channels* and has his point of view. The tension in watching is interesting and useful. If [that's missing], I doubt that I would watch TV often." Notice that Polina refers to the "right" to have diversity of viewpoint:

Vera (39, engineer/programmer): It would be a shame. We'd receive the identical information; it would not be interesting.

Mikhail: It's not worth closing it, because we get differently planned information; it helps reflection.

Aleksei (43, employee): I think they will open a new channel on its foundation, like TV-6 ... [it couldn't be closed down] of course not ... because the demand exists for objective information ... by society ... Come on, *the power will not go against society.*

Vera: *Well, before they could close it, but not now.*

Aleksei: *Not any more, of course.*

Galina (32, economist/manager): We like them [the anchors at TV-6] and we are also part of society. We also express our opinion, and so what if they [challenge] our point of view. They don't propagandize, but only present another point of view.

Andrei (43, military): Changing the name doesn't change much of the broadcasting and [all] the rest. I think they will stay.

This is a remarkable discussion in which participants who had experienced the Soviet system believe that finally they have attained their irreversible rights and the government could not go against the will of the people; it wouldn't. The other *Volgograd group of college-educated* is fairly indifferent. A 48-year old employee and a 22-year-old engineer have no feelings about TV-6; they don't watch it. Several say it's a shame. Anatoly (56, employee) fatalistically says "you lose something all the time, no matter what."

In the group with high-school education, the participants speak in an uninvolved voice about TV-6 and what is happening. Alena (25, artist) hasn't heard anything about it, and she does not receive TV-6. Natasha (37, blue-collar worker) has heard "something." Dmitri (33, unemployed) is fairly indifferent and calls TV-6 "something to watch," while Valery (38, blue-collar worker) calls TV-6 "not the most important channel." Throughout the discussion, Alena, who personally knows nothing about the qualities of TV-6 under attack, is passionately against shutting it down because of the unemployment it would create. She says quite eloquently:

Next to us, in the next entrance there are guys from TV-6 Volgograd. [They're] normal guys; they work normally; [they're] young. Overall these are still living people who work. They still put in their work, their resources. They do it for us; we watch it. To destroy is always simpler than to create.

When asked about freedom of speech in connection with the closure, she replies "I can't say." Others regard the reason for the threat to TV-6 is that some sort of struggle is going on probably related to politics and the competitors will remove them.

The *post-Soviet group from Volgograd* is both puzzled and strongly in support of viewpoint diversity. Discourse revolves around the silencing of journalists by the government. As Denis (21, student) put it: "they just don't want any competition." They also believe that Channels One, Two, and NTV are close to the President. Misha (24, student) raises the overarching question for society about the rights and the utility of minority views: "I think that we should listen to the opinion of the minority, because in this opinion you can find some use. In principle I hold the view that *all channels have the right to exist*." Denis replies: "and I don't even think that TV-6 *is* the minority. Many believe that the team at TV-6 will open a new channel if this one is closed down." Evgeny (25, in the military) raises a fascinating larger issue. Just at the time when Russia is trying to show off its democratic credentials, they "crush" TV-6. "I don't know why now, at least while they were showing that they have freedom of speech and thought and all the rest."

Rostov

In the first *Rostov college-educated group*, the discussion at first displays a proud indifference to the impending end of TV-6. Gennady (31, programmer) tosses off the remark: "Berezovsky will pay and it will all be fine." Alexei (43, employee) says whoever's sponsors pay more will get it. When the facilitator asks if generally they feel touched personally:

Alexei: No.
Gennady: No. I don't watch [TV-6].
Sasha (24, businessman): No.
Lilia (54, worker): No, of course not. It's a dirty story.
Ira (49, employee): How can it touch me personally? No, of course not.
Alexei: Again – No.
Lena (31, employee): No.

When the facilitator asks if the closure arouses any emotions, Alexei responds: "we don't know anything; therefore it doesn't touch me. I don't know what they are doing there. How can it touch us?" Most think it is some kind of political machination "behind the scenes" – not a good thing." Focus groups can trace the social interactions and changes of position or the introduction of new opinions and the following is certainly one of them, from a young bureaucrat. Anatoly (28, personnel officer in a prison) considers the precedent of closing TV-6: "people will begin to talk less."

Gennady has nothing but contempt for that fear: "Of course not. What are you talking about? There will be nothing." Sasha persists, probing still deeper into the issue of the station's closure providing the impetus for the disappearance of freedom in general: "There is direct persecution of Kiselev and his team. They're trying to take away the only independent channel that objectively evaluates the situation. In the long term it can grow into authoritarianism." Gennady rejects this extrapolation out-of-hand. Why? Because of the presence of a post-Soviet generation. "It's already a different generation, and they already think differently."

A number of participants in the focus group do not have such a rosy picture of the younger generation. In fact, they hardly think that young people will shoulder the values of anti-authoritarianism. These people see self-absorption and not civic involvement in the next generation.

Lena (36, teacher) puts it this way: "Youth doesn't give a damn about anything." Sasha: "they will be absolutely indifferent."

Gennady's thinking is conspiratorial and emotional. He is a person who gets most of his news from the Internet, suggesting that in him, at least, reliance on the Internet for news does not automatically confer the habits and values of democracy. On the contrary, although only 31, Gennady also does not believe that the majority in society should put up with minority views. He goes on at some length about the real meaning of TV-6:

Look, they closed NTV. Kiselev fought there. I'm saying honestly I wasn't sorry they closed it, and I thank God. Because a fifth column on television should not exist. [There was] some reporting from Chechnya in which they called our soldiers "federals" and the Chechens "freedom fighters." I bring up one example. I'm Russian and I'm in this country. I don't want any such channel to exist ... If TV-6 found its way and became a fifth column, let them close it.

Sasha also raises the TV-6 question to a more philosophical level: "I think it would be impossible to talk about any kind of democratic society and close an independent channel and bring it under control."

What is interesting about this discourse in this focus group, is that, as in society at large, the nay-sayers' harsh personal indifference to the ending of TV-6 is replaced by an about-face as the conversation continues and they rethink their casual dismissal to see larger, society-wide issues of great import. This is another example of the advantage of focus groups, of the way that the social setting interacts with initial ideas that haven't been thought through. Similarly, the emotional defensive nationalist position taken by Gennady, who is, after all, in touch with the latest information technology and its huge store of information, is sobering. Alexander (Sasha) counterposes the meaning of democracy. The clash of these two worldviews provides the observer with a battle about principles at the heart of the society in which they live. They agree that it can't be left to the next generation.

The other *Rostov group of college-educated* are much more at one in their criticism of the ending of TV-6 and of the precedent-setting force of the action and its capacity to affect the very freedoms this society has finally won. Several say that they don't understand the inside story and the intricacies of what's going on, but that doesn't stop them from calling it "persecution." When asked by the facilitator if there will be any consequences for society if TV-6 is closed, Vlad (40, engineer)

says "No." Misha (24, teacher, a graduate student) says: "No con-
sequences. What kind of consequences could there be?" Right away
Lena (26, teacher) says: "It will be even easier to close all the rest."
Mark (31, computer engineer) takes it further and more emotionally:
"Censorship! At TV-6 there's no censorship and now it will be everywhere. We, guys, look what we've come to ... There won't be any
more; they'll close it all ... What's the difference? It's all hopeless."
When asked by a fellow participant if he thinks TV-6 will be closed,
Mark answers: "Of course they'll close it." Mark is particularly concerned – and rightly so – that coverage of the war in Chechnya has been
drastically reduced on the state channels. "Notice that they don't show
news about Chechnya. Putin stopped it."

The high-school educated in Rostov don't see much connection
with the end of TV-6 and any societal value or impact at all. Julia
(28, technician) says: "Society loses nothing." Bogdan (22, does various
jobs) says: "I think it loses nothing." Sasha (31, director, youth club)
says: "It will be closed down as a channel – that is, the team will change.
It's completely possible." Julia indifferently mouths a saying: "Talented
people will always find their place."

So, they go on. It doesn't really matter to Nikolai (52, electrician):
"Nobody's irreplaceable of course." The ending of TV-6 has so little
connection with these less-well-educated that they see only the game of
musical chairs: NTV goes to TV-6 and onward; some stay; some leave.
What's the difference? Certainly none to them personally and they see
no societal interests in this uninteresting change of cast.

Finally there is the *post-Soviet group in Rostov*. They first comment that
the conflict is due to the team at TV-6, particularly those close to Evgeny
Kiselev, the head of the station. They consider it "personal," except for Ira
(20, student), who says: "I don't think that it's personal. I think everything is
tied up with economics and politics." The level of analysis about this case
goes no further than simply to name economics and politics, which is so
broad that it makes no real sense. Just five days before TV-6 will be taken
off the air, most of these young people quite complacently say that such an
ending could not possibly happen. In their words:

Andrei (23, economist): As an ordinary viewer, it's all the same to me,
    because they'll never lose TV-6.
Ira: Of course not. They wouldn't want to.
Oksana (20, student): Yes.
Ira: Yes.

Andrei: Yes, it will be unpleasant, but it won't happen.

Ivan (21, student): [It makes] no difference to me.

Nastya (25, housewife): It's absolutely no difference to me. He's [Kiselev] tolerated changes before this.

This is an uninformed group, lacking any political savvy about how things are done and what the political issues are. It offers blind acceptance of a naïve view that somehow Kiselev's political leverage is greater than Putin's. Their elders have a much wider knowledge and set of emotions and principles to apply. It is certainly possible that this ending of TV-6 is a matter of no interest to these young people and that is why they give almost dismissive answers. But even that shows the self-absorption and isolation that these young Rostov people have.

TV-6 closes down on January 22

Five focus groups took place just after the closure of TV-6. Nizhny Novgorod's all four groups were convened on January 23 and 24 and, in Moscow, the post-Soviet group met on January 28. We shall turn first to *Nizhny Novgorod*.

In the first of *the college-educated* groups, the participants traded stories about what it looked like when TV-6 went off the air. One said her Petersburg friends called to say that "Swan Lake" was being shown on the former TV-6 frequency. The ballet that was shown when Ostankino was taken over by *coup* plotters was now a part of Russian folklore. When TV-6 went dead, it was time for "Swan Lake" again.

The loss of TV-6 does not get much sympathy from this group and virtually no parallels are drawn with anything larger or more important. TV-6 does not seem to be a symbol or example of anything but itself. As Vladimir (59, retired) said: "So they closed it." Tanya (50, teacher) "It's not a loss." Antonina (24, graduate student): "It's just that now there are quite a lot of channels and to have TV-6, so that there are 15 buttons, [and that would make it a situation with] three channels, then it maybe would be felt." Sergei (28, occupation not given):

It's absolutely unimportant. Because I have a sister living in Chita. There are two channels there. Earlier I lived in Kazakhstan, and we had one channel: Channel One. Channel Two's signal didn't reach there. And such a region, believe me, where they get a total of 2–3 buttons, there are a lot of them ... So let's talk about what is real, like all revolutions, this is all done only in the capital.

When asked if this has anything to do with narrowing freedom of speech, he answers: "Nonsense!" Alexander, too, uses the growth in the number of channels to make his point: "So what, when you consider all the other channels." Antonina even thinks that in the competition for the deserted frequency, there could be better choices: "Nobody said they will be worse than TV-6." Sergei, closes: "[It's my view] that they think they can raise the flag, but, in fact, the people are so apolitical and so uninterested."

In the second group of *college-educated in Nizhny Novgorod*, the beginning of the conversation has the participants offering hypotheses about the origin of the action against TV-6. Olga (64, retired) says that she thinks it's because of Kiselev. Liuda (52, physician) talks about all the "underwater currents" that propelled the station's policy, its deficit, and adds: "and then the question arises: where does this advertising money go? Where? So that Kiselev flies his private airplane?" Kolya (45, general director) called it an "interesting channel, an individual channel, that is, a defined point of view." One may not agree, but "it was a point of view." Liuda says that it was to some degree different from other stations, "more contemporary," with a good many interesting programs.

When the facilitator asked if there was any connection to society's needs, Andrei says, "Of course not." Vladimir even finds the conflict healthy, in his Marxist language, he says "In a struggle something new is always born." Liuda: "There could be an even better channel." Only Marina is worried that the closure has caused the "[loss of], let's say, of faith that any points of view can go on the air without obstacles. Because this is after all freedom of speech to a certain degree." Alesha (52, teacher) says flatly: "I don't agree," and Liuda: "I also don't agree." Marina has no vocal support in the group.

At the end of this discussion Andrei says: "I was always interested about America's view of what is going on in Russia. Very often it generally coincided with that of TV-6." Liuda: "Yes, absolutely coincides with TV-6." Alesha finishes the session by saying: "Too expensive a pleasure."

Nizhny Novgorod's high-school-educated group knew about the conflicts over TV-6, but other than making guesses, including ousting Berezovsky as a central cause, they did not know what the real story was and showed some irritation that they were kept out of the loop:

Natasha (55, dentist): How can you have an attitude to what you don't know about? Simply the facts. I, for example, don't understand anything in this.

There were very strong comments in support of TV-6:

Slava (26, worker) said: The freest channel.
Zoya (64, on pension): Of course, I'd want it [TV-6] to exist, because there's
   more truth there …
Slava: The freest channel. They showed everything.

The discourse on human rights and freedom of speech are brought up
by Anatoly, who puts the blame squarely on Putin. Anatoly (23,
apartment TV repairman): "Well, Putin is infringing on freedom of
speech, to no purpose, it seems to me … They [TV-6] expressed
probably against him all the time, and he doesn't like it. He probably
wanted it to be a first/second channel." Olya (49, artist/designer):

I agree with that. Certainly they are infringing on freedom of speech, and they
probably want to dictate to people the correct line as before "the Party said."
Now there's no party, but there's a state line. There it's the power that
represents it to us. If there were on every channel the same thing, then that
means we will schedule programs for ourselves better, when there won't be
any choice, or other alternative to watch, some other news.

The session is ended by Viktor (62, on pension): "No, No. Nobody is
going to close TV-6. There will be sports for a while and a sale, but
Kiselev will participate in that, too. But they won't close it … they can't
close it." Viktor, like Gennady, does not believe that society should
take account of minority views. He also maintains, where Gennady did
not answer the question, that the state should step in to limit income
disparities. Of course, he is much older, living on a pension and not tied
in to the information society of the future. Perhaps that is what makes it
doubly surprising that his defense of the resuscitation of TV-6 is so
urgent.

The *post-Soviet group participants in Nizhny Novgorod* are confused about the reasons for TV-6's closure and, after the more dramatic
and public closure of NTV, see it as a pale imitation.

They are not particularly well informed or interested and neither
look for nor consider a possible link between this event of closure and
anything that affects more than the particular viewer. They talk only at
the level of their own gratification, and that is partly because there was
so little information in the public domain. Finding it impossible to say
anything concrete about the closure, because it all took place behind
closed doors, Kolya (20, student) summed it up: "It's a mess. It's only

by rumor that something took place or not. And in the end, they stopped the broadcasting and closed it down." Olya (23, translator) will miss TV-6; Lera (21, student) pragmatically says: "[It] depends what's substituted." When the facilitator asks if the absence of TV-6 reflects on society, Sergei (20, student) says: "It doesn't reflect at all." No one contradicts him.

The last focus group was the *post-Soviet one in Moscow*, convened nearly a week after the closure of TV-6. Here, large issues are raised that relate to the governance of Russia and to international relations. Oleg (25, worker/student) says: "You know, I agree there's pretentiousness there. But it's better to let [there be] at least some alternative to what is now going on." Lena (24, translator):

And really, does this accord with what Putin so strives for with the West? He builds bridges; he spends so much effort and time on finding a common language with Western countries. Isn't he handing them such a present? He specially closes the channel [so] that they have the opportunity to be up in arms about [it], not only about Chechnya, but also about the absence of freedom of speech in Russia.

The conversation changes to guessing at a reason for the closure – political, economic, a mix. Maxim (23, history teacher and graduate student) is pleased with the sports programs that have replaced TV-6. He finds them "a lot more interesting than TV-6. All this is total nonsense. TV-6 should have been closed long ago and Kiselev put in jail." Then, there is Igor (24, geological engineer), who never watched TV-6 at all, except once: "and I didn't like it at all." Igor surprisingly adds: "News of course is better. It's another alternative opinion ... There are people who watch. They need something to compare." Oleg responds about searching for alternative news ... to compare to other news: "Soon we'll be listening to Voice of America."

Into this rambling discourse, Ivan (21, student of jurisprudence) injects his opinion in the form of organized legal arguments:

About the closure of TV-6, there are two apparently contradictory points of view circulating. The first is legal, even economic. And the second is political. The essence of the legal or economic is the liquidation of unpaid obligations [as a reason to close down TV-6]. The political is well known: the President, the chief of state is trying to liquidate the opposition. In the given case the two points of view are not mutually exclusive; they supplement each other because the laws are the ability, the will, the conviction and the arbitrariness of power elevated and cast in law. In the given case the reasons are of course political, but they were cast in a legal form. It is an implement, an instrument of power.

Maxim, after the group speculates where the TV-6 personnel will go, refers to Ivan's argument: "It's useless to fight with the government. If Putin decided, then he decided."

Ivan states that in this case "The President has a clear position:"

Lena: What is his position, if I may ask?

Ivan: To liquidate the opposition.

Lena: Why does he need to?

Ivan: Because here *the source of power is the people, the opinion of the people.* And in the given case, it's necessary somehow to manage this opinion. After all, they will elect him and reelect him.

Lena: All right, what does Putin gain by closing NTV? This TV-6.

Viktor (22, tour manager): *A healthy opposition never hampered anybody.*

Ivan: But the liquidation of the opposition.

Lena: Why, why provoke so many problems for yourself? Over there the whole West is already wailing again. Gusinsky [and] Berezovsky are heroes in the West.

Ivan: The purpose of power is power. And in the given case power can get it [power] in the reelections if in the state there will be no oppositionist television, mass media which forms public opinion.

Lena: Where did you get that from?

Oleg: Isn't it easier to have a little opposition channel? Let's say just one. TV-6 alone. And it can always be quoted.

Lena: And then TV-6, this isn't power. It resonated now because they closed it. Otherwise it was nothing and nobody.

Maxim: I think there's just no opposition channel in Russia. All the existing channels ... TV-6, NTV, they're all bought by power. [Only] they have their politics. They just, so to speak, pull a blanket of oppositionism over themselves. Nobody tells the truth to [anyone]. Those liberal traditions that exist in the West, they're alien at the given moment; simply nobody takes it for something real. It's all an empty waste of time.

Ouster and change at REN-TV

When I first met Irena Lesnevskaya, a small ball of energy seated behind an imposing business desk, REN-TV was going to be a television station like no other. Impassioned, she spoke of the television scene in Russia, the cheap imports, the violence, sex, and moronic plots. Hers was to be a "channel for intellectuals." She spoke at length about this underserved population and that she alone would right the balance. I could not quite understand how a private station, dependent on the same pool of advertising money and investment as the rest of the competitive television world, could, frankly, survive catering only to "intellectuals." I applauded her for the feisty courage that never left her in the ominous years ahead. She was determined to steer clear of government financing; independence was a cardinal principle for her, and was tested very often in the industry that mattered most to the leadership.

She followed a different route for badly needed investment to prolong the life of the institution she and her son had created. Anatoly Chubais is a name well known to Russian politicians and citizens alike. He was a key figure in the privatization of state property and the deeply flawed "voucher" system, succeeded by the "loans for shares" giveaway, through which oligarchs were born and many ordinary people victimized. He harbored hopes for gaining the top office; founded a liberal party that kept him in the political game, and held appointive posts under Boris Yeltsin. He never got the top post; the fallout from the privatization schemes left him a very unpopular public figure. When he was given directorship of the state electric monopoly, Unified Energy Systems (UES), the largest electricity grid in the world, he made an investment in REN-TV that made up some 70 percent of the station's assets.

Times were changing under President Putin. Some oligarchs had their property seized and went into exile, and the media business was especially vulnerable to this kind of pressure. Nor were major natural resources to be in the hands of opponents of the President, as Mikhail Khodorkovsky [the once-powerful oil magnate charged with illegal financial maneuvers and given a stiff jail term by the Putin administration] learned. Chubais did not need tea leaves to speculate about his future; it was becoming plain. There was an apparent assassination attempt in March 2005. On May 25 of that year there was a disastrous power outage; four huge regions of Russia, including Moscow, were left with no electricity at all. Chubais, where the buck stopped, had put his deputy Arkady Yevstafiev in charge of one of the most critically important units of the organization: Mosenergo. Ten days after the power failure, President Putin went on television to say: "I'm pointing out to the chairman of the government the cynicism and obvious unprofessionalism of Mosenergo management." Yevstafiev was left out of the Security Council meeting (Chubais was not) about the causes of the blackout, and watching television, he got his first inkling that Putin's anger was directed at him, personally. Putin had also invited the Prosecutor General, Vladimir Ustinov, to the Security Council meeting. According to the reliable coverage of the newspaper *Kommersant*: "It looks like Putin wanted to warn all those present that it is necessary to check how UES pays taxes, spends investments and places money from the non-direct assets, such as real estate. The president was especially enraged by the fact that 'large pieces of real estate in Moscow, and especially in the center of Moscow for some reason belong to owners registered in Cyprus.'"[1] Chubais reportedly called Yevstafiev and told him to resign.

Although Chubais' move might be thought ordinary, he was, it appeared, attached to his loyal assistant and moved him into a high level at whatever bureaucracy he headed.[2] It was alleged that Yevstafiev was involved in a whole string of dubious moves; there was never a "last one." In the 1993 electoral campaign, an American public relations campaign was at the same time implementing an educational campaign about privatization and the use of the voucher. The television spot ended with "Your Voucher, Your Choice." But somehow ads, paid for by USAID, were changed to favor one of the parties: "Your Choice, Russia's Choice." When the scandal hit the front pages, all parties denied responsibility, and one name surfaced – Arkady Yevstafiev, then press secretary for Privatization Ministry chief, Chubais, who apparently told the American companies to change the spot. They denied acceding to this and although everyone blamed everyone else, it is likely the change was made by Russians. Mark Malloch Brown recalled that it was Yevstafiev who had instructed Sawyer Miller to change the tag line. According to Malloch Brown, in change of the public relations company's international practice, the company refused. USAID had granted Sawyer Miller the portfolio to

[1] K. Smirnov, "The President Found Weak Link in Chubais' Net," *Kommersant*, June 6, 2005, www.kommersant.com/doc.asp?id=583183.
[2] The following is based partly on E. Mickiewicz, *Changing Channels: Television and the Struggle for Power in Russia*, rev. and expand edn. Durham, NC: Duke University Press, 1999.

launch, explain, and run the new voucher system by which state property was supposed to become privately owned.[3] In spite of the scandal at USAID and in Russia, Yevstafiev was given the news directorship at the largest and most important television channel, Channel One. For Chubais to put his conduit there may have served his personal ambition and desire for control, but it did not serve the television public. But it didn't matter, Chubais left his position as Vice Prime Minister and, naturally, Yevstafiev went with him. In June 1996, elections were again coming up, and Yevstafiev and another activist operating in the grey zone were caught with a Xerox box filled with half a million dollars in cash. Chubais was a member of Boris Yeltsin's campaign committee and it was not difficult to guess where the money might be going. Amazingly, Chubais arranged for the resignation of those who had seized Yevstafiev and his cache. The criminal case was closed; no one ever proved to whom the Xerox box belonged. In 1997, Yevstafiev was one of those implicated in the receipt of book royalties, allegedly in the amount of $90,000 without having anything whatever to display as a book or a proposal. It was reported that he kept the "royalties" and the case was dropped because of an amnesty. In 2001, when Chubais went to head the electrical monopoly, he wanted his loyal Yevstafiev in control of the important Mosenergo unit. It was already filled as a patronage position by Moscow mayor Yury Luzhkov, who refused to be pushed aside. A SWAT team cleaned up the office for Yevstafiev to preside over Mosenergo:

Since the power crisis in the capital Anatoly Chubais has heard many reproaches. One of those was the lack of professional power engineers in the management of power systems in the country and in the Moscow region, in particular. It was this last argument that made a change in Mosenergo management inevitable.[4]

Putin's diatribe against the squirreling of assets out of reach in Cyprus is, according to *Russian Intelligence* a "carbon copy" of the threats he made against Khodorkovsky that, as we have seen, resulted

---

[3] Telephone interview with Mark Malloch Brown, July 1995. Reported in *Changing Channels*, see n. 2 above.

[4] V. Aglamishyan, "New Director of Mosenergo," *Izvestia*, June 14, 2005, www.mosenergo.ru/eng/index.php?id=31&news_id=983&theme=51&sessid=e697873437f8e953a7a2d32b4c54ba7.

in a stiff jail term.[5] Chubais himself was put under investigation by the Prosecutor General for negligence and abuse of power.

I summarize Chubais' checkered history and that of his associate Yevstafiev because it has a direct bearing on the last independent television news operation left standing. With Chubais' 70 percent of the shares and benign support, Lesnevskaya and Dmitri, could make a go of it in their independent, outspoken way. The circumstances may have changed for Chubais, perhaps only temporarily, but the President's language was ominous and, of course, elections were approaching. As in the United States, elections began to "approach" much earlier year by year and the informal campaign period opened earlier and earlier behind closed doors.

Chubais, perhaps prudently, put his 70 percent up for sale, and Lesnevskaya did not have the resources to buy it. REN-TV was bought by the German media company Bertelsmann (one-third of the shares) and by a Russian natural resources company close to the President: the pattern for the takeover of other media organizations. Severstal, a steel company, then sold 35 percent to Surgneftegaz, an oil company.

After twelve years of scraping together resources and refusing to be intimidated, REN-TV was approaching bankruptcy. Lesnevskaya knew, in any case, that the government was becoming concerned about her news programs, which were increasing in popularity in Moscow as the competition declined. At one point, she was seriously advised to focus on entertainment. She was not going to submit to anyone or bend her principles, however; she sold her shares, probably quite favorably, but it was still a profound loss that the single balanced and independent news had gone. Later, when the RTL division of Bertelsmann was approached about the principles of newscasting after Lesnesvskaya's departure, they said that they were minority shareholders and could not interfere with policy.

A content analysis by the Russian Union of Journalists and a Slovak media monitoring agency showed that in television news in March 2006 REN-TV had the only independent voice and was the only independent channel to devote less than two-thirds of prime-time coverage to political elites and, by contrast, had more time for

[5] www.russia-intelligence.fr/uk/iso_album/ria14.pdf.

dissenting political voices.[6] Clouding that picture are the observations of the long-time fighter for freedom of the press and speech, Alexei Simonov, head of the Glasnost Foundation. Simonov wrote that REN-TV was not among the most highly rated channels, though he called it "fairly influential," because of its independence, he added. As an experienced long-time influential man himself, he said about REN-TV that "it retains a certain amount of independence, but circumstances force it to look over its shoulder at other channels and avoid moving too far ahead of them."[7]

After the change, Olga Romanova, host of a news analysis program, was fired and several of her reports were pulled after she did one on a pro-fascist march in Moscow. When Romanova appealed to RTL's Moscow chief, Ralph Siebanaler, he said: "'When you have a change of management in a company, it happens unfortunately that parts of the former management team do not get along with the new team.'"[8]

REN-TV's stubborn fight should, however, be seen in perspective. The principle involved is important, but as a station it is on the periphery. It cannot be compared to NTV, even after the takeover by Gazprom. REN-TV was always an also-ran, bringing up the rear, but it kept its promises to its audience.

Although this case is significant, REN-TV was a minor – very minor – television station. In the regions, it often shared the channel with local programs and much lighter fare. It never had the clout of NTV. It is interesting that one – but *only one* – of our 158 focus group participants happened by accident upon the station, and thought it very good.

The discourse we hear from the focus groups is about why and how these two cases of television independence and divergent voices are really quite different from all that has gone before. They all know that reading some of the newspapers distributed mainly in the capital would be a good antidote, but subscription to this near-luxury is too

[6] BBC Monitoring, "Analysis: Survey Highlights pro-Putin bias on Russian TV News," May 3, 2006. Reprinted in *Johnson's Russia List*, 104, May 4, 2006, 10.

[7] A. Simonov, "Transformations of the Fourth Estate: The Media have become the Information Component of the State. How Media Freedom in Russia has Changed over the Past Five Years," *Nezavisimaya Gazeta*, October 7, 2005. Reprinted in *Johnson's Russia List*, 9263, October 10, 2005, 11.

[8] S. Kishkovsky, "Major Russian TV Station is Accused of Censorship," *New York Times*, January 2, 2006: C3.

expensive; takes too much dedicated time; and is so Moscow-centric, that the costs and benefits must be seriously considered.

Their preferred source is television: for convenience now, but soon not just in big cities or at work, other choices will be more convenient – such as the Internet when it enters many more million homes. In the meantime, the choices for accessing diversity would be first, as some of the participants say, to do what they did in Soviet times and dig for hidden clues. The shrinking globe and the Internet, wherever one finds it, is going to make it much more difficult to exclude all diversity for the large audiences that television attracts. The other choice is for the political leaders to think carefully about how much buying up independent stations really costs. They are all money-losing propositions, the rationale for which is that their function is to play a political role; they only look like normal television stations. Beyond this level of analysis, leaders might perform a more significant appraisal. Is their strategy of dominating the television screen, reporting in biased ways about elections, and making sure their messages reach the public really working? Do they have it right? Are viewers buoyed by the positive messages and mobilized to be active participants following the political script? It is apparent from listening to a collection of different kinds of people, in very different cities, that the strategy from the top may be producing the reverse results to those that were intended. If the other side of the screen were to be illuminated and audiences finally came into view, the whole house of cards of presumed effects would fall down and some serious attention to how viewers process the news would be in order. If average viewers and their cognitive systems were to be superimposed on the political fare they sit through, the match would be so off-center that the political leadership would either have to acknowledge a strategy of very high costs and low benefits or take much greater account of their viewers. Political figures are not the only decision-makers about television who are unaware of the skills of the other side of the screen: many journalists, public intellectuals, communications scholars, and others take that colorful variety of practices and values called "publics" and lump them together into a presumed grey mass, called "the people." That is a costly and losing policy.

7 | *The other side of the screen*

On the other side of the television screen viewers sit in rapt attention as the news unrolls. Some do. Others are making dinner, looking after children, and looking at the screen when something catches their attention. Some are working on the Internet, or sending emails to friends. So far, the picture could come from anywhere. It is what happens next that makes this very Russian case so intriguing. There are very few advantages that the people in Russia on the other side of the screen can claim. Control over what goes out on the screen comes from Moscow, as one after the other independent stations have been checkmated – usually by that persuasive charge of "insufficient funds." Russian viewers are intriguing because under these conditions they have developed some extraordinary ways to process the news – about which they care very much and always have done – in order to make sense out of it. Developing and enriching a sense of what is really happening on the news depends on what the viewers can bring for themselves. Most important of the instruments in their personal tool box is the capacity to effect a mental shortcut, so that what is given out as news can be made familiar, drawn out of the memory's storehouse of categories or schemas that not only fit this case but illuminate its real meaning.

The generating side of the screen that comes from Moscow and penetrates the entire Russian Federation with little true competition from local stations, especially in prime time, has its own notion of the minds on the other side of the screen. With only three national news networks its job of convincing viewers is much reduced from, say, what

This chapter is expanded from E. Mickiewicz, "Does 'Trust' Mean Attention, Comprehension and Acceptance? Paradoxes of Russian Viewers' News Processing," in K. Voltmar (ed.), *Mass Media and Political Communication in New Democracies*. London, Routledge, 2005 and reproduced with the permission of the Taylor & Francis Group.

it would be with 200 cable channels and endless possibilities in newer technologies.

We have seen in several different contexts that divergence is more common than congruity. At the all-important time of elections – when stations with an independent voice are closed down, bankrupted, or invaded – the messages of most importance to the broadcasters encounter viewers' processing that nullifies the intent of the message. In most domains of television news, the other side of the screen is full of cases of repudiation – alternative cases more convincing and personally tested than what is on the screen; and narratives of refutation that are so numerous that if Moscow did not insist on only one point of view with no downsides, they might actually limit the field of viewer-generated alternatives; they might be reduced to the usual "two sides" American viewers see. Two sides, an axiom of proper professionalism in American journalism, are only two (one of which is coming from the source of the policy – the government) out of what is actually a much wider spectrum.

The many meanings of "trust"

The way Russians talk about "trust" in television news is important for both Russian officials and for Western researchers. It turns out to be an extremely complex process for what seems a simple word that can be attached to surveys in several countries for purposes of comparison. It is also a warning sign: abstractions must be contextualized first and then translated into the nearest possible meaning, which may not be the "simple" meaning one started off with. In the focus groups what different people mean by trust is "dissected," contextualized, and reconstructed into the different meanings the Russian respondents intended.

In mass-surveys of public opinion, year after year, regardless of polling organization, the same question appears: Which news program do you trust most? The answer is consistent over time. By a significant margin, Russian respondents answer: Channel One's news *Vremya* [*Time*].[1] Viewers' trust of the official news may be one of the most potent assets for the government.

---

[1] Reprinted in *Johnson's Russia List*, 104, May 4, 2006, 9.

As a result of these answers, poll-takers can assume that consistent trust in one news program – run by the State – can provide information for modeling voting behavior, or the transition to democracy, and many other questions. It is also a variable that fits well into comparative longitudinal datasets. Channel One was the first national network in the Soviet Union. In Soviet times, *Vremya* was the only news program. The station always had the advantage of the most favorable technological infrastructure for virtually total penetration of the country. It was the first channel then and remains the first in penetration, and it is the most widely received news program in the country.

Russians watching news on Channel One

It would seem that there would be little disagreement among survey analysts about the meaning of trust. After the tape of a typical Channel One story, the one about the Novorossisk pipeline, the question of trust came up. It appears that the discourse permits multiple meanings for trust; it is not so clear how to interpret them without contextual clues.

The Novorossisk pipeline story is a prime example of state broadcasters' assumptions about their publics: that the message of upbeat tradeoff-free activity will be welcomed and assimilated. The government-controlled channel is the highest-rated program in all the cities, and Channel One figures at the very top, especially in Volgograd, where choice is more limited than elsewhere.[2]

The components of persuasion

McGraw and Hubbard (1996) summarize the steps necessary for persuasion: "(1) the recipients (constituents) must be *exposed* to the communication (the account); (2) they must pay *attention* to it; (3) they must *comprehend* it; and (4) they must *accept* the explanation as legitimate and credible."[3] Only then would the information be stored

---

[2] "Putin, Mass Media Top Positive Rating List – Poll," ITAR-TASS, May 23, 2006. Reprinted in *Johnson's Russia List*, 9276, October 23, 2005, 1.

[3] K. McGraw and C. Hubbard, "Some of the People Some of the Time," in D. Mutz, P. M. Sniderman, and R. A. Brody (eds.), *Political Persuasion and Attitude Change*. Ann Arbor, University of Michigan Press, 1996 (emphasis in the original).

and available for application to similar categories. Persuasion depends critically on assimilating the information from the television program and having it at hand, ready to be applied to the next case which one sees as similar or analogous; the accessibility heuristic is a powerful organizing or learning shortcut that citizens use.[4] As Graber has noted about her research in the United States:

Most political information is sloughed off ... because average Americans usually find it neither useful nor enjoyable. This explains why the majority of stimuli that people actually notice, including political messages, leave no long-term traces in memory and cannot be recalled even after a brief time lapse.[5]

The quality of attention

All of the focus group participants were *exposed* to the news story. But not all paid attention. Some became mental absentees; some lapsed into boredom; some were numbed by the load of facts, as the following discourse illustrates.

High-school-educated, Moscow

Natasha: I listened to half.
Katya: I think when you watch the information, the ordinary person simply takes time out ...
Maxim: Yes, you can go [and] put the tea kettle on.
Katya: These numbers – you can relax. There is something there, maybe, behind the picture, for whom this oil is interesting, but it's simply not interesting for us.
Olya: No sensations ...
Galya: They bombarded us with information.
Katya: They [weighed] us down.

---

[4] J. A. Ferejohn, and J. H. Kuklinski, *Information and the Democratic Process*. Urbana and Chicago, University of Illinois Press, 1990; Mutz, Sniderman, and Brody (eds.), *Political Persuasion and Attitude Change*; R. McDermott, "Arms Control and the First Reagan Administration: Belief Systems and Policy Choices," *Journal of Cold War Studies*, 4(4), 2002: 29–59.
[5] D. Graber, *Processing Politics: Learning from Television in the Internet Age*. Chicago, University of Chicago Press, 2001: 18.

Post-Soviet, Moscow

Oleg: It's overloaded with technical information. I don't think it's interesting for the viewer, how many millions of tons of oil are needed to fill this oil pipeline . . . It was interesting for me.
Igor: A little was interesting but there was a lot of water.

College-educated, Volgograd

Polina: I understood it a little distractedly . . . I didn't catch what took place.

Post-Soviet, Volgograd

Evgeny: Lots of information, badly done . . . A bunch of information piled on.
Misha: They just showed that it's such-and-such a length and the volume is such.

Post-Soviet, Rostov

Ivan: If I speak honestly, for the first 10 seconds I didn't understand what was [happening] on the screen. For example, if somebody is sitting, cutting carrots at home and watches [with half an eye].
Andrei: It will go right by.
Alexandra: Really everything takes place in Russia basically officially. The basic part [of the story] for reporters is cutting this ribbon.

The viewers talking here were not taking much in. Even Oleg (25, part-time college student, Moscow) who is interested in the event, finds the story "overloaded." Watching television is often a secondary activity; it serves as background while attending to something else. In an environment such as this, television must compete with other activities and, as one viewer put it, she looks up when something interesting comes on.

It was also characteristic of Channel One news that the format of the story appeared to trigger Soviet-era comparisons in the discourse.

College-educated, Moscow

Lena: It's like what we had on television before – as though all is data, here is so much arithmetic: so much here so much there, so much income.

Irina: It was done as an announcement.
Lena: Yes. Some kind of information announcement.
Natasha: Serious sums were named, therefore it can't be unimportant.
Lena: We can take this as a bulletin.
Igor: Reminds me of the old, actually, pre-perestroika [pre-Gorbachev] news.
Lena: Like a kind of accounting balance sheet.

College-educated, Nizhny Novgorod

Olga: It seems to me that it's too smooth. Too much, and it talked a lot of numbers.
Alesha: I think it was too drawn out for a news story.
Vladimir: The only, the one [piece of] information was that so many tons of oil were pumped in this. There wasn't any other information.
Olga: You don't even listen: numbers, such information.
Nikolai: Too many numbers; they're all empty. That is, it's necessary to separate them.
Olga: It doesn't say anything ... in Soviet times ... the story itself, I have in mind, the construction [is similar to Soviet times].

High-school-educated, Volgograd

Tamara: I think it's ORT [Channel One]. So much was said. It seems to me that they could even have shortened it, too much information; it was hard to stand it.
Natasha: That's their style.

Viewers who turn their minds off, or really do leave the room to make tea, nullify the first condition in the persuasion process. They are not genuinely exposed to the material. Others understand in different ways.

Trust, comprehension, and facts

Trust involves the audience's beliefs about the credibility of the source, a process of evaluation and perhaps a certain degree of positive affect toward the source.[6] In Russian, *doveria* can be translated as both "trust" and "confidence"; its root, *vera*, means faith. To avoid confusion, I consistently translate *doveria* as "trust," but it should be borne in mind that confidence in the station or story may also be intended. The

---

[6] McGraw and Hubbard, "Some of the People."

members of the Russian focus groups discussed Channel One's pipeline story right after they had seen it. It was natural that the apparently fact-filled story sparked discussion of what, exactly, a fact is. I say "apparently," because Russian viewers, used to such stories, have what might be called a graduated approach to the definition of "fact." At the simplest level, the discourse revealed that a fact is a narrowly delimited piece of information from a credible source for which the viewer has no means to *substitute a different, equally narrowly delimited piece of information*. The source is credible only in assigning a number – any number would do. In this definition of fact, the discussion appears to conflate fact and trust, and if a survey interviewer happened by, it would appear that the respondent trusts this story on this station, as the following discussion suggests.

Post-Soviet, Moscow

Lena (college-educated translator): In my view something was said, facts were given: who signed what, how many tons, etc. ... is this trustworthy information or not? It was trustworthy for me.

Katya (high-school educated, publisher's cashier): Trustworthy information – it's just that really it's an approach that is absolutely, purely standard and that's all.

Nikolai (post-Soviet college student, Nizhny Novgorod): It's objective from the technical point of view ... in principle nothing of the sort [clear contradictions] was said ... yes, they conveyed facts and that's all.

Vitaly (24, college-educated, employee, Volgograd): There's no basis not to believe.

Natasha (50, college-educated tax inspector, Moscow): What does it mean: this isn't true. What? [Should w]e doubt the percentages or the events? How can we judge, if we're not professional; we don't know, we are very far from it. We are average viewers; they give us information and we watch ... The comrades [others in her focus group] say it's not true; that it's necessary to present it somehow differently, as though it's show business ... They move[d] oil from one place; they received a budget, large amounts, billions of dollars, and from this money we'll do something there, we'll build, allocate, etc. Here it is concrete, purely economic.

High-school-educated, Volgograd

Alena (25, artist and fashion designer): Here there's only information that doesn't elicit suspicion. Yes, a pipeline and [things are] fine.

Andrei: They did their job.
Alena: They just did their job – that's also good. Really, is that insufficient? I don't consider that such information can be unobjective.

This, then, is how some of the participants in the groups express trust. In an issue that is not salient to them, they hear numbers about oil flow and revenue. These focus group members do not have at hand any numbers that contradict those given in the story. How can any viewer be in a position to dispute the numbers? Who has the knowledge to argue or deny, when the story consists entirely of measurements; when the event is made up of quantified features listed in sequence? It might be logical to expect that an acknowledgment of a piece of information as fact expresses trust, but that is not necessarily the case. It is an expression of a state of mind that says:

I don't care about this list of numbers; why would I have any to substitute for them? So, sure, I trust them; where on earth would I get anything to challenge them, as if I cared, and I don't. Why not these numbers? No reason.

That is a very unattractive notion of trust, and if a respondent to a mass-survey has this logic in mind, it can hardly be classified as trust in the usual sense. It is also likely that the numbers and the story will soon be forgotten. Lists of numbers are very difficult for viewers to process.

This is one caveat to bear in mind in analyzing cross-cultural opinion surveys, especially when the questions may have very different contexts across older democracies and countries in transition. There are also problems in analyzing surveys within older democracies; a study of survey analysis and survey instruments revealed a long series of weaknesses in poll-taking in the United States,[7] and different meanings of the same term should be included. For example, Hochschild (2001) notes that liberals will call themselves individualists when the term is defined as autonomy, while conservatives will identify themselves as individualists when the issue is self-reliance.[8]

---

[7] There is a critical study of the problems with mass public opinion surveys in G. F. Bishop, *The Illusion of Public Opinion: Fact and Artifact in American Public Opinion Polls*. Lanham, MD, Rowman and Littlefield, 2005.

[8] J. Hochschild, "Where You Stand Depends on What You See: Connections Among Values, Perceptions of Fact, and Political Prescriptions," in J. H. Kuklinski, *Citizens and Politics: Perspective from Political Psychology*. Cambridge, Cambridge University Press, 2001: 315.

On the other hand, much of the discourse about our story rejected this notion of fact. This kind of discourse questioned the status of a fact with no context. Such a "fact" is literally meaningless; it lacks a contextual dimension, without which a fact has no meaning. At issue is not whether Channel One's number or a different one is accurate, but what *any* number *means*, absent context. As the much greater part of the discourse shows, evaluation, comprehension, and retention were casualties of this mode of presentation and with them, trust, as usually understood. For these Russian viewers, it is from the *intelligibility* of the numbers that trust and comprehension are derived.

Their discourse reveals that for many it is impossible to comprehend the story to which they have been exposed and paid attention. Vladimir (59, unemployed, Nizhny Novgorod) argues that numbers by themselves have no meaning and therefore cannot be processed. If they cannot be processed, then they cannot be received and stored. In his group of Nizhny Novgorod, college-educated, the discussion includes, in addition, Liuba (24, teacher), Olga (61, pensioner), and Nikolai (45, company general director):

Vladimir: The only, the one piece of information was that so many tons of oil were pumped in ... There wasn't any other information.
Liuba: So many percentages.
Olga: You don't even listen, numbers, that kind of information.
Vladimir: I told you that a number has to be placed against something. If in this story, they put in some comparison with some other pipeline or something we already had, then we would have watched it differently.
Olga: Otherwise the story is not very interesting for the average viewer to watch.
Vladimir: Still, I'll stay with this. It is so imperative that there be numbers, if there is such information. It should always close with a number. And the number always has to be compared. One number ... never.

In Moscow, Viktor (46, merchant marine captain) and Igor (37, engineer) discuss the same fundamental requirement for context:

Viktor: They said a number there 20 billion, but if they said 30 billion, it's nothing to me, neither cold, nor hot.
Igor: Yes, it's practically impossible to evaluate.

In spite of the cascade of numbers and the unremittingly celebratory tone of the story, most of the viewers in the focus groups have not had their spirits lifted. Here in Moscow are Lena (housewife), Olga (pensioner), Igor (engineer), and Galina (supplier):

Lena: I'd say that I had no feeling. I'm indifferent, because really they just communicate to us what facts occurred. And maybe really they want to say that it's all good, but I don't know. I need to see a lot more factors to believe the advisability of this pipeline.
Olga: That's what I say, insufficient information.
Igor: Superficial information.

It is because of the inability of viewers to evaluate a story of this kind that often very little remains afterward. Some said they just shut down and sat inattentively. Others watched but could remember very little shortly after the story was shown. In Volgograd, Dina (20, high-school-educated bookkeeper) said that "literally in two minutes we forgot what it was about." And others watched but did not comprehend, as the comments below indicate. The first two, Galina and Natasha, finished high school; the rest have a college education:

Galina, Moscow: The overall purpose is not clear to me. Why did they do it? . . . Yes, to drive the oil to Europe. It's not clear to me here what's the main issue. Why is it done?
Natasha, Moscow: When I watched, it wasn't deposited into my head at all. I didn't understand it.
Maxim, Moscow: I don't understand what it's about. Is it about the storm or about some weather reports, or about oil?
Mikhail, Volgograd: What is all this for?
Marina, Volgograd: I didn't understand and further, so they showed us this story and afterwards does this oil do something for someone?
Misha, Volgograd: Why is it necessary to build [it]? I don't understand at all. They invested huge [amounts of] money.
Natasha, Rostov: In general nothing's clear, really. Somebody has most of the profit, how it will be divided; they said there a percent.
Olga, Rostov: Not clear at all.
Vika, Rostov: This information is simply for the average viewer, to look at it casually, to get acquainted . . . for the interested person no, it's like giving a toast [at a celebration].
Boris, Nizhny Novgorod: Honestly speaking, it also wasn't very clear to me in general, the whole news.

College-educated viewers appear to have greater requirements for source credibility than others. It was only in their discussions that the qualifications of the reporters came into play. These viewers look for specialized background and whether or not the reporter commands sufficient expertise to explain the event with appropriate depth and accuracy, factors important to a determination of credibility in Western studies.[9] In several conversations the story was contemptuously referred to as "amateurish," a surprising criticism to be leveled at the oldest, richest, and most widely watched channel in the country. If the story is thought to lack the necessary expertise, it cannot be trusted. Dissatisfaction with the level of knowledge displayed by the news story was expressed in better-educated groups, such as the following.

College-educated, Moscow

Olya: About the people who did the story – probably they are people far from economic issues.
Lena: Maybe dilettantes.
Natasha: A non-specialist did it.
Svetlana: It's for the average viewer who simply sat in front of the television set and watched.

Post-Soviet, Volgograd

Evgeny: Some information was too confused, it showed some technological moments. Maybe it's not professional

College-educated, Nizhny Novgorod

Vladimir: In any case, this reportage is unprofessional.

All the focus groups had been exposed to the story. Not all paid attention; some tuned out; some imagined themselves at home going to get something in the kitchen. Some did pay attention – the story threw out some very big investment and revenue statistics – and these participants then become candidates for the third stage in the sequencing of persuasion (accepting the frame), which is what the news was intended to accomplish. Some could not comprehend the story. They could not retain it long enough to be able to talk about it a few minutes later or, distracted by the different elements of the story, they failed to get the

[9] A. Lupia and M. D. McCubbins, *The Democratic Dilemma: Can Citizens Learn What They Need to Know?* Cambridge, Cambridge University Press, 1998.

main point, and it was not because they had not gone to college or lived in the provinces far from Moscow. For the viewers who had tuned out, failed to pay attention, did not retain the information, or did not comprehend the story, there was little likelihood that the message (the story) would be stored by the viewer and thus available to help understand or interpret new information and conditions. For those who did reach the last step, when the acceptance of the frame or point of view of the story is at issue, there is an asymmetrical split in the discourse. The smaller part accepts the story's facts, but on so narrow and fleeting a basis that it may be impossible to store in the memory. The larger part, at best, expresses an irritated and impatient dissatisfaction with the story for preventing them from applying their powers of evaluation. The discourse suggests that this evaluative process is something that is thoroughly familiar and ordinary for viewers, whether college- or high-school-educated. Russians expect to exercise it when watching the news and they know that for it they require context and comparative information. Failing to find it in the story, they find themselves unpersuaded. The pipeline event may be a big achievement of the government, but it may not be. They remain unconvinced by numbers. And assertions.

Longing for positive news ...

The Russian public tells the survey interviewers that they want positive news; they complain about the media's news menu of troubles, natural disasters, and accidents. Surveys demonstrate that respondents in very large numbers say that they are tired of, and repelled by, the dismal muck of contemporary Russian life on the television screen. In early discussions in the focus groups, in all four cities and among college-educated, high-school-educated and post-Soviet participants, there were a good many who disapproved of the tone and content of the constant stream of bad news. This discussion came up well before they saw this news story. They were invited to think about what they would want in a news program, and some expressed disapproval of bad news:

Katya (19, college student, Volgograd): I would try for more good, not unpleasantness or conflicts, or all kinds of war, but more good.
Lidia (63, high-school-educated pensioner, Rostov): Today they broadcast on the radio in the news program that in Moscow they expect acts of terrorism, chemical, all kinds. Why did they announce this? For what

purpose? To hype the situation and make people still more nervous? Why do they do this? I'd turn it off altogether.

Vitaly (24, college-educated, employee, Volgograd): I thought about it now, that first of all I'd take away most of the negative information, these catastrophes, sensationalism and so on. It doesn't seem to me to be interesting to the majority. I'd do sports and culture.

Marina (43, college-educated, employee, Nizhny Novgorod): If they gave information, for example, on vacations in various resorts or on theatrical programs and previews of shows. I think, this, when there's such harsh information, especially negative, that's horrible – terror, Chechnya, and crime news – it's awfully hard [on us].

At first glance it appears that in focus groups, as in surveys, we find the familiar distaste for bad news, and among some, a saddened resignation that bad news reflects bad times:

Lilia (54, college-educated, employee, Rostov): I would want less cruelty … though I know that right now life is pretty tough, but it would be nice to have more positive emotions.

Alexander (35, college-educated distributor, Volgograd): I completely agree [that there should be more good news on television]. I watch TV and I become sober, but our life, of course, is not so simple; times have changed.

… And rejecting it on television

That is not the end of the story. When viewers get what they appear to want – for example, when, later, they are shown this upbeat pipeline story – instead of approving, many reject the story out of hand. They do not believe it. A positive news story undermines its own credibility by invoking three different kinds of analogies for viewers. One comes from the new world of advertising that lends its techniques to the display of the government's achievements. Post-Soviet Mikhail in Volgograd likens the story to a public relations assignment: "I think what we saw was simply advertising – about what money is invested and how long it is and [how] it holds a million tons of oil. They wanted to show achievements and not what was lacking – showing everything everywhere is fine." For Mikhail's generation, advertising and public relations businesses are commonplace; they can't recall a time before the arrival of the spin doctors. Even in this failing city deep in the Volga heartland it is how he understands the unfolding of the benefits portrayed in the story. The more common analogy comes from the Soviet years: a positive story cues the paradigm of Soviet-era television news, and is shunted off into the category of deliberately distorted messages serving the state. Here are college-educated Muscovites, Viktor and Svetlana in one group and Lena, Igor, and Vladimir in a second:

Viktor: Everything is good.
Svetlana: And without depth, everything's very good ... I am used to doubting everything now.
Lena: It's not realistic.
Igor: Reminds me of old, really pre-perestroika [news].
Lena: Like a kind of accounting tally.
Vladimir: Like an accounting tally of the achievements of socialist construction.

Liuda from Nizhny Novgorod comments that: "When it all started, you know, it started so pompously, for some reason a question came up right away: what period is this? That is, in what time? I hadn't even heard the text yet, because I said to myself, it started so pompously: for me it's tied to that [time, the Soviet period]."

Third, a positive news story can cue corruption and planted news. A thoroughly positive message may be rejected as news, because it is seen as something commissioned or ordered up. Here is the discourse of a college-educated group in Volgograd:

Andrei: Whoever put in money into the construction of this pipeline, commissioned it [this story].
Vera: Without doubt.
Svetlana: Because everything's fine.
Mikhail: Because what they said was said with such satisfaction.
Polina: There were no difficulties in the construction.
Vera: [saying why she didn't believe it but others might] Basically those people who maybe have high-school education. Well, I have in mind old grannies and granddaddies. They believe it.

The suspicion of the focus group participants and so many others that corruption is pervasive and unavoidable, even for the smallest transaction, is disheartening. It produces an environment that taints the formerly great media heroes, as well. In the late days of Mikhail Gorbachev's administration through the first days of the partially competitive 1989 election, and through the rumblings of civil war and violence in Moscow in 1993, a recognizable group of anchors were heroes. They stayed up all night, when some rebels tried to take over the television building; they provided a continuous connection to the public, for the rebels had counted on help from the provinces. As Boris Yeltsin wrote in his memoirs: "television saved Moscow." Then the heroic phase ended, privatization was hurriedly and corruptly carried out and became only more widespread up and down the status ladder and across the country. This environment, and the common knowledge that money had played a big part in the kind of news transmitted cast the anchors famous for their courageous past exploits in the same mold that had created the current environment: being rich meant that one had to be corrupt; there was no other way to get there. The achievements of an earlier time faded fast and the current environment became the referent.

Then and now: same anchor, loss of integrity. In short, as the audience becomes more and more news savvy, the position of journalists – the respect and admiration for the reform revolutionaries – changed to an expectation of corruption and self-inflicted loss of autonomy for money. The rapid, massive changes in the economy, the crony capitalism that the few at the top invented, have for our participants rendered *any* obvious wealth suspicious. Recall the military man from Volgograd (Andrei, 43, college-educated); he remarked: "You know, in our time, I don't respect people who earn money by any means whatever: with the use of filth. [How] is not important." It is not envy or greed, but vengeance and anger. Many building projects in the provinces have been burned down because of these emotions. Marina Goldovskaya, the well known documentary film-maker, made a film called *The Prince is Back*, in which a poor family with an old pedigree came back to Russia from Ukraine to the crumbling, dilapidated family seat, determined to rebuild it and make a museum: Napoleon had stopped there. When it was nearly finished, under the most trying of conditions without running water or electricity, and took shape, the neighbors burned it down in a determination to bring them down to their own level.

With corruption so pervasive at all levels in Russia, viewers take it for granted that many people, and much of the "news," are "bought." The conversation between Andrei, the engineer from Nizhny Novgorod, Olga, the bookkeeper, and Kolya, the general director, was illuminating. Andrei said: "Capitalism is the ability to sell yourself"; Olga (47, bookkeeper) agreed: "Any person can be bought; it's only necessary to know the price." Kolya adds: "everybody sells himself, unfortunately. We all sell ourselves … it depends on how much money." This is the present. The past, when the iconic anchors had no real money to make and displayed their altruism, has disappeared under the weight of the massive corruption that has hit the media very hard. One focus group member had said, about another television news issue, that the bought or planted news was "commissioned, but objective." What he meant by this was that everyone knew what was going on; none was fooled, even though the top officials kept thinking that the undifferentiated mass of viewers were too dull-witted to merit serious attention and perhaps any change of strategy.

While consuming positive news stories, viewers reject them as patently unbelievable. They neither trust nor recall their contents. And each population stratum says *it* isn't credulous, but *others* down the status ladder would be. Young Moscow urbanites say *they* understand but their elders wouldn't; their parents' generation say *they* understand, but someone in a provincial city would not. From Volgograd and Rostov, the adults say *they* understand, but rural people would not, particularly the lowest rung on the status ladder, the rural elderly.

The Russian public laments the negative sides of their lives; television is only a conduit. They wish their lives were different, but they know that a buoyant portrayal lacks verisimilitude.

Russians demand contextual information and comparisons. They do not recall or trust stories in which numbers are cited unless there is a context in which those figures may be compared, or relevant other dimensions included. Pseudo-events, which flatten the context to foreground privileged actors, are often viewed as "ordered" (*zakazukha*) or "commissioned." Happy news is distrusted. Russian viewers recognize that much, or even most, televised news and public information is ordered, and they add that information to their personal analytic navigational system. It is this system of cognitive shortcuts that has been demonstrated above. Some of it is a holdover from the past; some responds to new stimuli from a new set of institutional actors. The complexity of the cognitive instruments is visible in all of our cities, even where there is little political competition and a narrow media choice, and across the different levels of education. Russian viewers weigh the manipulative intent in messages. In producing what they intend to be persuasive messages, media elites' assumptions about reception diverge in important respects from the process by which their Russian publics understand the news. Russians, as we have seen, have an array of mental shortcuts, salient experiences, and traditions of expending effort to enlarge the context of the news, and an awareness of the rarity or impossibility (almost in a post-modern sense) of objectivity. They are also aided by the miscalculations that elites make in constructing and disseminating messages intended to provide a definitive frame, when they underestimate viewers' processing capacity and fail to recognize the negotiated nature of information reception.

Overall, this has been a picture of audiences working hard to expand what they expected and knew to be a truncated, insufficient, limited amount of news. It was up to them, they indicated, to add the missing dimension.

The case of TV-6

The comments from the sixteen focus groups reproduced here are drawn from the various discourses among the different types of focus groups. One of the most interesting current events that came before the focus groups was the closing down of TV-6. There were deep divisions in the discourse, and an overall sense of lack of access to the truth of what had happened behind closed doors, in the same way as they said they had no access whatever to information about corruption at high levels.

In a mass survey taken by the Foundation for Public Opinion on January 24, 2002, respondents were asked: "How do you feel about the decision to liquidate TV-6?"

I include these findings, because they include both expected and unexpected findings. The bars in figure 7.1 are labeled "total," "Muscovites," "Putin," and "Ziuganov" (Ziuganov, the Communist candidate). Moscow is really very different from elsewhere in Russia. Partly this is because the density of reception is very high but, more important, Muscovites have their own, different, way of looking at life. Indeed, some of the Muscovites in the focus groups as we have seen, made it plain that they had no empathy for natural disasters elsewhere in Russia (it was their own lack of preparedness). One woman said that she lived on an island called Moscow, and neither knew nor cared about the rest of the country. That there is also a powerful material difference in Moscow can be seen from any trip to Russia.

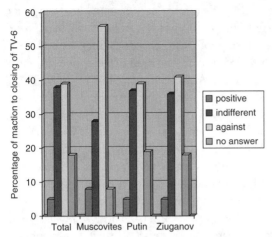

Figure 7.1 Channel TV-6: positive, negative, or indifferent?
Notes: Survey of 100 population points, 44 regions and republics of Russia. Interviews at home and in the field between January 19 and 20, 2002, with 1,500 respondents. There was a supplementary survey of the city of Moscow, with 600 respondents. The sample margin of error was 3.6 percent.
Source: Zakrytie TV-6, January 24, 2002 survey, Foundation for Public Opinion.

The other interesting feature of this survey is the similarity in the responses of the Putin and Ziuganov supporters. Partisanship rarely divided the discourse in the focus groups. Surprisingly, perhaps, almost no one's politics had any effect on their ideas, satisfaction, or dissatisfaction with the media. There were very few examples – as when a female pensioner wanted to resurrect the military–patriotic programs of Soviet times and to have mandatory education in the old values, for example.

There were differences among post-Soviet young people and their elders, among the participants' level of education, among those in Moscow and those in other cities. During the period when official pressure was being put on TV-6, some voices rose to claim a new, inherent human right: the right to a diversity of viewpoint. Theoretically, the presence of a human right is an entitlement: it must be met. Assertion of this inherent right had little effect on the Russian power structure, but it displayed a changed group of viewers. True, they were a small minority of the participants in the focus groups but, as one college-educated viewer said: "A corner has been turned."

Polina (23, housewife): after saying that each channel broadcasts its own way, goes on to say "The person has the *right* to watch all four channels" (italics mine, throughout this chapter). She has staked a claim on the basis of rights – in this case, the right to viewpoint diversity on the air. In the same group, Alexei (43, employee) asserts: "[it couldn't be closed down] of course not ... because the demand exists for objective information ... by *society* ... *Come on, the power will not go against society*." Vera (39, engineer/programmer): "Well, before they could close it, *but not now*," and Alexei adds: "*not any more, of course*." The post-Soviet group in Volgograd is attuned to what they believe must have been a fundamental change of rules and the political culture. The Soviet era, they assume, is over, and the new political order has been built on rights inhering in individuals. These rights are also, when considered together, of great importance to society as a whole. The need for diversity of views on television has become a right and the existence of that right carries with it what in democratic theory would use a different metaphor: If the principals (the voters) support that right, it cannot be overturned by their agents (officialdom) – the few who draw their power from the population.

The post-Soviet group in the same city speaks the same way. Misha (24, university student): "I think we should listen to the opinion of the minority, because in this opinion you can find some use. In principle I hold the view that *all channels have the right to exist*." Denis (21, university student): "And I don't even think that TV-6 *is* the minority." Evgeny (25, military): "[Just at the time when Russia is trying to show off its democratic credentials] they crush TV-6. I don't know why now, at least while they were showing that they [had] freedom of speech and thought and all the rest." Again there is the assertion of rights: in these comments we see freedom of speech and all that belongs to that category of right, and the right of the majority not to be driven by an unseen minority against the will of that majority.

To regard the continuation of a television station as a category of right is really quite remarkable. It is not just individuals who have the right to alternatives in news broadcasts: it is a right of society. The individuals in our group frame their arguments as large-scope rights that apply to all of society, existing for the benefit and the good life of society, not just the self-gratification of atomized individuals. The participants link two rights: freedom of speech and freedom of society to have diversity of viewpoints.

When focus group participants contributed tradeoffs (see chapter 4), most of them were related to the lives of the individuals offering them, and most of them were limited, personal, and stubborn, taking one position or another. Some displayed an integrative reasoning that permitted them to see the benefit and reasonableness in both sides of an argument and to try to devise a solution that could take both into account while improving society as a whole. This awareness of new human rights, at present very much in the minority among all groups, showed a similar willingness to consider their own ideas and solutions at the societal level and to see how they might benefit society as a whole.

Higher education makes a difference

Going to college produces significant differences. Participants with high-school education perceive little "connective tissue" between the elements of Soviet television. Some of their preferences are articulated as anti-contemporary practices, some bring up a universally loved children's program, but there is little effort to provide an overarching logic or rationale that could connect the elements of Soviet television as a whole. Socialization in patriotism appears to be unrelated to socialization about foreign countries, and the role of the Party – with the exception of staging long and boring Congresses – is not so prominent. The structure of programs is important to high-school-educated participants the quality of film, sports, and diction; but they seem to be recalled in a void. It may be the case here that the "boring" news and other public affairs programs simply did not become memories; devoid of emotion, or even of understanding, they cannot be summoned and are not available in processing the life of their pasts and developing connections. When we look at issues of policy tradeoffs, even though in Russia they are concealed and only the positive side is presented in the news, we see the same advantage the well-educated have in integrative reasoning, in abstract reasoning, and the ability to place observations within a society-wide context.[10]

---

[10] G. Baker-Brown, E. Ballard, S. Bluck, B. De Vries, P. Suedfeld, and P. Tetlock, "The Conceptual/Integrative Complexity Scoring Manual," in C. Smith (ed.), *Motivation and Personality: Handbook of Thematic Content Analysis.* Cambridge, Cambridge University Press, 1992.

The configuration of blame

In her study of the sources of protest in Russia, Javeline (2003) finds a connection between protest potential and how blame is attributed.[11] She writes that "the ability to make specific attributions of blame for a problem" is a key component in the likelihood of protest action" (2003: 223). Further, such protest will be at the local level, since that is where blame can be shown to be tied to the problem.[12] When the focus groups talk about television, they talk about national television, and they blame Moscow and the Kremlin (meaning the seat of government). There seems to be no intermediary authority able to act to improve or solve the problems of these individuals. It is a very long stretch from an ordinary bookkeeper in Volgograd to a complaint to the President. Local officials cannot be a substitute, since they are seen as inserted by Moscow and, besides, viewers understand the media, especially television, to be a business like any other and so part of the web of corruption. The nomination of governors by the Kremlin was legislated in 2004.

However, approaching elections can be a stimulus for action on the part of those left out. In May 2007, demonstrations against the continuing reduction of political choice broke out in Moscow. Led by ideological opponents Garry Kasparov (the chess champion) his political opposite the far right Eduard Limonov, and the moderate former prime minister, Michael Kasyanov, there were two "Dissenter Marches" in Moscow, two in St. Petersburg, and two in Nizhny Novgorod. Large numbers of riot police were out in force and easily and brutally ended the event. From what the focus group members say, Moscow, the Center, the Power, as it is variously called, is too remote to impose change, and the Kremlin's preferences permeate deeper and deeper into local politics, no matter whom the elections produce as leader from a small field. The trio of "Dissenter" leaders have much building to do to gain grass-roots support.

---

[11] D. Javeline, *Protest and the Politics of Blame: The Russian Response to Unpaid Wages*. Ann Arbor, MI: The University of Michigan Press, 2003.

[12] Ferejohn and Kuklinski, *Information and the Democratic Process*; Mutz, Sniderman, and Brody, *Political Persuasion and Attitude Change*; McDermott, "Arms Control."

Short time horizons and uneasy lives

The strategic necessity of watching television remains. In chapter 1, Katya (23, cashier for a publisher) said that she would not miss a single edition of the news on television, because: "in recent times in Russia, something happens and not only in politics and economics, but even simply elemental catastrophes and so forth, crises, conflicts, etc. In principle I need these data to know what's going on." Julia (20, student, in Moscow) had a nerve-wracking sense of the time horizon for existence; she watched the news, because "suddenly the country is destroyed while we're sitting." For others it has become the norm to watch television, to be prepared for the unknown inside the family or at work, and to try to reduce the uncertainties by working hard at processing what is given, even though it may be far from the full story. It is difficult to live with such short time horizons; it interferes with planning one's life or career, and it blunts the will to act.

Heuristics at work

Russians use strategies to extract meaning from extremely limited political information on their television. As we noted at the beginning of this study, it would be wise not to lose sight of the findings of psychology research literature in the United States, which considers the less successful aspects of heuristics. Lack of knowledge may impede citizens from making a policy choice consistent with their interests: the voter determines what is in her interest by her use of heuristics, but sometimes comes up short. Kinder (2006) reminds us that "when we take shortcuts, we sometimes end up in the right place – but sometimes get lost. In taking cues from elites we can get lost because the elites themselves may be mistaken ... Thus, heuristic processing can lead to erroneous conclusions."[13] While acknowledging this caveat, other social science studies consider the use of heuristics, as Russians seem to do (without naming it as such) – as an aid that enables citizens to judge policies and other choices with respect to their own interests when they lack the knowledge on which to base those choices.

---

[13] D. R. Kinder, "Belief Systems Today," *Critical Review*, Special Issue on *Is Democratic Competence Possible?*, 18(1–3), 2006: 205.

Ordinary people use capabilities they have to expand the diet of news they get:

[D]rivers use the trajectory of oncoming headlights to draw accurate inferences about the future locations of other cars, and consumers use brand names to draw accurate inferences about particular qualities of many consumer goods.[14]

What we saw in our focus groups were policy alternatives, advice on avoiding natural disasters, what must be done to develop trust in the media, and a clear-headed resignation in the face of policies concealing tradeoffs (as most do) that would make their lives more difficult.

American research literature asks increasingly "not whether citizens are judging political matters badly, but whether they are capable of political judgment at all – good or bad."[15] In one experiment, choosing in conformity with one's values and interests went from 53 percent if only one side of the argument was displayed, to 75 percent when both were. Even among the least informed it went from 30 percent to 84 percent.[16] As the authors point out: "our findings will apply just so far as there are incentives and opportunities for opposing points of view to obtain public expression [what we have termed viewpoint diversity]."[17] Recognizing the need for diversity of viewpoint as a new human right shows how important it has become for some of the Russians in our groups.

Much of the theory underlying how the Russian groups were set up and the interpretation of their discourse has come from work done outside of Russia, and a number of disclaimers are necessary. American research designs and respondents simply cannot be compared to this study: the methodological differences are enormous and do not permit comparisons of findings. The institutional, economic, political, historical, and other environments, and the socialization that occurs within them, also mean that any attempt at comparison should start with new,

---

[14] A. Lupia, "How Elitism Undermines the Study of Voter Competence," *Critical Review*, 18 (1–3): 217–232, p. 227.

[15] P. M. Sniderman and S. M. Theriault, "The Structure of Political Argument and the Logic of Issue Framing," in W. E. Saris and P. M. Sniderman (eds.), *Studies in Public Opinion: Attitudes, Nonattitudes, Measurement Error, and Change.* Princeton, Princeton University Press, 2004: 135.

[16] Saris and Sniderman, *Studies in Public Opinion*: 152–153.

[17] Saris and Sniderman, *Studies in Public Opinion*: 156.

specially designed projects that control for these differences, if that is possible. What has been most illuminating throughout this study has been the insights we get of how the human brain works.

Some heuristics used in Western research involve the insights we get of how incrementalism can be built into budgeting; of the position of interest groups, the availability of the heuristic to be used in analogous situations, and of what values the political parties traditionally stand for. Political party labels can be especially helpful heuristics, mainly because they combine political parties with long histories and differences in ideology. If, in this study, the availability heuristic is seen to be employed frequently among Russian viewers, it is because it *is* used very often and because, in the Western literature on heuristics, it appears to be the most powerful heuristic of all.

Changes in election rules

Few of the heuristics described above would be of much help to Russian viewers. The obstacles to making real sense of a news story are therefore more formidable for them. Russians do not have political or policy lobbying groups arguing their positions.[18] There have been micro-parties in national elections (where three dozen or more parties are not unusual, one of which, such as the CEDAR party for the preservation of the environment, might be dedicated to a cause), but they are never a serious political alternative and, in any case, the odds have changed in favor of large, rich parties under the patronage of the Kremlin. Although this is not a study of the end-point of understanding news – behavior in elections themselves – the changing environment in Russia suggests that it will be more difficult in the future for diversity of viewpoints to be represented in parliament. Russian electoral rules followed the German practice by decreeing a 5 percent threshold of votes for a party to be able to send deputies to parliament but from the 2007 elections the threshold will be 7 percent, which is considered hard to overcome. So more parties will not get seats: the votes will be apportioned among the winners; and all who voted for parties failing

[18] There are numberless, including foreign-funded, nongovernmental organizations (NGOs) working to improve the environment, stop trafficking in women, save and improve water quality, and form civil society. They are small and usually regional and there is an explicit prohibition against any kind of assistance from these groups in political lobbying.

to meet the 7 percent threshold will have wasted their votes. As I noted earlier, the formation of genuine political parties in Russia – parties that are wholly autonomous, can put forward competitive programs, build strength at all levels of society, and have staying power – has not been very successful. Hale's (2006) study of political parties in Russia is deeply pessimistic, and lays out a map of the Kremlin's tightening control of what otherwise might be a space for parties. There are party substitutes, also tied to the Kremlin, that perform some of the functions of parties, but real incentives or a "market" for parties has not developed.[19] Hence, one of the most commonly used heuristics by which Americans match up their interests with a policy or candidate is not present in Russia. The party label may define the party, but the chances of entering parliament are smaller than ever before.

And yet, even with minimal (and always threatened) diversity of viewpoint, one example of public expression of personal values and interests should be recognized, even though it has not yet entered the history books. The "against-all" vote, as we saw in chapter 3, survived for decades in the Soviet era, because it was so modest, buried in the ballot paper and attracting a minuscule fraction of voters. Typically, the "against-all" voter was only slightly less marginal a citizen than the "no vote" citizen who stayed at home after the fall of the Soviet Union, when voting was no longer mandatory. "Against-all" was only a single-digit percentage figure in national elections, but in the early 2000s it changed its composition and its strength. From marginal, older, rural voters, the composition of "against-all" voters became young, urban, and economically well situated. The "against-all" vote won urban and regional elections or caused a runoff, and its continuous growth worried Moscow. In preparation for the 2007 parliamentary elections the option of voting "against-all" was removed from the ballot by a vote in the Russian parliament.

In preparing for the 2007 elections, the Russian parliament also changed another part of the electoral system. A system in which half the deputies were elected by party-lists and the other half by single-member districts was converted into a fully party-list ballot. This meant the end for some well-known political figures, feisty and articulate – usually for a liberal rather than a conservative cause – who had

---

[19] H. E. Hale, *Why Not Parties in Russia? Democracy, Federalism, and the State*. New York, Cambridge University Press, 2006.

been elected as individuals: without them, the range of discourse in the pre-2007 parliaments would have been even more constricted than it was. In the run-up to the 2007 parliamentary elections, the Russian legislature converted all voting to the party-list system and abolished the single-member district.

Russian viewers' adaptations of cue sources

Russians do use a heuristic: the identity of the television station. When there were still four main news stations in Moscow their labels provided a shortcut to political meaning, which is why we concealed all the logos when we asked about specific stories. Viewers could get information from those labels, as chapters 2 and 3 demonstrate at least with respect to some policies. During electoral campaigns, the stations adopted such similar, incoherent – and, to the viewers, repellent – formats that the station label lost its utility. The argumentative TV-6 was removed; the formerly argumentative NTV was taken over and tamed. Even if the news program was often sparse in content and unspecific, with viewpoint diversity it could at least provide an increase in news for Russian viewers.

However, another heuristic, also identified above, remains very powerful: the availability heuristic. All Russian viewers keep some experiences, emotions, values, "at the ready"; they are able to summon them up unconsciously to explain a current news story. What is not available – because it was not understood in the first place, or had no meaning to the individual, or appeared heavy-handed in its intent to persuade – could not be used and was tossed out. At the opposite range of the spectrum, Russians are particularly adept at bringing to bear on their consumption of news other stored categories or schemas of emotions, values, and events that matter very much to them and that may serve as useful analogies or reflections. We have seen that these Russian viewers expand terse stories into broad disquisitions on development versus preservation of the environment. Because the government and its closest allies present similar stories on all of the three national news stations from which they habitually seek information, the activity of "filling in" what has been left out is particularly important. Russian viewers work hard to discover the news, and when they cannot directly compare broadcasts to find discrepancies, they operate on the basis of the availability heuristic.

Dissatisfaction among viewers may affect them as individuals but, more probably, as a family unit at home around the dinner table or having tea. The focus group participants say repeatedly that the will of Moscow or "the Center" – not necessarily an individual office-holder – is reaching ever closer to controlling lower-level local political structures by "planting" their choices. Focus group participants speak of regional elections and predict the victory of the candidate who is "pleasing" to Moscow. Between their ample set of often highly emotional attitudes and the Center, where the decisions are made, viewers seem to see a void, impassable unless their elected representative should become accountable to the people who voted.

The individual and society at one

For most of the viewers in our groups, life is so circumscribed by work and family, and supported by such low levels of income, that they must forgo even movies. Outside Moscow, life is difficult, even for college graduates. The television set in the center of the room (or in every room in the house, as one viewer proudly announced) is the third activity in daily life – work (including housework), taking care of children, and television. Even many young people are reduced to this trio of activities.

Russian viewers are sophisticated, work hard viewing several different news programs or checking with friends and relatives, and have a powerful instrument in the heuristics they have developed. Beyond that, however, these focus group participants displayed more: they often showed integrative reasoning, in that they clearly saw tradeoffs in projected policies and recognized that different values were attached to each. They tried to take a society-wide view and retain as much as possible of the benefits of each choice in the tradeoff process. The members of the focus groups displayed another quality, rare even in democratic states: a minority recognized in the end of TV-6 a loss to Russian society as a whole. None of the viewers praised TV-6 for its superior skills and television product. Rather, TV-6 gave another view, and they recognized how important it was to have a diversity of viewpoint, even if it was a diversity of self-serving interests.

In taking this stance, they had two points in mind: one was that diversity of viewpoint was vital to *society as a whole*, the other that their comments did not advance solely personal interests. Viewers who spoke on these subjects insisted that diversity of viewpoint had become a human right and, as an inherent part of the human being, created an entitlement that should be implemented. There were several viewers who said that the "power" would not go against public opinion; they would not shut down what society valued. "Those days are over," one of them said. Such unmet rights may lie dormant, but having become a "human right" they do not vanish. We also saw earlier that for other members of the focus groups the very definition of "objectivity" is *viewpoint diversity*. It may be external diversity, with one station on one side, and another station on the other, but these viewers can handle that.

The discourse of some focus group participants also displays xenophobia, bigotry, complacency – and, especially among the condescending young in Moscow – the sense of having no connection whatever to the country beyond their "island, Moscow."

The voices that came out so strongly in the focus groups do not expect to see the changes they hope for in any near future. The young, the post-Soviets, are more attuned to their professions than to comparisons with the Soviet past, for which they mainly have contempt, having not grown up with it. But they are clearly not a monolith. As these young people age, we do not yet know what will happen in a demographically shrinking Russian society, and how they will go about constructing their own new values.

Some things do conflict with the actions of the leadership: the television menu does not suit most viewers; the news is particularly badly presented and condescending, and its format is the least likely to be assimilated by viewers; the election stories are particularly disliked and are generally seen as confused and repellent. The younger generation has a very negative view of television on the Soviet model and, even though they didn't see it, their assessments are harshly negative. Older people conflate a carefree childhood with a children's program on television; they wish that the happy feelings it evoked would return. But neither group has a nostalgic longing to replace what they see now with the earlier Soviet model. Some years after the dissolution of the Soviet Union, our Russian focus group members had not lost their astonishing sophistication in expanding what the news story had deliberately left out or, while there was still diversity of views, what the opposition station had exaggerated beyond credibility. Diversity of viewpoint emerges as one of the most-sought-after features of television news. It *defines* objectivity and therefore enhances trust; it expands knowledge to such an extent that it is possible to function as a citizen in a democratic society. The capacity to consume a diversity of viewpoint is also part of what it means to be "human": for that impassioned group it is an inherent right, an entitlement, and must be implemented throughout society. In the end, it was taken away, but two features probably remain: the wish to reinstate viewpoint diversity as soon as possible, and the wish to assure its availability throughout society.

Chapters 1–6 of this book show Russian viewers deprived of viewpoint diversity in the one mass-medium on which the vast majority of citizens is dependent. Their preferred upbeat news stories on the state-connected stations depict a world so unlike how people understand the news that they are effectively ignored or subjected to the mental short-cuts of which Russians have a significant supply. Even without viewpoint diversity, the same methods serve the viewers, and it can be how far their probes can take them. Russian viewers with any level of education are impressive, with a formidable armory of ways to get at the news. The impetus for such a lot of work – comparing news stories, analyzing them, discussing them in social groupings – may well be the sense of threat, unease, and unpredictability they have lived with for so long. Political leaders and broadcasters persist in imagining an undifferentiated, unsophisticated mass on the other side of the screen: in fact, this country's viewers have remarkable abilities, and unique motivation, and these will not disappear any time soon.

Index